# BORDER WOMEN

CULTURAL STUDIES OF THE AMERICAS
Edited by George Yúdice, Jean Franco, and Juan Flores

# BORDER WOMEN

## *Writing from La Frontera*

Debra A. Castillo
and
María Socorro Tabuenca Córdoba

Cultural Studies of the Americas, Volume 9

University of Minnesota Press
Minneapolis / London

Published by the University of Minnesota Press
111 Third Avenue South, Suite 290
Minneapolis, MN 55401-2520
http://www.upress.umn.edu

Library of Congress Cataloging-in-Publication Data

Castillo, Debra A.
    Border women : writing from la frontera / Debra A. Castillo and María Socorro Tabuenca Córdoba.
        p.    cm. — (Cultural studies of the Americas ; v. 9)
    Includes bibliographical references and index.
    ISBN 0-8166-3957-4 (hc : acid-free paper) — ISBN 0-8166-3958-2 (pbk. : acid-free paper)
    1. American literature—Mexican American authors—History and criticism.    2. American literature—Mexican-American border region—History and criticism.    3. American literature—Women authors—History and criticism.    4. Women and literature—Mexican-American border region.    5. Mexican-American border region—Intellectual life.    6. Mexican-American border region in literature.    7. Mexican American women—Intellectual life.    8. Mexican American women in literature.    I. Tabuenca Córdoba, María Socorro, 1955–    II. Title. III. Series.
    PS153.M4 C33 2002
    810.9'9287'08968—dc21

                                                                                    2002009357

Printed in the United States of America on acid-free paper

The University of Minnesota is an equal-opportunity educator and employer.

12  11  10  09  08  07  06  05  04  03  02          10  9  8  7  6  5  4  3  2  1

*Para Aydé y Clementin de Coquis*

*Para mi familia en Tijuana/San Diego
—Queña, Pili, Gude, y Maru—de Debbie*

# Contents

# 1. Reading the Border, North and South

Very few places have been subjected to as much verbal abuse as the border between the United States and Mexico.
> —*Rolando J. Romero, "Border of Fear, Border of Desire"*

In a recent essay, Etienne Balibar comments that he first became aware of the equivocal and vacillating nature of borders during an afternoon of beer and chocolate with a fisherman from Pátzcuaro. Borders, the French philosopher learned, do not always work in the same way, and people bring different baggage with them when they cross. The man explained to Balibar why his attempts to cross the border into the United States always met with failure:

> because, he told me, "there is a letter missing" in Tarasca (his maternal language); "hace falta una letra, entiendes amigo." This letter, lost from time immemorial, can never be recovered. And this letter is the one you have to have to cross the northern border.

Balibar goes on to comment that this impossible recuperation of the missing letter, and with it the ability to cross into the United States, is nonreciprocal:

for never in his life will the gringo tourist recover the letter that is missing in English, or French, or German, and nonetheless he will cross the border as often as he wants for as long as he wants, to the point that it will lose its materiality. (227)

There is much to ponder in this anecdote, about imaginary and material borders, about Mexican immigration and gringo tourism, about the relative weight of the words of an indigenous Mexican fisherman and a French tourist/philosopher, about the way in which the northern Mexican border serves from the one side as a definitive barrier and from the other as an inconsequential (immaterial, metaphorical) line. The fisherman's missing letter almost too neatly fits into an allegorical articulation of current theoretical discussions of culture as something constructed through discourse. From this perspective it becomes all too easy to reimagine his confrontation with the northern border as a dissonance in signification, a site of discursive contestation. Thus, while it may seem that the literary-critical establishment has in recent years developed an allergy to fixed taxonomies, our profession has not yet been able to escape entirely from the ancient art of the catalogue, as if we too were looking for a missing letter that will provide a metaphorical key to break through an intellectual barrier/border. Metaphors like the "migrant" (Hall), "nomad" (Bradotti), "frontier" (Grossberg), "hybrid" (Bhabha), "circuit" (Rouse), "fringe" (Burgin), "margin" (Hutcheon) help to make possible an alternative cognitive map in the contemporary social space.

Furthermore, these discussions of the individual's interaction with this abstract space, often vaguely defined with the equally metaphorical term *border,* have served as points of departure for powerful contemporary theories that attempt to explain modern sociocultural phenomena.[1] In this respect, too, the interplay between Balibar and the fisherman, between Balibar and the reader of his academic essay (in its original French or translated English), also bears upon a concern forcefully articulated by Bruce Robbins:

the gendered and classed privilege of mobile observation in a world of tight borders and limited visibility corresponds to a traditional self-image of criticism itself. . . . It is an article of our contemporary faith that . . . intellectuals and academics are not detached but *situated.* (248–49)

Reading together Balibar and Robbins reminds us how equivocal this situatedness can become for the western intellectual, who has access to the facile border-crossing ability denied his interlocutor. Robbins continues:

> The anticosmopolitan jargon of the authentically particular and the authentically local provides no escape from or political alternative to the realm of the professional. It simply conceals the exemplification, representation, and generalization in which any intellectual work, professional or not, is inescapably involved, its own included. (251)

It is simply too easy for us intellectuals to read the metaphorical potential of the missing letter without taking into account the very real material conditions of a closed border/barrier.

Undoubtedly, the theoretical discussion on the metaphorical border owes its most enduring debt to Gloria Anzaldúa's much commented on and cited 1987 *Borderlands/La Frontera.* It is in part due to her influence that the idea of "the border" has become very prominent in a number of academic disciplines since the mid-1980s, especially in the United States, where this image has served as a popular locus for discussion on the breakdown of monolithic structures. Scholars working in border studies have attempted, in Anderson's words, to "dismantle the patriarchal and Anglocentric confinements of the term 'American,' specifically as it relates to 'American literature'" (1). In this sense, Anzaldúa's border, like Balibar's and unlike the Mexican fisherman's, evokes the intellectual project of a discursively based alternative national culture while gesturing toward a more heterogeneous transnational space of identity formation.

The notion of the border has been used recurrently in the theoretical and critical arena in order to illustrate a privileged site of operations. Yet, for those involved in border studies on the Mexican side of the border, it is difficult to conceive of the border simply as a metaphor at the very moment in which we are seeking conceptual frameworks for the analysis of border literature. If the U.S. theoretically conceived border serves as an objective correlative for discussions of U.S. dominant culture and its resistant spaces, the Mexican border region, in a parallel manner, helps address the question of how and where to relocate discussions about mexicanidad. From the Mexican side, however, the borderline itself retains a stronger materiality than is typical in U.S.-based commentary, a not-unexpected result of the differential in ability to simply cross to the other side. Far too often, as for the Pátzcuaro fisherman, the geopolitical border looms as a puzzling barrier against which Mexican nationals' dreams are dashed and broken. At the same time, if border literary expression in Mexico is someday reduced to simply being a metaphor, it will be necessary for us to find the direction of such metaphors and the degree of scientific truth they may contain. By saying this we do not mean to imply that the border is "the possession of one or the other side" (Bruce-Novoa, "Metas monológicas, estrategias dialógicas," 13). But it is important to indicate that in order to think of the border "as a line shared by the inhabitants on both sides [in order that it be] open to transit" (ibid.), it is important either to take both sides—the United States and Mexico—into consideration or to be specific about which side one is going to talk about or study and to recognize the material and metaphorical differences involved in such transnational analyses. Otherwise, the "intellectual colonialism" from which the Mexican border has suffered to this day will be perpetuated to the detriment of both its primary referents—people in general or flesh-and-blood artists—and its literature.

In this book we propose to look at such questions through a reading of women's writing, including authors from both sides of the border across the region from Texas to California. When writing this book we intentionally chose to focus on short stories and fragmentary texts, not only because they are by far the most vital and exciting products of the new border narrative by women, but also because they speak most forcefully to the necessary rethinking of border theory from within the border area. Homi Bhabha has said that the border serves to place the polemic of culture in the realm of "the beyond." "The beyond," as he explains, is not a new horizon, nor does it pretend to leave out the past, since we live in a moment of transit, when time and space traverse each other to produce complex figures of difference and identity: past and present, in and out, inclusion and exclusion. This social space any longer corresponds to "the abstract cohesion of a compact national State . . . which can be defined because of its relation with a specific territory, neither to the oppositions between centers and peripheries, since our world does not work that way" (*Location of Culture*, 1–4). With human mobility, migration, or diaspora, either from rural to urban areas, from small cities to large metropolises, or from the Third World to the First, the concept of culture as an internally coherent autonomous universe can no longer be sustained. It is, then, important to rethink our habitat (home, city, country, world) not as a static place with peoples who enjoy fixed identities, but rather as dynamic territories and peoples with multiple identities.

If we agree that we are in a moment of "the beyond," or "the time-of-the-now," it becomes even more vital to rethink the importance of those immobile origin narratives and to observe the moments or processes that are produced in the articulation of cultural differences. Those spaces will be, in Homi Bhabha's terms, the places of the in-between, the interstices from which we can elaborate other strategies of being, which will allow us to create new places of identity, collaboration, and subversion in the precise moment of defining society itself. In his introduction to *Rethinking Borders,* John C. Welchman speaks about how crucial the theme of the border has become for many exhibits, intellectual projects, and conferences. However, he quite rightly indicates that in many of those cases a convincing critical framework has yet to be established for the border discourse. One of the signal goals of his project is precisely that of outlining this underexplored critical framework and developing a coherent perspective on the proliferation of border theories and practices that have constructed a new scenario on the debates regarding postmodernity, cultural studies, and postcolonialism.

What we define as "border theory" or "border writing" in the United States almost always refers to concepts such as these, rather than to any particular geographical area, though the U.S.-Mexico border is frequently called into reference in the margins of such arguments as the most salient test case for such theoretical analyses. South of the border, these terms allude more specifically to the region's literary output. Nevertheless, despite the increasing theoretical attention to the border area, literature from the Mexican border has been seriously understudied, both in Mexico, due in large part to its marginal geographic position within the country, and in the U.S. academic arena, where the rising trend of Chicana/o-based border theory has effectively captured the bulk of critical attention.

Thus, when one examines studies on border literature, two very distinct perspectives come into view: the Mexican perspective, which focuses on the literature produced within the region, and the U.S. perspective, which focuses on more abstract theoretical concerns with typical gestures in the direction of Chicano/a and Latin American literature. Despite numerous elements that would seem to suggest the affinity between U.S. and Mexican border theories and literatures, the asymmetry between the United States and Mexico also marks the differences between the two cultural projects. The border as perceived from the United States is more of a textual—theoretical—border than a geographical one. U.S. Chicana/o scholars use the border metaphor to create a multicultural space in the United States in order to erase geographical boundaries. They use the real geopolitical border to construct an alternative Chicano/a discourse and to denounce centralist hegemony in the United States, and sometimes—more rarely—in Mexico as well. Strikingly, however, the global phenomenon of transnationalization turns binational and local when we turn our gaze to the border zone. Despite the efforts of theoreticians to develop their analyses in an even-handed manner, the cultural products of these two countries fall into a distinct power differential, as is also true of the political realm. U.S. border literature occupies the dominant space, and Mexican border literature falls into a subordinate one. While there is no doubt that Chicano/a literature serves as an expression of a minority culture within the United States, nevertheless when it is put into the perspective of a transborder literary project, the disparity is clear. What and who crosses the border and what does not applies to literary texts as well as persons. In a balance of relative privilege the Chicano/a scholar's resistant text, with its limited distribution network within the U.S. dominant culture, is in a position of clear and distinct advantage when compared to the extraordinary difficulties attending Mexican border writers both within the Mexican dominant establishment and with respect to international border theoretical discussions. Added to this already complicated scenario, we could also speak of the disarticulation of Mexican literature, and the tension between dominant and border cultures within the two countries, which adds another layer of contradiction and complexity to the discussion.

When we turn to Mexican border literature, one of the more striking aspects of the sparse scholarship is its general lack of attention to such theoretical issues and, on the level of textual analysis, a tendency to ignore women's literary production. While women have been extremely active, only recently have they begun to be noticed as authors of significant creative works in the most important border cities (Tijuana,

Mexicali, and Juárez). What scholarship has been published on writers from the border has tended to study work by their male counterparts. The sparse creative writing workshops up until very recently have limited their support to men, and kept a distance between the male writers and those women who wanted to join the workshops. Public and private institutions did very little to support literary work, and the spaces for publication were reduced to a few literary reviews, which most of the time limited their pages to works by male writers. These boundaries excluded women writers from the opportunities to present their writings to the general public. Yet, in terms of a transborder literary theory, the women's work is far more compelling than the more publicized men's; in general, women authors tend to leave behind old literary and social conventions in order to conceive innovative writing forms, and to posit new subjectivities.

Since the mid-1990s, however, it has become possible to talk about a handful of Mexican women who are gaining visibility locally as well as nationally and, incipiently, internationally. Their writings are still primarily published in local newspapers, chapbooks, and magazines, and while it is tempting to speculate about the interaction of publishing outlets and creative efforts, the end result is a distinct preference for short forms. In their prose works, these authors favor vignettes, short stories, chronicles, and short novels; whether by choice or necessity, however, these short forms have come to define a particular quality of Mexican border writing by women. Interestingly enough, these emergent voices, while often very different from those of their Chicana counterparts, address analogous concerns, allowing us to read these women from both sides of the border together for a more nuanced exploration of the theory and practice of border writing.

A common trait with all of these writers is their tight imbrication of an awareness of how these issues of cultural location affect perception of the geopolitical border, along with a carefully calibrated exploration of the other, personal border of gender roles and gender consciousness. Thus, for example, Rosina Conde has declared that even before taking cognizance of the geographical border, the first border she was made aware of was the border of gender. Likewise, Rosario Sanmiguel claims in an interview that she does not remember living in a world without borders:

La frontera es un espacio muy violento. Te golpea por todas partes. El hecho de estar junto a los Estados Unidos y tener a la Migra vigilándonos todo el tiempo. La frontera es como la habitamos y como caminamos por todos sus espacios. Nos permea por todos lados. Ahi nos confundimos y nos mezclamos todos: ricos y pobres, mexicanos, chicanos y gringos, cholos y chorchos, hombres y mujeres, homosexuales y heterosexuales; primer mundo y tercero. La frontera es violenta, pero fascinante. Cuando descubres todos sus rincones, no te puedes separar de ella.

[The border is a very violent space. It strikes at you from every angle. The fact is that the United States is right next to us and the Migra is constantly watching our coming and going. The border is the way in which we dwell and walk through all its spaces. We all swarm through the air and intertwine: rich and poor, Mexicans and Chicanos, cholos and preppies, men and women, heterosexuals and homosexuals, First World and Third World. The border is violent but fascinating. When you discover every nook and cranny, you cannot stay away from it.]

In their exploration of these personal and political borders, the authors' living spaces are subverted and the characters rearticulate the home, the office, the streets, the hotels, the brothels, and even their own bodies. They transgress the traditional chronotopes of patriarchal literature through focusing on the narrative voice of a female subject (Díaz-Diocaretz, 91). Here, too, reading together the Mexican women with their Chicana counterparts provides a fruitful dialogue about the relationships of daily life and domestic space to a larger national reality, about the shift in perception provided by a doubly marginalized character—female and border dweller—with respect to the local cultural enclave, to the reinterpretation of dominant national culture, to the rethinking of transborder dynamics.

One dominant characteristic of both Mexican and Chicana texts is that they privilege orality. Their language is direct, and their speech is taken from everyday life. The narrative or lyric voice does not hesitate to express, when necessary, her sexuality or eroticism. Such characterizations can be found on a continuum between two poles: the individual and the social. On the one hand, the Mexican women frequently write about the exploration of the female body through the desire for the other, and/or the communion with the other; on the other, they often imagine their characters' interactions with the bars and brothels that define one of the most well-known social problematics of the region, with the tensions of migration to the North, with experiences of harassment as undocumented workers, and with the fearful interactions with the border patrol. These topics will also serve as a framework to discuss the exploitation of prostitutes, maquila workers, and undocumented women. At the same time, the Chicana writers frequently provide a complementary discussion of these social spaces, now from within— and resistant to—pressures of U.S. dominant culture. Here the tensions of migration are imagined from the other side, from the permeable border of assimilation and the more-difficult-to-transit spaces of racial discrimination.

Nelly Richard's excellent essay, "Cultural Peripheries: Latin America and Postmodern De-Centering," elaborates not only on the way in which the centers concentrate wealth and control its distribution, but also how those centers have had enough authority to confer and validate meaning on people, places, and things. Consequently, in order to decenter the centers, Richard considers it essential to incorporate the rhetoric of the other within the concerns of progressive intellectuals. Likewise, she emphasizes that it is fundamental to achieve the democratization of the mechanisms of cultural meaning which depend on the dehierarchization of those discourses that comprise the production circuits of critical discursive exchange. For Richard two types of forces impel dehierarchization: those that move theoreticians and critics of the so-called alternative postmodernity, who have decided to "use privilege to destroy privilege." The second force is that of the people who have emerged from the borders. For these people to use the border as a place of enunciation allows them to shift the constraints that cross the boundaries of cultural systems of distribution when they unveil the arbitrariety and the vulnerability of discourses of the center. Says Richard, Latin America

> uses (abuses) the postmodernist model in international competition (the parodic quote) in order to auto-consecrate itself postmodernistically as both pretender and impostor in the ceremony of the precedences and successions of the First World, in order to auto-consecrate itself as the usurper of the role of master of ceremonies. (220)

It is precisely this task of dehierarchization and reelaboration that we propose in this bifocal, binational study of women's writing. What remains in question is to what degree border writing in general duplicates the kind of "tricks of meaning" Richard adumbrates in her lucid discussion of the postmodern peripherical use of pastiche.

## THEORIES ABOUT THE U.S. BORDER

Harry Polkinhorn, one of the most prolific U.S.-based critics of border writing, considers border literature to be a discourse that cannot be confined within theoretical frameworks. For Polkinhorn, border writing stresses the importance of an *otherness* whose locus is to be found in a nonplace of transition that gives rise to either a game or a struggle between two or more languages and cultures. While Polkinhorn focuses on Chicano/a literature, the border as a geographical region becomes particularly important in his essay, "Alambrada: Hacia una teoría de la escritura fronteriza," in which he states that "the only way to understand the border is to cross it" (31). The perspectives of this critic, the way he views the border—and/or what makes it a border—occurs through looking from North to South. "Crossing the border" seems to provide simply a pretext for a more distanced reflection that will allow him to better evaluate the expression of his points of view on Chicano/a literary production. At the same time, Polkinhorn's metaphor of a war fought against contending centers of power is clearly indicative of a centralist bias. In this struggle, he imagines that Chicano/a literature and that of Mexico's northern border participate in analogous, if not identical, situations.

He considers border literature—Chicano/a literature in his case— to be subversive because it is a "bastard" form. Chicano/a literature is thought to be illegitimate because it has taken root in a transformation of linguistic code and an unawareness of Chicano/a identity and parentage, an unawareness of an external "we." According to this critic, this misbegotten offspring threatens the status quo. He views narrative identities in Chicano/a literature as being imprisoned between opposing forces caught in a no-man's land between the United States and Mexico that produces fragmented and marginal literature.

Polkinhorn sees the wire fence separating the two countries as a barrier that does not allow Chicano/a literature to cross over to the Mexican side. On the U.S. side, however, this no-man's land has extended its limits northward, far beyond its former confines. This reconceptualized image of the border is not particular to Polkinhorn but has become a commonplace in contemporary Chicano/a criticism, to the degree that the borderlands "become a Chicano Eden, the original paradise" (Romero, "Postdeconstructive Spaces," 230). It is no longer a matter of Mexicans, Cubans, Puerto Ricans, and Nuyoricans struggling separately against hegemonic centers of power within ethnically exclusive fields of conflict. Today a self-concept of Latinity is readily being embraced, academically and politically, by Chicanos/as, Nuyoricans, Latin Americans, and Spaniards living in the United States. Consequently, any discussion within the United States on "the border" addresses a much broader field of ethnic, class, and gender differences.[2]

Walter Mignolo's *Local Histories/Global Designs* offers one of the most complete and theoretically powerful surveys of recent discussions of the idea of the border in U.S., Latin American, Caribbean, European, and former British Commonwealth thought. Mignolo condenses his major contribution to this extensive body of theory through use of a metaphor: "By 'border thinking' I mean the moments when the imaginary of the modern world system cracks" (23). Later, he clarifies that this crucial organizing concept for his project derives not from a Platonic universal, but rather from the concrete and specific histories of the Spanish intervention in the Americas, and especially the fraught history of U.S.-Mexican and U.S.-Caribbean relations since the nineteenth century (67). Mignolo throughout this book is concerned with two seemingly contradictory impulses: first, to anchor his highly theoretical and "global" studies in local Latin American and U.S. minority practices, as well as in the special perspective derived from intellectuals like himself who move between two languages and two cultures, and, second, to track the effects of globalization, which in his study are notable for "creating the condition for and enacting the relocation of languages and the fracture of cultures" (293). Finally, for Mignolo, the most crucial insight of his discussion of what he alternatively calls border gnosis or border thinking is that this structure offers him the opportunity to imagine the possibility "of theorizing from the border (border as threshold and liminality, as two sides connected by a bridge, as a geographical and epistemological location)" (309).

It is precisely in this respect that Claire Fox raises a warning flag, and her book, *The Fence and the River*, has as its explicit goal a critique of the abstract or metaphorical concept of border so frequently evoked in theoretical discussions like Mignolo's. Fox comments that "even though the U.S.-Mexico border retains a shadowy presence in the usage of these terms, the border that is currently in vogue in the United States, both among Chicano/a scholars and among those theorists working on other cultural differences is rarely site-specific." Most typically, Fox finds, the concept of border is used to mark "hybrid or liminal subjectivities" in general, and when spatialized, "that space is almost always universal" (119).

Guillermo Gómez-Peña is perhaps one of the most well-known U.S.-based artists whose primary stock-in-trade has been his status as the authentic border subject-cum-postmodern native informant. Yet, Gómez-Peña creates precisely this sense of a generalized, deracinated borderness in his performances, and local referents are excluded in the analytic deployment of these same performances by writers and critics from both sides of the border, people like Néstor García Canclini and Homi Bhabha, who have picked up on Gómez-Peña's articles and performances as archetypal representations of the border self. Eduardo Barrera succinctly summarizes his concerns about this issue:

> The artist's texts are the product of his fascination with the border's synchronism. It would be naive to think that they have not been influenced by post-structuralist bibliography. Gómez-Peña fabricates his border by drinking from the same theoretical watering holes as the academics who test their arguments with his texts. This quasi-incestuous relationship has turned into a vicious circle which excludes primary referents. Gómez-Peña's border turns into the Border of García Canclini and Homi Bhabha, and the artist turns into the Migrant. (16)

The U.S.-Mexican "border" popularized by Gómez-Peña displaces the actual physical border and all it contains. The release of his video *Border Brujo*, his performance of "The New World (B)order," and the publication of *Warrior for Gringostroika* (1993) have led audiences to think that the border represented by this artist is truly "the" U.S.-Mexican border.[3] Notoriously, at the same time, local Mexican artists reject his vision with the comment that his border in no way corresponds to theirs. This opinion was expressed, for example, in interviews with culture researcher José Manuel Valenzuela and writer Rosina Conde. Conde's comment is particularly apposite, as she belonged to the Border Art Workshop/Taller de Arte Fronterizo (BAW/TAF), which Gómez-Peña founded. Conde left the workshop, she says, because they wanted to present a border art much different than ours, but this was not the problem since art can be represented in a number of forms. The problem was that they wanted to impose their will. They wanted to turn us into pseudo-Chicanos/as, or into a fronterizo/a that did not represent us. They wanted us (the Mexicans) to agree with their proposals just to get an audience. This was not right as it was a matter of each one of us making his or her own contribution while respecting other individuals and cultures, but this did not turn out to be the case.[4]

Gómez-Peña's colonializing gesture can be interpreted using one of Rosaura Sánchez's concepts from "Ethnicity, Ideologies, and Academia." Sánchez discusses the ideological strategies that mainstream culture uses to mystify the relationship between minority cultures and itself; by means of such mystification strategies, U.S. cultural imperialism extends itself beyond the geopolitical boundaries of the United States. However, "being affected, influenced, and exploited by a culture is one thing and participating fully in that culture is another" (81). If we relate Sánchez's example to "the border" as metaphor, we can note that the efforts to erase the borders and the appropriation of categories such as that of the migrant, and even of the border itself, facilitate the erasure of the physical border, along with its flesh-and-blood migrants, writers, and readers, as well as the artistic expression that is produced on the Mexican side.

It is important to recognize that recent interpretations of the border in the United States have been innovative in their attempt to equate the border with the boundaries of the Americas, boundaries that are in a state of transformation and are therefore culturally unstable. Notwithstanding, in practice, it is also true that the United States, after the signing of NAFTA, has reinforced its geopolitical border with Mexico and, consequently, social and cultural exchange has become more difficult than it was before. As a result, the performances of Gómez-Peña, rather than offering "alternative reality" or creating an internationalist dialogue, have mistakenly projected the mere image of a migrant while displacing the flesh-and-blood referent. The latter "is left alone and exploited by a very real blockade and Resolution 187 after his or her existential surplus value has been extracted" (Barrera, 16). In the same fashion, Gómez-Peña's artistic portrayal of the border suppresses numerous other artistic representations of the border and makes them disappear.

The work of Gómez-Peña has also influenced cultural criticism in

Mexico. For example, Néstor García Canclini does not consult the works of writers and artists from Tijuana in order to carry out his work on "hybrid cultures" in that city. Instead, he focuses on Guillermo Gómez-Peña's performances and on his polemical essays on border life. In light of the fact that Guillermo Gómez-Peña is perceived as an "outsider" in Tijuana's cultural circles, it is ironic that hegemonic critics such as García Canclini validate Gómez-Peña by accepting the latter as "the fronterizo" while presenting Tijuana as the representation of *the* hybrid space.

Unfortunately, such intellectual colonialism, as seen in the work of Gómez-Peña, is not the only factor responsible for the lack of specialized criticism directed toward literary production on the Mexican border. The reconceptualization of Chicano/a critical discourse from the mid-1980s to the present decade has also had an impact. This change has favored an attempt to capture a global perspective of the border in an effort, as proposed by Héctor Calderón and José David Saldívar in *Criticism in the Borderlands,* "to remap the borderlands of theory and theorists" (7). That book does, in fact, make a serious effort to disarticulate the borders of the monolithic discourse of American literature in favor of a more expansive definition that will give greater currency to the work of Chicano/a writers and other writers of color in the United States. Nevertheless, from the point of view of an effort to look for a binational border theory, their book again falls short, in that it concerns itself solely with U.S. local concerns: its criticism on the borderlands is restricted to the U.S. side of the border.

One more example underlines this point. Perhaps because of her zeal to erase borders, Emily Hicks uses terms such as *biculturalism, bilingualism,* and *bi-conception of reality* as foundational concepts for her analysis in her book, *Border Writing* (xxv). This is a laudable and intriguing proposal, yet in presuming that all border residents who read "are informed by two codes of reference" (226) and, therefore, capable of being categorized as uniformly bilingual, she runs the risk of excluding a large number of primary referents. For example, there are few bilingual writers on Mexico's border with the United States and even fewer who are bicultural. Nor are there many readers in the region who can be characterized as either bilingual or bicultural. Thus, Emily Hicks's border writers and readers are either ideal types, or they are seen through a Bakhtinian theoretical perspective on "border culture," according to which any and all readers and writers are border residents; therefore they are bicultural in the broadest and most inclusive sense of the term *culture*.[5] In Hicks's attempt to erase borders and present us with ideal types of creators/writers, she obscures the social, cultural, and economic policies that affect very real human beings who inhabit the borders.

In the Chicano/a attempt to decolonize the border, there is still a trace of "a longing for unity and cohesion" (Romero, "Postdeconstructive Spaces," 229), as can be noted in Gloria Anzaldúa's search for a mythological space in *Borderlands/La Frontera*. In the same way that Gómez-Peña has been legitimated as "the migrant," critics have made Anzaldúa "the representative" of "the border." In Anzaldúa's work the border also functions primarily as a metaphor, in that the border space as a geopolitical region converges with discourses of ethnicity, class, gender/sex, and sexual preference. Nevertheless, Anzaldúa's book, despite its multiple crossings of cultural and gender borders—from ethnicity to feminisms, from the academic realm to the work of blue-collar labor—tends to essentialize relations between Mexico and the United States. Her third country between the two nations, the borderlands, is still a metaphorical country defined and narrated from a First World perspective. Her story is less ludic than that of Gómez-Peña, and more anchored in real referents, but these referents are defined solely in terms of an outcast status. Anzaldúa's famous analysis does not take into cognizance the many other othernesses related to a border existence; her "us" is limited to U.S. minorities; her "them" is U.S. dominant culture. Mexican border dwellers are also "us" and "them" with respect to their Chicana/o counterparts; they can in some sense be considered the "other" of both dominant and U.S. resistance discourses.

In contrast with Hicks, *Borderlands'* perspective more closely approximates the everyday life of the primary cultures of the valley of Texas. For Anzaldúa the border space is a place inhabited, from an Anglo perspective, by strange and mulish persons. Here the Texan brand of capitalism has made its mark by dispossessing the valley's inhabitants. In her book Anzaldúa articulates a cultural and social wall between white Americans and Mexican Americans, again in contrast to the diffusion of borders as observed in Hicks, or in Calderón and Saldívar's work. Gloria Anzaldúa is critical of U.S. authoritarianism, and in her writings she challenges the hegemony of monolithic U.S. discourse. It is in no wise the same, however, to belong to an official minority within the United States as it is in Mexico. Anzaldúa and Gómez-Peña speak from the interstices of U.S. dominant culture and they have self-authorized their hybrid discourse in the social construction of difference. Nevertheless, upon becoming authorized and canonized voices of that difference, they are ineluctably allied to the practices of political and economic power on an international level, even given the fact that—ironically—their writing and their performative actions resist such practices. In contrast with Gómez-Peña's appropriation and promotion of his "unique migrant self," Anzaldúa writes about been tired of being "repeatedly token[ized]" (*Making Face, Making Soul,* xvi), since there are a lot of women of color living in the borderlands.

If we were to follow out the implications of such arguments, if we cross the border literally as well as metaphorically, we would have to note that because of the comparatively fewer social, economic, and political advantages enjoyed by Mexico's northern border states, Mexican writers in the region do not possess the publishing resources available to minority groups in the United States. This means that it is not the same to be a minority and have to resist the center in the United States as in Mexico. For example, small independent publishing houses, such as Azar Publications of Chihuahua, Between Lines (Entrelíneas), Earrings and Bracelets (Aretes y pulseras) of Tijuana, and Puente Libre Editores of Juárez, or government-supported presses, such as the Autonomous University of Baja California, UNISON, and the Autonomous University of Juárez, while publishing and disseminating literature from the border area do not have the resources or the recognition, range of design possibilities, press runs, or distribution outlets of even such "minor" publishing houses as Aunt Lute Press, Kitchen Table Press, Third Woman Press, and Arte Público Press in the United States.

As can be observed in this brief review, the border as perceived from the United States is more textual and theoretical than geographical, whereas from the Mexican side the geopolitical referent never entirely disappears. While we could say that each side has a "missing letter" that makes crossing difficult and challenges comprehension, the different cultural and political factors that influence intellectual and artistic production remain ineluctably tied to economic issues and local conditions of relative privilege and deprivation or discrimination. Carl Gutiérrez-Jones concisely pulls together both the trends and the stakes:

[S]tepping away from this specific conflict enough to resituate ourselves in the context of the various border culture theories considered here, it seems apparent that such theorization will of necessity concern itself with the institutionalization not only of disciplinary techniques manipulating desire but also of particular epistemological constructions of what can and cannot be "legitimately" known. Several avenues might be pursued as critics delve into these dynamics; one might, for instance, pursue an anatomy of the institutional practices that would sustain the anti-immigrant epistemological stance. However, as the theoretical trends noted suggest, even greater attention will need to be paid to the mediation among diverse "subject-affects" and specifically situated institutional designs. (111)

In both *The Dialectics of Our America* and his later book, *Border Matters,* José David Saldívar sets out to traverse a space impregnated with Latinity by which Latino and Latin American writers of diverse backgrounds set out to articulate "a new transgeographical conception of American culture—one more responsive to the hemisphere's geographical ties and political crosscurrents than to the narrow national ideologies" (*Dialectics,* xi). Saldívar's methodologically rigorous and thorough studies offer important points of departure for our work in this book, while at the same time these revisionary projects are clearly set within the context of rethinking U.S. literary and cultural studies. In them, he strategically explores and explodes the melting-pot myth with a more subtle rereading of the historical and cultural record to take cognizance of migrant flows from Mexico, the Caribbean, and Central and South America, and their impact on U.S. national culture, asking, for instance, the crucial question: "what changes, for example, when American culture and literature are understood in terms of 'migration' and not only immigration?" (*Border Matters,* 8). In both books Saldívar proposes that it is difficult to theorize in general at present because current theory is not written from a critical "distance," but from "a place of hybridity and betweenness in a global border composed of historically connected postcolonial spaces" (*Dialectics,* 152). In addition to his reflections on being in a hybrid space of interpolation, the global borders he defines are more real to a position of articulation from within the border area; after all, the U.S.-Mexican border is indeed a place in which (post)colonial spaces are historically connected.

Like Saldívar, who knows that in order to study the border it is necessary to take both sides into consideration, Rolando Romero reminds us of the need to specify which side(s) of the border is (are) been analyzed in any given study. In his judiciously wrought "Border of Fear, Border of Desire," for example, Romero examines cultural and political texts from both Mexico and the United States and traces out the institutional structures undergirding typical theoretical gestures and informing common metaphors. As he notes in his conclusion to the article, "the conflicting views of the border suggest that most of the critics project their own assumptions and Utopias. Under the guise of a quest for knowledge, the researcher invests the Other with non-existent cultural signification" (62). Romero's cautionary words are well taken. As he reminds us, "we will not be in a position to recognize the allegories of the self in the narrations of the border" unless we make the effort to unpack the metaphorical overdetermination of such now-standard metaphorical usages.

## LITERATURE FROM THE MEXICAN BORDER

If, generally speaking, the projection of a borderlands theory represents for many Chicano/a writers and thinkers the imaginative return to a metaphorically conceived Mexican/Latin American cultural tradition which serves as a source of empowerment, this tradition is accessed more often through memory and secondary texts than through actual visits to the Mexican side of the geopolitical boundary line. This tendency toward a metaphorical, rather than literally based appropriation of border experience underlies one of the crucial differences with those border dwellers who live on and cross over between the two nations on a daily basis. For such people, it is difficult to see the border as a metaphor or as a utopia, although at the same time there is a deep awareness that repetitive movement does not guarantee a more correct perception or a clear-cut representational model.

In Mexico the study of what is referred to as the literature of the northern border began in the mid-eighties. The emergence of this literary form, as well as its analysis, derive from a coincidence of specific political factors, reinforcing our perception that in order for this cultural movement to exist there needed to be more than a talent pool; certain minimal material resources had to become available. Francisco Luna and Rosina Conde, among others, agree that interest in border culture and its literature evolved at that time because of the obsession on the part of Mexico City authorities "por reforzar el fardo romántico de la identidad nacional" [to reinforce the romantic notion of national identity] (Luna, 79), to "cultivar y nacionalizar a los estados fronterizos, dándose de conocer lo que consideró la esencia de lo mexicano" [cultivate and nationalize the border states by revealing the essence of what it was to be Mexican] (Conde, "¿Dónde está la frontera?" 52) or, more crudely and probably more accurately, "por darles chamba a los cuates" [to give jobs to their buddies] (M. Villarreal, interview) through the Border Cultural Program (Programa Cultural de las Fronteras). These three responses clearly indicate the range of reactions to the program: to shore up a conflicted sense of national identity, to civilize the barbarians, and to continue centralized corruption by other means. At any rate, border literature was given a significant boost dating from 1985 with the influx of federal money to support cultural projects.

However, the conceptualization of this project is fraught with contradiction. If the central government's concern is primarily seen as one of "nationalization," it follows that the inhabitants of the northern states were still largely seen in the mid-1980s as an uncultured and potentially disruptive hybrid group, dangerously threatened by absorption into the U.S. culture next door. The centrist dominant discourse, then, would be geared toward promoting a process of homogenization with a very specific political agenda. At the same time, to remind us that the agenda is "romantic" in nature is to also evoke the centrist persistence of thinking in terms of tired clichés held over from nineteenth-century models of nation formation. To hint that the unspoken agenda was to provide opportunities for typically corrupt political appointments is also to voice the resistance of many border inhabitants to the process of centrist totalization.

What might be the political stake for then-president Miguel de la Madrid in maintaining a country distinguished as "muy mexicano" [very Mexican] through promoting regional cultural development? What would inspire such a program of wanting to reinforce an abstract Mexicanness at precisely this point in history? De la Madrid's border program was created in 1985, when Mexico was still suffering the effects of the 1982 crisis and the hegemony of the ruling party, the PRI, was being threatened, particularly by powerful conservative politicians in the north. As a political project, then, the program served to authorize and to include the all-too-often forgotten (and increasingly important) border population within the horizons of "lo nacional" [the national], and also—in this area of heavy investment in foreign industrial plants—helped to buttress with visible projects the rhetorical position that "el país no estaba en venta" [the country was not for sale] to transnational interests. The official project, then, to use Bhabha's terms, seemed to require "an originary narration of fulfillment" (*Location of Culture*, 51). It needed to sketch out the absent subject and make him/her present; it needed to identify itself within the concept of the savage border or to identify the savage with the civilizing force of national culture in order to impose upon the border another discourse, transforming and normalizing it within the national classificatory system. It is not too exaggerated to suggest that, in anticipation of NAFTA legislative approval, the border culture program projected a Mexico both educated and united in order to counteract national anxieties about appropriation or absorption by the United States.

A number of authors born in the border region, or whose work has been produced in that area, have refused to allow themselves to be considered border writers, specifically as a rejection of the political project underlying the Border Cultural Program. For Rosina Conde, for example, to accept the label "border writer" would be to accept as well the stereotype that the official project attempted to institutionalize and in fact perpetuated through the mechanisms of the state (Nelson, 1). José Javier Villarreal and Minerva Margarita Villarreal believe that being catalogued as border writers has the very real effect of preventing them from ever entering into the hallowed canon of "Mexican writers." Rosario Sanmiguel, on the other hand, considers that recognizing herself as a border writer means accepting as well her marginal position within the national literary scene:

> El día que me publique una editorial fuerte y que mi trabajo se difunda como el de Campbell o Gardea, dejaré de ser de la frontera para ser del centro; la frontera y lo fronterizo es estar fuera del ejercicio del poder. (interview)

> [The day that a large press publishes my work and it is distributed like that of Campbell or Gardea is the day that I will stop being from the border and begin being from the center. The border and borderness means being outside the exercise of power.]

From both sides of this discussion, then, the label "border writer" becomes a highly charged, ideological issue. At the same time, all these writers consider literature from the northern border to be their own particular contribution to national literature. They do not see the task of addressing a border reality as an imposition—after all, they had been writing and commenting on this region, and had been meeting to read and discuss each others' works, long before the federal government stepped in with a new program to allow them to achieve some minimal local visibility and distribution for their works. Although official patronage through government programs was largely designed to put a "chastity belt on Mexican nationality in order to protect us from foreign influence," and border residents were forced "to adopt a role dictated to them which was based on false premises" (Luna, 80, 52), other social factors, combined with the government's program, contributed to enabling literature to gain wider currency more quickly in northern Mexico than it had in the past.

While resistance remained in some quarters, most writers from the border region took advantage of this brief transformatory period to negotiate and to authorize their own cultural projects through making use of the possibilities opened by these official channels. They took advantage of the centrist rhetoric to make present a movement that had been gestating in limited circles in the region for many years, but whose projects in a larger context were stagnating for lack of official support. Francisco Amparán has made it clear that many of the pre-1968 writers (1955–60) who had been born outside Mexico City took this project seriously, remaining in their places of origin and forming local literary workshops. Gabriel Trujillo Muñoz agrees. Trujillo notes that the workshops helped poets to become more aware of their potential and to acquire more critical perspectives. Humberto Félix Berumen, in "El cuento entre los bárbaros del norte," discusses other factors that rapidly opened new avenues for the development of literature in the northern border states: a burgeoning middle class, the demand for educational and cultural services, the association of writers who decided to produce and publish their work in their places of origin, the presence of a market of readers, and the increased diversity of local publications.

In general, the consensus is that the literature of the northern border states experienced dynamic and significant growth during the eighties. The emergence of regional literary forms was clearly indicative of a tendency to reject the federal government in Mexico City and to affirm regional interests, as paradoxical as this may seem in light of support programs subsidized by the federal government. Of course, the centralist policy of "domesticating the barbarians of the North and teaching them what culture is" demonstrates a total unawareness and lack of respect for the officially designated narrative other while ostensibly favoring the region by promoting forums on northern border literature.[6] Similarly, the Mexican government's promotion of decentralization and the promise of NAFTA during the 1980s, although presented as panaceas, have resulted in consequences such as the population boom along Mexico's border with the United States. This result is all too closely related to the processes mentioned by Amparán and Berumen, which are, as we saw previously, reflected in the perspectives of Conde, Luna, and Villarreal. Nevertheless, considering the lack of autonomy of Mexican states, it would be naive to believe that any artistic-cultural phenomena could be promoted without the previous blessing (or curse) of the Mexican government. That is to say, one can hardly discuss the manifestation of artistic production in the northern states without acknowledging the fact that the matter first passed from one desk to another within the federal government's bureaucracy in Mexico City.

One of the most visible products of this infusion of funds were the series of books published by the Consejo Nacional de la Cultura y de las Artes (National Commission on Culture and the Arts). These books have become the official version of the regional literatures from the border states and for that very reason have been controversial. Berumen, for example, says that the idea behind the project was a good one, but that the volumes themselves are insufficient to give a sense of the depth of literary cultures in the region ("La literatura," 20–21). Especially controversial was the government's tendency to appoint volume editors from Mexico City, frequently giving the job to people with little direct knowledge of the literatures they were supposed to anthologize.

The prologues of the volumes from border states which make up the collection Letras de la república[7] offer little discussion of literature dealing specifically with the border area or with the emergence of "border literature." Nevertheless, these prologues all have certain elements in common: particularly, they all signal the need for the region or state to be recognized by the community itself and they describe an effort to seek redress for exclusion, neglect, and abandonment by Mexico City.

These prologues also agree that the period of the greatest publication and promotion of each state's literature began in the late eighties, and that cultural magazines and workshops have furthered literary production in the region. These anthologies discuss a "testimonial vocation as it relates to natural and human landscapes" and an "interest in structuring a discourse in which contradictions of cultural identity" can be resolved or given priority (Cortés Bargalló, 63). They also speak of a sense of regional autonomy and identity that subsists in a tense relationship with Mexico City's efforts to promote a homogeneous (but implicitly centrist) concept of "Mexicanness."

Ignacio Betancourt, Patricio Bayardo, and Chicano critic Francisco A. Lomelí are among the first scholars to begin to sketch out informed analyses of border literature. Betancourt, in a very brief article, comments on various works by both Mexican and Chicano authors. Although the conclusions reached in the article are suggestive rather than fully developed, Betancourt's work is interesting because his concept of the border includes both border regions and, consequently, their literatures: specifically, Chicano/a literature and the literature of Baja California, Mexico, in which Betancourt is an active participant.[8] Bayardo, in *El signo y la alambrada,* surveys the literature of Baja California as well as providing a historical explanation for the permutations of culture in the California border space from 1848 (when the United States took control of upper California) up through the 1980s.[9] Although we do not share his traditional and monolithic vision of Mexico, he nevertheless deserves recognition as one of the first thinkers to carry out a systematic effort to understand the uniqueness of Mexican border life without stereotyping it.

In the seminal article "En torno a la literatura de la frontera: ¿Convergencia o divergencia?," Lomelí develops his concept of the border as a dynamic site of socioeconomical, cultural, and political exchange and resistance, and as a unifying element between Mexicans and Chicanas/os. He also talks about Mexican border literature and comments on two Chicano authors. He mentions some of the difficulties of defining "border literature" because of the particularities of this geopolitical space and the cultural differences among the inhabitants on both sides of the border. Lomelí's essay is of great value since he makes very clear why it is important to rethink the category of "Literature," directly confronting the kind of bias so succinctly captured in Mexican writer Carlos Montemayor's declaration: "La literatura de la frontera

norte (es) un mito, un error" [Mexican Northern Border literature is
a myth, a mistake] (27). Lomelí argues that scholars and writers who
adopt Montemayor's position in effect only take into consideration an
"official" literature, which is of course canonical literature or "good"
literature, disregarding any national, regional, or gender-conscious literatures. Lomelí discusses the significance of the broader and more nuanced understanding of what is called "literature" and the valid claim of
the border(s) literature(s) to be reread and evaluated in an appropriate
context.

Still, the study of this literature is in its early stages since very few
critics have done substantive research and most of the work is descriptive. Sergio Gómez Montero, Humberto Félix Berumen, Gabriel Trujillo
Muñoz, and Francisco Luna agree on most points of discussion, and
these four authors have served as the most consistent commentators on
the literature of Mexico's northern border region. These essayists have
suggested that in order to study the literature of northern Mexico, one
must not view either its literature or geography as a massive whole.
The region is made up of diverse topographies, natural resources, and
climates. Urban development differs significantly from one state to the
next. Consequently, contrary to the concept of "border literature" in
the United States, "la literatura de la frontera norte" is a phenomenon
set into motion differentially by the unique cultural factors existing in
different places.

These authors believe that the literature of Mexico's northern border emerged and coalesced during the 1970s. This holds particularly
true for the more important urban centers of the border states. Literary
production—and, on most occasions, publication—takes place in cities
located on the border or in other important urban centers in Mexico's
northern states. Narrative and poetry stand out as the most widely employed literary forms. Among the diverse themes of both genres, the
border's geographic realities (mountains, the sea, the desert, the borderline, urban centers) are fundamental. The colloquial and vernacular quality of the language permits the portrayal of the region's typical linguistic
characteristics; however, bilingualism and code-switching are not common practices in the literary works they study. The re-creation of everyday life is given priority, and the representation of urban space is one of
its unique traits, without falling prey to the provincial costumbrismo of
the past.

The authors producing this literature were born, for the most part, since the 1950s, and their work began to be published in the 1980s. They can be placed into three different groups: (1) those who have produced a body of well-established work that is recognized both in Mexico City and internationally, including Gerardo Cornejo, Jesús Gardea, Ricardo Elizondo, Alfredo Espinosa, Rosina Conde, Daniel Sada, José Javier Villarreal, and Minerva Margarita Villarreal; (2) those authors such as Mario Anteo, Francisco Amparán, Inés Martínez de Castro, Luis Humberto Crosthwaite, José Manuel Di Bella, Patricia Laurent, Margarita Oropeza, Rosario Sanmiguel, Federico Schafler, Micaela Solís, Regina Swain, and Gabriel Trujillo Muñoz who have managed to establish solid reputations within the national literary scene; and (3) those writers who participate in creative endeavors that are not widely recognized outside of their local communities.[10] It is worth emphasizing that not all border writers write about their regional contexts or experiences; a number place their writings at a distance from the region's temporality and its sociological conflicts.

One of the principal impediments to potential literary delimitation is the lack of critical studies dedicated to the analysis of the diverse literary expressions found in individual genres. At present, narrative has far more often been the subject of research than other genres, although poetry is the form most preferred by authors. This critical gap is probably due to the fact that the narrative has been the literary form that has received the most attention both nationally and internationally. Theater has received virtually no attention, in spite of the fact that there are writers and critics in Mexico's border states dedicated to dramaturgy. Although institutions of higher education have personnel involved in literary research, little is done to promote conferences specifically designed to further critical analysis of contemporary regional literature. With the exception of the meticulous studies on literary-cultural production carried out by the Department of the Humanities in Hermosillo, Sonora, and in the Autonomous University of Baja California, which has a professorship in regional literature, no other border institutions have permanent seminars or courses dealing with contemporary regional literature.[11]

Defining the territorial limits of the "northern border" is another difficulty we face. In his works dealing with border narrative Berumen includes both those writers who live and work in urban centers as well as those who live 900 kilometers to the south of the U.S.-Mexican border.

One of the arguments used to justify these limits is Berumen's contention that one must not approach the region from the vantage point of its administrative characteristics when discussing literary phenomena, but rather its sociocultural traits. This is perhaps Berumen's least convincing argument, since there may very well be more differences than similarities. However, among Berumen's great achievements, it is worth mentioning the periods he has established for the contemporary narrative, his analysis of literary phenomena as sociocultural processes, and, most especially, his inquiry into the role of labeling or classifying these phenomena as "border literature"—*literatura de la frontera*.

In addition to thinking about the region's growth and development, its cities, and the idiosyncrasies and regionalisms of its inhabitants, one must also consider the border discourse of the last two decades in terms of its relevancy to the inhabitants of the region in general, and to its writers in particular.[12] It may strike one as odd that Fernando Martínez Sánchez, in his prologue to an anthology on Coahuila, considers this state to fall within the limits of what is referred to as border culture, or that the cities with the greatest literary production in the state, Torreón and Saltillo, are located 700 and 400 kilometers south of the border. This oddity points up the question of the border region's geographic limits and the place of articulation of its writers vis-à-vis traditionally recognized northern cultural centers such as Monterrey and Chihuahua. The discussion has gone principally in two directions: on the one hand, the literature that is produced in these two cities is not considered as being marginalized from Mexican national culture, given the support that the writers and the urban centers have enjoyed (despite the tension between Mexico City and Monterrey that Minerva Margarita Villarreal stresses in her anthology *Nuevo León, Brújula solar*). In considering the literary-cultural patronage of border cities before the 1980s, Monterrey and Chihuahua, although lacking Mexico City's resources, do compete for and obtain more support from the capital than does the border area, and they have more resources to begin with. On the other hand, there are those who would argue that—the political economy of culture aside— given the distance of the two cities to the south, accurate assessments of the degree of "borderness" cannot be reliably made by anyone living so far from the border that they seriously question whether or not they actually live within the border region.

The two preceding perspectives can be termed *regionalist* and *es-*

*sentialist*. The proponents of the first perspective have drawn attention for commentary that has been critical of cultural institutions in Chihuahua and Monterrey because of their favored status in receiving official patronage.[13] This perspective reflects an antagonistic relationship between those who reside in the relatively more dominant urban centers in the north and those who live on the border. Hence Humberto Félix Berumen's suggestion that the border be divided in terms of its socioeconomic characteristics turns out to be unconvincing. The essentialist view would establish a fixed border literature in which border writers would all be cut from the same cloth. In this taxonomy, border writers, in order to be considered as such, would have to reflect solely on matters having to do with the border.

Is border literature about, on, of, or from the border? In Mexico, for whom have the terms "the border's literature" or "border literature"—*literatura de la frontera* or *literatura fronteriza*—been coined? There is still a great deal of confusion on this matter. Academics tend to assume that border literature is comprised of those Mexican works that focus on regional themes. The origin of this misunderstanding lies in the fact that writers from Mexico City who write about the border are generally included in literary analyses of northern border literature, often to the detriment of less well-known writers from the border area who may or may not use local referents in their work. Danny Anderson, for example, posits that the perspectives of Laura Esquivel, Carlos Fuentes, Ricardo Garibay, Ethel Krauze, and Paco Ignacio Taibo II, among others who write about but not from the border, have provided a historical storehouse of "representations which help one to distinguish the uniqueness and the often responsive nature of literary production on the border and in border states" (6). It is also certain that by relying exclusively on these more canonical works one is likely to engage in a Gómez-Peña–type intellectual colonialism. This colonialism is made manifest when one accepts the works of these writers as representative of the border, instead of seeking out other texts by writers from the area. As a result, those authors who write from the border find their work displaced from public consciousness in favor of the latest thematically related "border" book by a well-known centrist writer. It is, therefore, signally important to make the distinction between the border as expressed in literature as opposed to the literature actually produced on the border. The differentiation helps prevent the erasure of Mexican border writers and their writings in favor of works by either well-known Mexican or Chicano/a writers.

When studying the introductions to the Letras de la república collection, a number of peculiarities characteristic of northern border literature can be noted. If we accept the validity of the border division suggested by Berumen as well as the posited ecotonal community of Gómez Montero,[14] the prologues, as a whole, seem to be discussing a regional literature far more comprehensive than each state offers individually. The region proposed as the northern border region brings to the forefront of critical discussion Mexico's decentralization and the North's creation of new artistic forms. It reflects a literary movement whose textual reconstruction began in the late 1970s and is gaining literary currency today. With this in mind, we can begin the articulation of a textual border, analogous to that defined in Chicano/a literature, in which a Mexican geographic space would also acquire a generalizable value, not in relationship to the United States or the rest of Mexico or Latin America, but in terms of the bonds existing among the border states. In this rearticulation, the main differences between the literature on the two sides of the border may very well persist: for Chicano/a literature the border is an abstraction, an inexhaustible utopia, a "Garden of Eden." In Mexican border literature the topic of the border occupies an ordinary space, a place that is infrequently represented in writing. It is, in this literature, more than a trope or locus amoenus. It is part of a literary regional movement that, like the border itself, is in a state of constant development: dynamic and forever changing.[15]

MEXICAN/CHICANA WOMEN WRITERS

It is the purpose of this book to contribute to the rethinking of border theory and border practice through a nuanced engagement with texts by women writers from both sides of the U.S./Mexico border, emphasizing the contributions of writers whose work, in Spanish, English, or a mixture of the two languages, calls into question accepted notions of border identities. Each chapter reads a different border writer and uses her work as a point of departure to re-elaborate a more binationally sensitive and feminocentric border theory.

Chapter 2 focuses on Alicia Gaspar de Alba, who was born in El Paso and wrote her collection of short stories, *The Mystery of Survival*, in the 1980s as she moved from El Paso to Juárez to other cities in both Mexico and the United States. Her work, both in this collection of stories and in her poems, is less easily recoupable to the emerging Chicana canon than that of fellow creative writers like Helena Viramontes or Sandra Cisneros, partly because her aggressively bilingual style poses a serious course-adoption dilemma to the primarily Anglophone institutional structure for most such courses in the United States. Thus, the theoretical question that engages us in this chapter is precisely that of the place of a binational, bilingual writer in the national literary consciousness. Two of the eleven stories in *Mystery of Survival* are written entirely in Spanish. Another sequence of stories, focused on the curandera Estrella González, rely for their impact on a de-exoticized acceptance of the powers of this traditional healer. In each case, the weighted choice of Spanish or English or Spanglish in these stories evokes the tensions of living in two languages and two cultures, languages that conflict not only with each other, but also with the presumed cultural underpinnings that, in the border zone, are frequently highly charged. Gaspar de Alba's narrative is marked in a particular manner by her own social commitment, her own imbrication in a border reality that has left the northern border of Mexico out of official histories of that country, and at the same time has left Chicano history out of official histories of the United States. Doubly set adrift from official historiography, the Chicana writer attempts to piece together an alternative, rooted, genealogical tale.

Of all the narratives written in Northern Mexico in the last decade, that of Rosario Sanmiguel is surely among the most significant, and chapter 3 of this book is dedicated to her collection of stories, *Callejón Sucre y otros relatos* [Sucre Street and other stories]. These stories respond forcefully to the demand for a border literature that is firmly anchored in the language and the landscapes of her home city, Juárez. This urban environment is the point of reference for all the stories, and the main characters frequently play out the domestic dramas between mothers and daughters. At the same time, this polyphonic text captures the social diversity of languages, individual voices, and multilayered social discourses from both sides of the border. While the stories make no programmatic effort to define a border identity as such, the subjectivities described in them could be understood nowhere else. Nevertheless, Sanmiguel's stories sit oddly against the body of border theories common to the U.S. cultural context and it is, perhaps, only because of work like hers that we can begin to explore the reasons why this is so. As noted above, what we understand as border theory tends to be written from north to south—that is, from the United States to Mexico—and the gesture of crossing borders serves most often in such studies only as a pretext for the articulation of wholly northern projects. Sanmiguel's stories, however, are firmly located on the southern side of the border. When she narratively crosses to the other side, south to north, her specific geographical and social contexts inevitably provoke a necessary, bifocal alignment of theoretical presuppositions as well.

Contemporary theorizing about the autobiographical form serves as a point of departure for our discussion (chapter 4) of two border narratives that implicitly insert themselves into this ongoing discussion. Both Norma Cantú's *Canícula* and Sheila Ortiz Taylor and Sandra Ortiz Taylor's *Imaginary Parents* explicitly play with the borderlines of presumptions about the autobiographical genre in their playful, fragmentary adaptations of this form. In either or both cases, the narrative always comes back to the tensions between traditional conceptions of autobiography and the particular circumstances defining an interstitial or fronterizo cultural space. It is telling that both of these autoethnographies require physical displacement from, and return to, the borderlands in order to open a free space for creation, and that one of the most crucial defining characteristics of these two fronterizo texts is their encoding of border life as constant movement, either realized or potential.

Reading Tijuana-based Rosina Conde's works (chapter 5) requires yet another shift of attention. For this border writer, the consciousness of liminality extends itself to all realms of experience. Conde's work directly addresses the traditional dichotomies of Mexican fiction and inscribes the border existence as a particularly privileged location—simultaneously strange and familiar—to explore the gender- and regionally bound nature of discursive constructions of Mexicanness itself. Her explorations of the intimate spaces of daily lives of border dwellers offer themselves at the same time as a political release from erasure on the national cultural scene as they also effect a rejection of sexually marked repression in relationships both ordinary (portraits of stress lines in working-class and middle-class families) and liminal (her delicate explorations of the insistently border-inflected worlds of assembly plants, prostitution, and striptease).

Chapter 6 offers a U.S.-based parallel to Conde's reinvention of Mexican identity. This chapter studies Californian Helena María Viramontes' collection of short stories, "Paris Rats in East L.A." The power of Viramontes' collection rides to a great degree upon the cusp of the near-oxymoronic double meaning of "homely"—both homelike and unattractive—and that in the interstitial slippage across the discursive boundaries between places and people both loved and unlovely we can locate the parameters of Viramontes' own homely theorization of a specific contemporary Chicana consciousness. The streets and houses of East L.A. are all the home her characters know or can imagine, and they deal comfortably with their stridencies, since those streets and those interiors are their intimate domestic spaces. The ten-year-old budding "home girl" of 1963 is today's Chicana feminist, and in delving into the roots of Champ's story Viramontes reconstructs the historical and cultural conjuncture that led to today's Chicana's sense of cultural and political agency.

In *MotherTongue,* the prize-winning novel about the tortuous relationship between a Chicana Sanctuary worker and a Salvadoran refugee, which we study in chapter 7, Demetria Martínez offers the reader a theory and a poetics for rethinking the construction of ethnic discourse and national identity at the conflicted intersection of various simultaneously held, and often mutually contradictory roles. Martínez puts us all, herself as well, in the position of observers upon the recent events in El Salvador and on the U.S. Sanctuary movement, contemporary history that is already and too soon fading in our collective memory. Both the Salvadoran man, who has solid reasons for needing to change his name and hide his identity, and the Chicana woman, whose identity is split between her U.S. life and her Mexican heritage, suffer from traumas that are both political and linguistic, and so in their mutual love they hurt each other as a reaction to the pain and estrangement they both feel. What makes this book so compelling is that its delicately poetic concern with the gendered quality of language and of complexly nuanced human relationships carries as well an implicit call to reconsider personal decisions involving political commitment.

Recent discussions about that archetypal postmodern border city, Tijuana (cf. García Canclini)—whether philosophical, anthropological, critical, or fictional—tend to focus on typical themes or narrative tics: the flexible geography that makes Tijuana both an island and an analog for the postmodern condition, the theme of the city as a Hollywoodesque set for a Wild West movie, the puzzlement over how to understand the role of the maquiladoras and the area's industrial boom, the awareness of a vast movement of people both north and south at this busiest of the world's borders, the uneasy concern that Tijuana is both a pop-culture commercial construct and a degraded utopia, a persistent and nagging phobia about feminization, and about female sexuality. Chapter 8 examines Regina Swain's collection of short stories, *La señorita Superman y otras danzas* [Miss Superman and other dances], and María Novaro's film *Jardín de Edén* [Garden of Eden] and discusses how both of these narratives provide explicitly border Mexican, explicitly female-gendered takes on these issues. What Swain does in these brief stories is to trace critical nodes in these contradictory and complementary discourses, recovering their concealed or forgotten genealogies, and setting them side by side in a text where everything and everyone is dangerously, disruptively out of place. Likewise, Novaro's film reelaborates the Tijuana border space. Even though Novaro is an "outsider" to the border region, in her film she grants the city a different image from that projected from Hollywood since the 1930s or Mexico City's film industry since the 1940s. Like Swain's stories, Novaro's film concentrates on the imbrication of the Tijuana border area with her inhabitants' search for identities and dreams.

As these texts intimate, theorizations about the border cannot be consolidated into a singular, hegemonic structure, but rather need to maintain an alert attentiveness to the nuances of multiple voices and positions. Short, fragmentary retakes and seemingly discontinuous snapshots offer, perhaps, our best hope of more positioned and polyphonic border theories. In shuttling back and forth across the real and metaphorical borders between countries, books, languages, and institutions, we hope to be able to provide at least a suggestion of some of the missing letters that will contribute to the evolving study of border theory and border culture.

# 2. Bilingual

*Alicia Gaspar de Alba*

El pueblo que pierde su memoria pierde su destino.

*—Mexican proverb*

As we commented in the first chapter, many recent discussions of border theory in general, and Mexican-U.S. border theory in particular, have a curious undertone that profoundly shades how we read border texts and predetermines to some degree what texts enter into this dialogue and thereby constitute the newly forming canon from which we choose our examples. From the Mexican side, one aspect of this phenomenon is the displacement of writers *from* the border—who, subject to small press runs and inadequate distribution, are less well known and tend to be associated with "regional" themes—by centrist writers *about* the border (Carlos Fuentes' *Frontera de cristal* and Laura Esquivel's *Como agua para chocolate* are salient recent examples) and by border writers displaced to the center of the country (Silvia Molina's *La familia vino del norte*) whose work is widely read and distributed, while also fitting more neatly into dominant culture constructions/inventions of borderness. On the U.S. side is a notable privileging of English-dominant oppositional Chicana thinker-poets like Gloria Anzaldúa in course syllabi, elite journals, and texts by high-powered theoreticians like Homi Bhabha. In many of these works, concrete border consciousness is otherwise unfortunately slight, and reference to Spanish-language border texts and theory even slighter.

Even in well-informed current discussions, Mexico's northern border's remoteness and relative isolation from the two contemporary dominant national discourses (Mexico, U.S.) offer intriguing opportunities for speculative projection from both the Distrito Federal and the District of Columbia. And while these two sets of discussions often occur in a parallel manner, in the best of such work border theorization necessarily requires a transcultural dialogue between these two dominant cultural discourses *and* between the resistant voices within these two dominant cultures by which border culture is invented, projected as an imaginary space, and reread in the engagement between texts. Thus, from both sides of the U.S.-Mexico border, the region has been submitted to intense scrutiny both as an apocalyptic space of a rejected past/present, which is often nevertheless a perversely attractive one (particularly true in popular culture and media representations), and as the best hope for a utopic project for the future (in high theory recuperations of the metaphor of the border as well as in some government projections). While we cannot hope to sort out the complexities of these practices here, we would like to signal the processes by which border theorization seems to require a transcultural dialogue between dominant cultural discourses in which the border culture is invented or imagined. We will then read a pair of short stories from Alicia Gaspar de Alba's bilingual collection, *The Mystery of Survival,* and conclude with a few speculations on the implications of such works in U.S. and, marginally, Mexican canon construction.

Let us look first at the utopic image familiar to us from so much border theorization. In their introduction to *Border Theory,* David Johnson and Scott Michaelsen summarize recent contributions to the astonishingly popular theoretical formulation of border studies. They note the hundreds of conferences, articles, and books organized around this topic, making it what they call "one of the grand themes of recent political liberal-to-left work across the humanities and social sciences" in the United States. They continue, in a perceptive and pointed conclusion:

> In the majority of this work, interestingly, the entry point of "the border" or "the borderlands" goes unquestioned, and, in addition, often is

assumed to be a place of politically exciting hybridity, intellectual creativity, and moral possibility. The borderlands, in other words, are *the* privileged locus of hope for a better world. (2–3)

Johnson and Michaelsen are absolutely accurate in this summary, and only add to it that, interestingly enough, the general direction of this liberal-to-left work exactly inverts the traditional dominant culture (both U.S. and Mexican) stereotypes about the border as a place of deplorable cultural mixing, intellectual and creative vacuums, and immoral depravity: the equal and alternative apocalyptic vision. In these more recent theoretical recuperations of the border, the characterization as a "locus for hope" can occur precisely only to the degree that the U.S.-Mexico border's concrete location is undermined and the border region becomes u-topic, a floating signifier for a displaced self.

This finding is also consonant with the conclusions in Walter Mignolo's influential article, "Posoccidentalismo: El argumento desde América Latina" [Postoccidentalism: The argument from Latin America], the Spanish version of what will become one of the key points in his later book, *Local Histories/Global Designs*. In the version aimed at a Spanish-speaking audience, this Latin Americanist scholar proposes the generation of a border epistemology from the various Third World spaces in order to help reconfigure understandings of the legacy of colonialism in the Americas writ large. Mignolo rejects the U.S.-European-based "orientalist" postcolonial model in favor of the concept of "occidentalism," which he borrows from Venezuelan scholar Fernando Coronil, expanding Coronil's project to a revised epistemological underpinning for the analysis of the colonial enterprise. In this effort, the metaphor of the border serves a crucial role. Mignolo recurs to the old Sarmientian opposition of civilization and barbarism and, tying it to a brief excursus on Anzaldúa, calls for the revindication of "la fuerza de la frontera que crea la posibilidad de la barbarie en negarse a sí misma como barbarie-en-la-otredad; de revelar la barbarie-en-la-mismidad que la categoría de civilización ocultó; y de generar un nuevo espacio de reflexión que mantiene y trasciende el concepto moderno de razón" [the force of the border which creates the possibility for barbarism to deny itself as barbarism-in-otherness; to reveal the barbarism-in-the-self that the category of civilization occulted; and to generate a new space of reflection that maintains and transcends the modern concept of reason] (157).

Following upon Mignolo, critics like Abril Trigo wax even more abstractly poetic: "la frontera es marca de la Historia, la frontería habilita memorias fragmentarias; la frontera sutura (a) la epistemologia moderna" [the border is the mark of History, the borderlands habilitate fragmentary memories; the border sutures modern epistemology] (81). For writers like Mignolo and Trigo, the border most aptly serves as a foil to define the self, which at the same time suggests its containment within the boundaries of a single human body and allows it to partake of a free-floating unanchoredness. Its fluctuating quality makes it a perfect objective correlative for concepts ranging from liminality and psychic repression to a figure for a Foucauldian heterotopic space. To the degree that border theory approaches the inaccessible edges of pure transgression, it dissolves into an indeterminate quality: something like a transcendental grammar or mathematical formula. Says Trigo: "la frontera es sólo una función" [the border is only a function] (72), and later: "es fácil, sin duda, incurrir en la fetichización de este no-lugar fronterizo en tanto *locus* privilegiado de producción de conocimiento" [it is doubtlessly easy, to incur in the fetishization of this no-place borderlands as a privileged locus for the production of knowledge] (79). In this manner, Trigo takes a debatable statement ("la frontera es sólo una función") and assumes it as the grounding for further extension: functionality as a privileged site, but only if the border is understood as a metaphor rather than a specific place. However, one could argue, *pace* Trigo, that if indeed the border can be reduced to a mere floating functionality, then the oxymoronic quality of a no-place (utopic) space as an alternative site for knowledge production offers not an alternative epistemology, but only a slightly disguised version of the west's most traditional reasoning. This unrecognized complicity with older forms of knowledge production is one of the more worrisome qualities of much abstract theorizing and points not only to an evacuation of concrete meaning, but also to an unconscious complicity with rejected structures such as the civilization and barbarism model evoked by Mignolo, or the fetishization metaphor deployed by Trigo.

If the border is insufficiently actualized as a conceptual tool in works like those of Mignolo, Trigo, and García Canclini, it poses another kind of problem for the work of other well-known border thinkers, where the concept of the borderlands can be too easily recuperated into a certain type of cultural nationalist discourse. Johnson and Michaelsen ask: "Of what use, finally, are concepts like 'culture' and 'identity' if their invocation, even in so-called multicultural contexts, is also exclusive, colonial, intolerant?" (29). On the U.S. side, the contributors to Johnson and Michaelsen's border theory volume quite rightly question, as the editors note, "the *value* of the border, both as cultural indicator and as a conceptual tool," finding "the identity politics of border studies' most prominent instantiations naive and wanting in quite similar ways" (29, 31). Benjamin Alire Saenz trenchantly argues this point in his critique of Anzaldúa's canonical text, *Borderlands/La Frontera,* which he sees as a dangerously escapist romanticization of indigenous cultures, offering little of practical value to today's urban Chicanos/as (85–86). This problem is, of course, not unique to Anzaldúa; Johnson's article in the same volume describes the process by which Octavio Paz's definition of Mexicanness is produced by crossing the border into the United States and fetishizing that act of crossing as a psychic journey in understanding the national and personal self as a cultural product. Says Johnson:

> On either side of the border, on both sides of the border, there is one cultural identity; however it is defined, in whatever terms it is disclosed, it is nevertheless *one*—it is *our* identity. And even if on either side of the border there is more than one cultural identity, each one will be located within the horizon of a certain discretion; each will be found in its own place, bordered by the dream of its proper univocity. Such is the effect of Paz's border. . . . "[W]e" will only find ourselves there, awaiting us on the other side of the border. (133–34)

Johnson's reading of Paz reminds us of striking similarities between the Mexican thinker's 1950s meditation on Mexicanness and Mignolo's 1990s discussion of border epistemology as a play of self and other. Despite generational and ideological differences, for both Paz and Mignolo the most salient quality of the border is that the act of crossing serves the psychic function of reflection. The border itself becomes a mirror, exacting knowledge of the self and the other but, most important, a reinscription of the self in the other, of knowledge of the self.

This highly abstract and metaphorical theoretical approximation to border theory is not widely accepted by border writers and artists. One concrete example of the operations of this presumed univocity, this unrecognized intolerance, as projected from the Mexican side is provided by the history of the Border Art Workshop/Taller de Arte Fronterizo (BAW/TAF). Founded in 1984 by performance artist Guillermo Gómez-Peña to bring together Mexican and U.S. border artists, Chicanos and non-Chicanos, many of the Mexican nationals dropped out. Explains Chicano artist David Avalos:

> [S]ome resistance to the BAW/TAF came from Tijuana artists. They said, hey, we don't think that the border is this wonderful place of exchange. We can't dispense with our nationality, so we can't join the parade. . . . The BAW/TAF has the perspective of the USA, as do so many of the notions of border that we consume. (198)

Other critics have succinctly pointed out how Gómez-Peña's phenomenal success in the U.S. academic scene as the representative border artist/thinker—when, ironically, in the border area he is considered an outsider to their cultural circles—has created the conditions for conjoining dominant cultural discursive practices that define "hybridity" and determine the value ascribed to this project in the metaphorized community. What is needed, these border critics suggest, is that such well-received and respected writers rethink more thoroughly the epistemological status of their own discursive practices. Too often, these theoretical reimaginings, overtly resistant to their respective U.S. and Latin American dominant cultures although writing from within them, define an ideological longing projected onto a specific space that must remain, in this theory at least, both diffusely utopic and concretely sited (but incompletely known). The actual border, so distant from mainstream centers of theory production in both the United States and Mexico, offers itself all too neatly as the very metaphor of this desired fluidity for thinkers who have lived with their backs to its concrete reality.

In contrast with the liberal-to-left theory producers, the alternative and more apocalyptic popular culture concern about the border figures an anticipated future that is also and at the same time a refused past. In using the word "refused" here, we are using refusal as both a noun and a verb (Trinh Minh-ha has already made this connection in another context; "Acoustic Journey," 6), as well as an inadequate suturing: re-fuse, fusing together two disparate materials that continually come unstuck. The border in this sense reflects those stereotypes about itself that each society has refused, while readmitting the stereotypes about the refused other; it also reflects the border as a well-known site of refusal—the literal and figurative dump for each society's urban, industrial, toxic, and sexual wastes. And yet, because the refused (repressed) always returns in some future moment, because the refuse is inextricably linked to the most personal and private details of modern life, dominant cultures' refusal is doomed to shadow itself, past and future. Trinh says:

> If, despite their location, noun and verb inhabit the two very different and well-located worlds of designated and designator, the space between them remains a surreptitious site of movement and passage whose open, communal character makes exclusive belonging and long-term residence undesirable, if not impossible. (6)

To speak about the border in such a context is to empty it out, retaining the projected residue of a refused and powerful violence. Cities like Tijuana and Juárez almost too neatly conflate symbolic geographic and moral exclusions from the healthy body of the state. From both sides of the border, these cities represent that tacky and vile and threatening thing that middle-class morality must resist and cannot stop talking about. This latent violence is echoed even in the U.S. tourist imaginations, where the border frequently figures as a sort of cinematic Wild West outpost, and in centrist Mexican conceptions, where it persists as a convenient trope for provincial cities full of violent men and lawless women.

In her discussion of the sexual interface of colonial encounters, Ann Laura Stoler offers a helpful point of departure for an analysis of this trope. Her work focuses on what she calls the "analytic slippage between the sexual symbols of power and the politics of sex," and asks the important questions: "Was sexuality merely a graphic substantiation of who was, so to speak, on the top? Was the medium the message, or did sexual relations always 'mean' something else, stand in for other relations, evoke the sense of *other* . . . desires?" (346). Despite, or perhaps because of its shocking physicality, control and manipulation of the sexualized trope serve both central Mexico and U.S. dominant discourses as a salient instrument of textual authority in constructing and controlling discussions about the dangerous attractions of a degraded border reality.

When we turn back to the border with these insights in mind, it is striking how consistently in these discussions images of sneaky invading hordes are linked to phobias about female sexuality and disguised in dominant culture's fears/celebrations of social change. Striking, too, is the consistency in evocations of a historical amnesia tied to figures of a refused and denied historicity. These issues are given particularly sharp attention in those works by Mexican- and U.S.-based border writers whose works grapple seriously and directly with the consequences of a doubled linguistic and historical heritage.

Both U.S. Spanish departments and the Latin American literature programs in universities have been slow to grasp the possibilities for exploring literary expression like Alicia Gaspar de Alba's in which the play between two languages and two cultures is at the core.[1] It is neither surprising nor particularly original to note that literary canons prefer sharp delineations, both linguistic and national. Using the example of the *Heath Anthology of American Literature* as a typical instance of the ideological underpinnings of canon consolidation, Johnson observes:

> Mexican literature, on the one hand, will be written in the shadow of the border; U.S. literature, or so-called American literature, on the other hand, will also take place there, but on the other side, on *our side*. . . . The borders separating these two literatures remain necessarily secure. . . . The *Heath Anthology* extends the notion of American literature only as far as English allows it: there will be no text, no "literature" included in the *Heath* that does not appear in English. There will be no text produced on the other side, *el otro lado*. . . . [T]here will be no American literature in any other language, in any other place. (147)

The same point can be made with respect to the Mexican literary establishment, which has generally relegated border writing to some space outside the canon of national literature in that country. Certainly it is true that border theoreticians tend to explicitly reject this monolingual and hegemonic vision in favor of a more fluid model that asks for a consideration of the borderlands as a binational and bilingual space of physical crossing and cultural translation. Yet frequently, actual literary and cultural practice remains firmly within national boundaries. If we use Héctor Calderón and José David Saldívar's *Criticism in the Borderlands* as an instance of this unexplored national bias even in explicitly contestatory texts, we note that, in effect, the book dedicates itself to disarticulating the borders of the monolithic discourse of American literature. Nevertheless, the distribution of planes on this global map is tied only to the local: to the United States. Their criticism on the borderlands restricts itself to the borders of the U.S. sociopolitical system. Johnson and Michaelsen would agree. In their terms, such analyses define a practice by which "a border is always crossed and double-crossed, without the possibility of the transcultural" (15).

Two of the eleven stories in Gaspar de Alba's *Mystery of Survival and Other Stories* are written entirely in Spanish. One, "El pavo," focuses on a child's anticipation of the mainstream U.S. holiday of Thanksgiving; the other, "Los derechos de La Malinche," offers a poetic meditation on that much-discussed indigenous woman from the early-sixteenth-century conquest of Mexico by Spain. Another sequence of stories, focused on the curandera Estrella González, rely for their impact on a de-exoticized acceptance of the powers of this traditional healer. In each case, the weighted choice of Spanish or English or Spanglish in these stories evokes the tensions of living in two languages and two cultures, languages that conflict not only with each other but also with the presumed cultural underpinnings that, in the border zone, are frequently highly charged. This tension is heightened by the interlinked nature of the stories, which gives them, as Cordelia Candelaria has already noted in her introduction to the volume, the quality of a "loosely woven novel" (3), creating even more of an awareness of the jostling of different voices and different languages against each other. In effect, as the counterposition of the Thanksgiving and the Malinche stories suggests, at question in Gaspar de Alba's work is a deeper interrogation into the nature of historical origins for national and cultural identity claims. Gaspar de Alba's narrative is marked in a particular manner by her own social commitment, her own imbrication in a border reality that has left the northern border of Mexico out of official histories of that country, and at the same time has left Chicano history out of official histories of the United States. Unable to find a secure position for herself within the histories of either Mexico or the United States, the Chicana writer attempts to piece together an alternative tale, only to come up against the flotsam and jetsam of haunted shadowtexts from both sides of the border (the Pilgrims, the conquistadores) that tend to substitute for other forms of historical reconstruction.

The twinned themes of memory and destiny are repeated over and over in the book, in Spanish and in English, often associated with some variation of the proverb that serves as epigraph to the collection and appears textually in the first story, stenciled onto a whitewashed wall in Querétaro: "el pueblo que pierde su memoria pierde su destino." The child narrator in that story asks her mother what it means, and her mother impatiently responds: "I don't know. . . . Mexican proverbs don't mean anything anymore" (12). Pointedly, the loss of meaning has a good deal to do with the loss of language and with the willed memory loss involving the mother's refusal to acknowledge her daughter's abuse at the hands of her stepfather. This intentional forgetfulness, this encrypting of memory, results in the creation of the Pandora's box, or memory piñata that serves as one of the book's leitmotivs. By the end of the volume, with "Facing the Mariachis," one of the linked series of stories involving the curandera Estrella González, the author adds to this discussion the nuanced and explicitly female alternative genealogical tale involving a recuperation of memory through the deliberate creation of the child/ future storyteller, Xochitl, implicitly conterposing Xochitl to Malinche as alternative textual strategies.

In the classic telling of the Malinche story/myth, the indigenous woman betrays her people to the Spanish conqueror by serving both as interpreter and mistress for Hernán Cortés; "malinchista" in Mexican usage evokes the sense of an unpatriotic betrayal of the nation to foreign interests. Octavio Paz's seminal analysis of Malinche as the icon of Mexicanness focuses on this psychological trauma of a national identity based on a foundational betrayal that is both political and sexual. As Paz notes, the cry, "¡Viva México, hijos de la Chingada!" recognizes the implicit underlying connection between the nation and Malinche as the figure of the raped indigenous woman, between the Mexican male force and the children born of violence. In this reading, Mexicans, metaphorically born to the rape victim ("la chingada"), wake up to find themselves victims of the evil betrayer, and so have no recourse but to commit violence, including sexual violence, against women and against their fellow man so as to shore up a sagging and threatened identity as the possessor of a powerful and inviolable male body. And yet, as Paz says, in these paranoid constructions of gender and sexual norms, while "la Chingada" is ineluctably associated with the mother, her very passivity leaches her identity and her name; she is nothing and no one; "es la Nada" [she is Nothingness] (68, 72). If in the complexities of national myth the nation is both mother and whore, then national pride and perceived deficiencies in the national character derive from a common cause. Moreover, if racially inferior and sexually available women are to blame—literally or metaphorically—for society's problems, tacitly national pride is also bound up in the admission that nothing can be done to improve the situation since the powerful, handsome, yearned-for father is always already gone.

Chicano, and especially Chicana, critics and writers including Norma Alarcón, Gloria Anzaldúa, and Ana Castillo have turned this negative image of the indigenous woman on its head, rewriting her story as that of an empowered woman. Cortés called Malinche "mi lengua" [my tongue], and the Chicana recuperations of the power of her native tongue and her indigenous body offer an iconic example for the potentiality of a woman who escapes the confines of the home and allows herself to speak. Thus, the image that in Mexico figures shame and betrayal becomes in Chicana theory a figure of pride and empowerment, as well as a metaphor for the bilingual resistances of the contemporary Chicana woman who is faced with a second colonial threat through the pressures of U.S.-Anglo culture and the English language that threaten to efface her from the national imaginary. Alfred Arteaga sees this recuperation of a usable image for cultural consolidation as a particularly urgent project in the fraught cultural contact zones of the border region:

> For Mexicans and for Chicanos subjectivity is reproduced anew in the self-fashioning act of heterotextual interaction. But this sense is more acute for the Chicano than for the Mexican because the Chicano derives *being* not only from the Spanish colonial intervention but also from Anglo-American colonialism: for not only was Mexico conquered by Spain, but Northern Mexico by the United States. (27)

At the same time, Arteaga quite rightly points out the stress points in current poetic and theoretical reelaborations of the myth of the Malinche, especially in its most celebrated forms where, ironically, prominent Chicana lesbians (Gaspar de Alba would be included in this distinguished body) fall back into a heterosexual metaphor of national and textual production: once again, as in Paz, textual production devolves back onto the absent authority figure, the white father.

Gaspar de Alba offers her take on this vexed international and interlingual problematic genealogy, exploring the issue of a usable past by way of aggressively feminocentric tales that nevertheless must cede their authority to the "barbudos," the Spanish and gringo male-dominant heterotexts. Her poem, "Malinchista, A Myth Revised," places the native woman in the context of an impossible power struggle between two figures of male domination, both of whom access speech by means of homicidal violence. On the one hand, the indigenous priest derives his power of sacred speech from the ritual sacrifice of human messengers who mediate between the gods and their earthly servants. For the priest, Malinche's unmediated power of speech is sacrilegious and incomprehensibly terrifying:

> The high priest of the pyramids feared La Malinche's
> power of language—how she could form strange syllables
> in her mouth and Speak to the gods without offering
> the red fruit of her heart.

Strikingly enough, Gaspar de Alba's Malinche discerns no substantive difference between this literal sacrifice of human hearts on Aztec altars and the figurative ripping out of indigenous life by white men in their violations of body and soul following upon the successful conquest. On the contrary; the priest and the conquistador are strangely identified by the analogy in their violent practices, and both are relegated to a secondary status in the history in which they imagined they would figure as central images:

> . . . history
> does not sing of the conquistador who prayed
> to a white god as he pulled two ripe hearts
> out of the land. (212–13)

Unlike her male counterparts, if ambiguously, La Malinche/La Llorona in this poem retains her power, no longer as the embodied Speaker but as the haunting presence whose indecipherable shriek captures the imprinted cultural aftershocks of the violent convulsion that reshaped an American empire during the colonial period. She is both the nurturing mother who curves her body protectively around a much-beloved newborn child and the horrific ghost of a murderous child killer who returns to the scene of her crime to cry of vengeance. Malinchismo, Gaspar de Alba suggests in this moral tale, is redefined not as the act of a betrayer but as the reaction of one who has been betrayed; the horror that perverts the mother's nurturing instinct derives from another's violent action against her. Malinche is a potent force in this revised myth, but she is potent less as an embodiment of contemporary resistances to patriarchal power than as a historical reaction, as a figure of past abjection.

The short story "Los derechos de La Malinche" picks up on and expands imagery the author had begun to explore in the more concise format of the "Myth Revised." From the poem, she draws the central thread of the tale, the imagery of heart and speech, and the metaphor of the cactus so crucial to both variations on the tale. In the story, however, the writer adds both a contemporary focus and a binational message, with her emphasis less on the act of betrayal (though, of course, the story cannot avoid this retelling) and more forcefully on the woman's proactive recognition and assumption of her rights.

"Los derechos de La Malinche" opens *in medius res* with the voice of the female narrator raising at the very beginning the question that, while suppressed, will haunt and destabilize the whole of the succeeding text: "No me voy a disculpar. Después de tantos años, hasta nuestra lengua ha cambiado. Es posible que ni me entiendas. Es posible que mis palabras todavía estén coaguladas" [I am not going to ask for pardon. After so many years, even our language has changed. It is possible that you don't even understand me. It is possible that my words are still coagulated] (47). Economically, with these few and tightly constructed phrases, Gaspar de Alba outlines the central problematics and metaphorics of this story: the response to an implicit demand for contrition, the problem of communicating across languages, the image of the blood clot that stands in for a choked narration. The narrative voice, abruptly interrupting the English flow of the majority of the stories in this volume, begins aggressively refusing to ask forgiveness. But forgiveness for what? For a traitorous reputation? A linguistic transgression? A sexual one? The uncontrite voice in refusing to ask nevertheless evokes an unstated history in which such forgiveness would more typically be begged for—and perhaps grudgingly given. And yet, in the very next sentence, we are invited to wonder if indeed "disculpas" are exactly what are at issue here—perhaps we misunderstand. After all, the language has changed: "our" language has changed. But which language? The historical Malinche originally translated Maya to Nahuatl, and later, as her abilities grew, Nahuatl to Spanish. The narrator in this story shifts to Spanish in an Anglophone context and a predominantly English-language collection. And yet, the story is there, on the page, stubbornly written in Spanish, defiantly non-U.S. oriented in its metaphoric base; there, as María Lugones has said in reference to her own use of bilinguality in her theoretical texts, to be understood or to be missed, so that in both sharing an understanding and in having to skip over the text because of linguistic inability there is an important meaning.[2]

This contestatory stance introduces a narrator who is simultaneously a contemporary woman and that much-maligned and celebrated indigenous figure. In its historical evocation of the conquest tale, the story details a change of language and change of name through involuntary baptism and the imposition of a foreign spirituality: Malintzín becomes Malinche and then Marina in the wholly unwanted, terrified gesture of "el vendido" [the sellout] who tosses his "gotas de ácido" [drops of acid] in her direction in an attempt to control her (50–51). This cultural rape is paired with sexual abuse; indeed, sexual intercourse with the conqueror follows immediately upon baptism. Moreover, this doubled violence figures the narrator's entry into the space of narration. In the overlapping of colonial and contemporary times, of Malinche and her modern counterpart, these two elements of a spurious catholicism and sexual abuse remain paired. Thus, the modern woman refers elliptically to sexual abuse by her father in the sordid surroundings of a movie matinee, through a parody of the Lord's Prayer: "tú, padre nuestro que estás en el cielo . . . me alzabas la falda y me dabas el pan de cada día" [you, our father who art in heaven . . . lifted my skirt and gave me our daily bread] (52). Likewise, the Spanish conqueror's entirely expected use of Malinche's body is paired with the modern woman's distaste for the pressured sexual relations with her gringo boyfriend, and both experiences are dismissed with the same phrase: "lo que pasó con al barbudo no fue más que otro tributo a otro conquistador" [what happened with that bearded man was no more than another tribute to another conqueror] (52).

Yet, at the same time as the colonial Malinche and her Chicana counterpart dismiss complicity in their own abuse, they are profoundly aware of the social context in which the colonial woman, like the modern abuse victim, is made responsible for her victimization. The opening sentence of the story, with its implication that typically forgiveness would need to be given for the unstated offense, offers a clear index to this social construction by which the woman is sullied (in social terms) by the abuse visited upon her. Moreover, the bloody clot of words—an unspoken story, in another tongue—reminds us that at least at one level the rape victim is expected to keep silent and suffer in shame for her violation.

For both women, the first sign of this impending conquest is a linguistic catachresis, followed by physical disgust and vomiting:

Malintzín se empezó a marear. Le venía un ataque de palabras raras, palabras que no conocía, palabras secretas de las diosas. No quería que el extranjero escuchara su canto. . . . Se le convulsionó el estomago y echó un líquido amargo a los pies del barbudo. Ya le venían las primeras sílabas. (51)

[Malintzín began to get nauseous. An attack of strange words came upon her, words she didn't know, the secret words of the goddesses. She did not want the foreigner to hear her song. . . . Her stomach convulsed and she threw up a bitter liquid at the bearded man's feet. Then the first syllables came out.]

Derrida is on the right track when he theorizes, in a discussion of Kant, the relation of the aesthetic category of the sublime and the physical experience of vomiting, and his conclusions are apposite for reading Gaspar de Alba's story as well. In his analysis, disgust in some sense stands in for that which is unassimilable. Vomit is the reappropriation of negativity by which disgust lets itself be spoken:

What it [the logo-phonocentric system] excludes . . . is what does not allow itself to be digested, or represented, or stated. . . . It is an irreducible heterogeneity which cannot be eaten either sensibly or ideally and which—this is the tautology—by never letting itself be swallowed must therefore cause itself to be vomited. Vomit lends its form to this whole system. ("Economimesis," 21)

Derrida concludes: "The word vomit arrests the vicariousness of disgust; it puts the thing in the mouth" (25).

Both literally and metaphorically, then, what the white man puts into the indigenous woman—his words in her ears, his water and semen in her body—provokes disgust at that unassimilable presence that nevertheless figures the hegemonic discourse that must somehow be taken in and made one's own. It is, as Derrida and Gaspar de Alba intimate, too much to be swallowed and therefore must be thrown up. At the same time, the colonial woman needs to hold back the pressure to give her words into the conqueror's ears, to give anything of herself or her culture to him. Thus, while disgust and vomiting give form to the system, the retention of some quality of the unassimilable creates blockages—the blood clots that choke narrative even while they retain the chameleonic power of the native woman's unspoken, unspeakable secrets.

Derrida's analysis of the sublime strikes a chord with Kristeva's parallel reading of the coming into consciousness of the "I," which she sees as constructed through the expelling of the sign of the other's desire. Thus, if Derrida's reading helps us to see how Malinche accesses her various languages, Kristeva defines the consolidation of the self through violation:

> During that course in which "I" become, I give birth to myself amid the violence of sobs, of vomit. Mute protest of the symptom, shattering violence of a convulsion that, to be sure, is inscribed in a symbolic system, but in which, without either wanting or being able to become integrated in order to answer to it, it reacts, it abreacts. It abjects. (3)

Kristeva further notes the essential connection between this coming to consciousness of the self and an awareness of personal death: "it is thus that *they* see that 'I' am in the process of becoming an other at the expense of my own death" (3). Nevertheless, what "I" knows and what "they" see—the irreducibility of the body and the inevitability of its decomposition, both figured in the disgusting qualities of vomit—must be repressed (the exactness of the folk wisdom already adduced linking La Malinche and La Llorona is never clearer than in this respect). Fear, too, must be thrown up, driven out. And yet, of course, it always haunts us:

> it shades off like a mirage and permeates all the words of the language with nonexistence. . . . Thus, fear having been bracketed, discourse will seem tenable only if it ceaselessly confront that otherness, a burden both repellent and repelled, a deep well of memory that is unapproachable and intimate. (Kristeva, 6)

While for the colonial woman nausea is provoked by the need to contain the words of power in the face of an alien threat, in the modern woman's experience the immediate need is to eject the foreign presence from her body, to rid herself of an invader who is nonetheless at this point, nearly five hundred years after the conquest, deeply of her own body and blood—the father to whom this story is explicitly addressed:

> Te eché en seguida. Abrí la boca sobre el excusado y te dejé salir. . . . No me voy a disculpar. Cuando me avisaron de tu embolia, sentí una gran calma. El coagulo de palabras en mi garganta al fin se empezó a deslizar, al fin pude soltar la sangre de tu recuerdo. (50)

[I got rid of you immediately. I opened my mouth over the toilet and allowed you to leave. . . . I am not going to ask for pardon. When I was told about your embolism I felt a great calm. The clot of words in my throat finally began to break up, at last I was able to get rid of the blood of your memory.]

Here the death of the father, and the visit to the grave that frames the narrative, serves to free up, finally, the clotted narrative. The language may have changed from the words of power Malinche caught back in her throat, but in any case the vomiting up of that unassimilable presence of the disgusting allows narrative to take shape.

Another form taken by resistance to the master discourse is even more closely aligned with the symbolic import of the story's title than the image of vomiting. Says the modern woman at her father's grave, "He venido a traerte tunas" [I came to bring you prickly pears] (47). The prickly pear is, of course, a sweetly delicious native fruit, but one whose delicate heart must be carefully uncovered because of the cactus spines covering the protective outer peel. If, in this story, what is foreign and cannot be assimilated causes disgust and must be vomited, it would seem that the cactus fruit would stand at the opposite pole as a native source of pleasure and nourishment. Nevertheless, Gaspar de Alba's use of this fruit, with its blood-red secret core and prickly exterior, rests on a different and feminocentric metaphoric turn. At the end of the story the modern narrator clarifies: "Estas tunas son los derechos que me violaste, las palabras secretas que me tragué" [These fruits are the rights of mine which you violated, the secret words I swallowed] (52).

Here, too, there is a carefully articulated genealogical thrust, as the modern woman's evocation of the blood-red fruits echoes the colonial woman's resistance to the force of the conqueror, her strategy for a silent opposition to his violation. The enforced silence, the secret that also becomes the defining quality of her identity and her resistance to cooption, are figured in the internalization of the image of the prickly pear, by which the narrator and her foremother define those alienated rights, those coagulated narratives, that constitute them as excluded subjects from the masculinist-driven national enterprise. These women are raped and discursively rendered abjectly apologetic or voiceless precisely so that their tongues will not be disseminated within this hegemonic structure. Yet, paradoxically, their exclusion creates the possibility for not only rhetorical rendering of difference but also real oppositional strategy. Says Santiago Castro-Gómez:

> Observarse *como sujetos excluídos* conllevaba la posibilidad de desdoblarse, observar las propias prácticas y compararlas con las prácticas de sujetos distantes en el tiempo y el espacio, establecer diferencias con otros sujetos locales y producir estrategias de resistencia. (210)

> [To observe *as excluded subjects* carries with it the possibility of unfolding, of observing one's own practices and comparing them with the practice of subjects distant in time and space, of establishing differences with other local subjects and producing resistance strategies.]

If the prickly pear is what the modern woman swallows, and, in the unclotting of the narrative, it represents the blood she spills on her father's gravestone, this metaphorical connection becomes even more deeply layered through reference to the colonial tale. There is a homology of mouth and genitals in this story, already established in the parallels between rape and vomit, violation and secrecy. Both sites on the body become overdetermined loci of what is forced on the woman, what is resisted, what is spit out in silence. In this resistant narrative, the prickly pear serves an important function in a wincingly graphic attack on the master's power:

> La Malinche no dijo nada. . . . Esa noche, Marina se preparó bien. Con la ayuda de Coatlicue y Tonantzín, se irritó las paredes de su sexo con el pellejo espinoso de unas tunas, dejando que el jugo rojo de la fruta le chorreara las piernas. . . . Cuando él se encontró en aquella hinchazón, en aquel nido de espinas donde su miembro se había atrapado como una culebra, sus gritos le salieron a borbotones. Nunca se había sentido Doña Marina tan dueña de su destino. (51–52)

> [La Malinche said nothing. . . . That evening, Marina prepared herself well. With the aid of Coatlicue and Tonantzín she rubbed the walls of her genitals with the spiny peel of some cactus fruits, allowing the red juice to flow down her legs. . . . When he found himself in that swelling, in that nest of spines where his penis was trapped like a snake, his shouts escaped in torrents. Never had Doña Marina felt so in charge of her destiny.]

This is not a utopic tale, however. For both Malinche and her modern counterpart, defiance is reactive: a refusal to submit passively to a conquest that has already taken place. "Los derechos de La Malinche" begins and ends at the father's grave, suggesting that in this circular narrative the feminine voice, whether clotted or free-flowing, is still doomed to repeat the structure of violation and vomit. Furthermore, the unclotting of narrative offers purging (vomiting) of the father's memory—but it is still the father's story, like the father's gravestone, that frames the tale and dominates its telling. Survival, when that survival is marked by the inescapable presence of the father's grave serving as the only opening onto narration, offers no clear, proactive solution for the future.

How then do we get beyond the abject? How to break the folkloric link of Malinche/Llorona, which discovers a perverse vomiting of the lover-father and his words/works? Or, to put it in other terms, how do we rethink the heterotext in the service of the feminine? Gaspar de Alba hints at one possible alternative poetics in her much anthologized poem, "Making Tortillas," which seems to offer an implicit response to precisely the kind of blockage we have been tracking in her Malinche poem and story. The secret, she tells us, is to refuse the premises of the patriarchal model, so damaging to women's self-construction:

> Tortilleras, we are called,
> Grinders of maíz, makers, bakers,
> slow lovers of women.
> The secret is starting from scratch. (*Beggar on Cordoba Bridge,* 45)

"Starting from scratch," in genealogies as in cooking, is in effect what Gaspar de Alba does in her most powerful Malinche poem, "Letters from a Bruja." This poem in some sense restages the colonial encounter, echoing and giving force to the mysterious "palabras secretas de las diosas" [secret words of the gods] alluded to but repressed under the father's narrative in "Derechos." Reading this poem, positioned from the perspective and in the voice of La Malinche's mother, reminds us that the ontological question undergirding our analysis to this point—that is, "Who or what is the self?"—is a question inevitably positioned from the perspective of the father's law. It is, at base, a man's existential question, rooted in patriarchal concerns about the integrity of the "I" and the primordial quality of the self's desires. Gaspar de Alba does not deny the power of this historically established framework, but her bruja defamiliarizes it. In "Letters from a Bruja" Gaspar de Alba estranges us from that male-oriented ontology and asks not "who am I?" but "who can I engender?," where the focus is not on the invasion of the self by the violating other and the vomiting out of the unassimilable foreign presence, but rather on the female genealogy that serves as patriarchy's necessary complement: not father right, but the rites of the goddesses. What Gaspar de Alba provides in this almost allegorical lyric recuperation of the female genealogy is not just another renegotiation of tired concepts but a strategic operation to usher in a reconceptualization as well as a reinscription of the linguist/cultural project.

The bruja in this poem is terrifying and wonderful. She forces us to rethink the hoary legend of La Malinche from the perspective of deliberative, feminocentric action, as part of a resistant heritage of strong women, neither self-abnegating nor abject. Following Natalie Melas, we could say that Malinche's witch-mother's poem, when (dis)placed into the context of a patriarchal model,

> produces a version of incommensurability which differs from our received definition of the incommensurable as "that which cannot be measured by comparison for lack of a common measure," suggesting instead a definition along the lines of "that comparison which cannot measure because its equivalences do not unify." (275)

The unity here is not that of spiritual or physical violation, but rather of blood and bone, of women physically conceived and spiritually engendered in women's bodies and from women's knowledge.

There are two parts to the "Letters from a Bruja" in *Beggar on Cordoba Bridge*. The first "letter" is addressed "to my daughter," explicitly identified as Malinche:

> But tonight my scorpion's blood boils
> with the heat of the lion . . .
> and you are conceived, hija,
> from the worm of incest,
> Already your seed bears the gift of darkness.
> Already your name washes up
> on the salty foam
> between my thighs: Malinche . . . (46)

The second "letter" is addressed to Malinche's daughter who, five hundred years after the Spanish conquest, has learned to speak in yet another tongue, neither native American nor imposed Spanish, but the English of the new conquest. This girl child will inherit the grandmother's words and powers, which will spill forth from her mouth not as vomit but as generative potential:

> I wind stories in your native
> tongue to frighten you . . .
> We are together only
> to hunt each other down.
> I have waited five hundred years for this.
> In fifty more my bones will rattle
> around your neck. My words will foam
> from your mouth. (47)

The bruja in this poem is something other than and beyond conventions of either the abject or the beautiful. Even sitting in the mud, she cannot be mistaken for anything except a figure of enormous potency, akin perhaps to the goddesses Coatlicue and Tonantzín evoked only parenthetically in "Los derechos de La Malinche," but here given voice and centrality. Likewise, if abjection and vomit are a form of rejection of death, an expelling of fear, here the strong woman makes fear an integral element of the learning process; death is not bracketed off as the uncanny presence of a monstrous decomposition, but brought home and made part of the self in the homely/uncanny string of bones around the granddaughter's neck. The scorpion that accompanies the women in this family line may sting, but the poisoned words carry weight and power. The women in this poem do not wait for phallogocentric authorization to enter the symbolic realm; that patriarchal trap has been long since recognized. Instead, they draw from "the gramarye of your blood" (47) an alternative sacred and erotic structure.

The bruja's power is evoked as well in "Facing the Mariachis," the last story in the volume, *The Mystery of Survival and Other Stories*. Here, too, Gaspar de Alba comes closer to a structural alternative to narrative-as-vomiting, one that still retains its stubborn anti-utopic quality. This narrative tells the story of Mercedes, a Mexican woman who unburdens herself of a guilty secret to her supportive and understanding husband, José, a Chicano. Mercedes was raped at fourteen and forced to marry her rapist, an abusive curandero's assistant, subsequently giving birth to a deformed son she describes as a monster. With the assistance of the curandera Estrella González, she poisons first her child, and later her abusive husband. Yet this secret crime is for Mercedes only the prelude to another, greater secret—the payment that the curandera demands for her assistance in the double murder is for Mercedes to give birth to a girl child created by the old woman with the application of her mysterious powers. Thus, Mercedes has allowed herself to be made pregnant through the offices of the curandera with the daughter who, according to the wise woman, will represent the living memory of her culture. This secret of a pregnancy without male intervention is the deeper crime that Mercedes is unable to confess even to her loving husband. The story ends as Mercedes, nauseous with the burden of her unconfessed guilt and her new pregnancy, haunted by the wails of her dead son, leans back in her husband's arms as the mariachis play "El niño perdido" at his request.

If we can say that the Mexican proverb "a people that loses its memory loses its destiny" serves as the organizing theme of this volume, the final story in the collection offers a critical rereading of this project. Mercedes' child, Xochitl, is the narrative voice explicitly structuring the whole of this loosely knit sequence, and she is directly associated with the memory piñata that will rescue the destiny of her people from oblivion. In conjuring this child, the curandera rubs an egg over Mercedes' womb and repeats, in Spanish and in English: "Your womb shall be the piñata. The piñata shall carry the memory. When the piñata breaks, the memory will be the destiny of she who comes" (100). Her immaculate conception is quite obviously meant to echo the Christ story, and Xochitl's birth is tied to a recuperation and rewriting of the immemorial founding tales of western society as a strategy for future redemption.

What Gaspar de Alba provides in this almost allegorical tale is not just another renegotiation of tired concepts, however, but a strategic operation to usher in a reconceptualization as well as a reinscription of the linguist/cultural project intimated in the whole of this collection. The prehistory of Xochitl's conception and birth forces us to rethink the whole of the volume. There are two crucial steps involved in this breaking and reconstruction of previous presuppositions: (1) the revelation of the originary crime; and (2) the conception of a child without male participation.

Josefina Ludmer helps us understand the import of a fictional structure organized around and through focus on a murder, and her study of
this issue is applicable point by point to Gaspar de Alba's story. In her
"Mujeres que matan" [Women who kill] she writes,

> El delito en la ficción puede afectar al conjunto de diferencias porque en
> realidad funciona como un instrumento (teórico, si se quiere) que sirve
> para trazar límites, diferenciar y excluir: un línea de demarcación que
> cambia el estatus simbólico de un objeto, una posición o una figura.
> (781)

> [Crime in fiction can affect the body of differences because it really func-
> tions as an instrument (theoretical, if one wishes) that serves to trace
> limits, to differentiate, and to exclude: a line of demarcation that changes
> the symbolic structure of an object, a position or a figure.]

This quality of structural and symbolic difference underwriting crime
narrative and distinguishing it from other narrative forms is given another twist (what Ludmer calls "torsión") when the murderer is a woman:
"la cadena de mujeres que matan cuenta otra vez cada vez que un grupo
nuevo, un sujeto-posición diferente, se abre camino entre los intersticios
de los demás" [the chain of women who kill tells once again each time
that a new group, a different subject position, is opening a path in the
interstices of the others] (793). In Gaspar de Alba's story, this exploration
of theoretical positionings, this opening into a new and different subject
position, explodes onto the page with Mercedes' revelation of her murders of her monstrous child and of her abusive first husband with the
collaboration and complicity of the curandera Estrella González. This
criminal twist permanently alters our perception of the stereotypical, self-
abnegating Mexican housewife and forces us to reread the entire volume
again, so as to reevaluate the other stories of women's relationships to
abusive men, from Malinche's time to the present, from another perspective: that of justifiable rage and deliberative action.

Ludmer notes that this symbolic and narratological twist in fiction
about women who kill often finds an analogy in the distortion of the
juridical field. Like the murders to which Mercedes confesses, women's
crimes tend to be domestic, private: the so-called crimes of passion. Ludmer comments that these women, in their narrative representations at
least, are seldom prosecuted by the state and infrequently brought to

"justice" in any formal or informal sense. For Ludmer this double torsion acts both as a distortion (of the narrative underpinnings of crime fiction, of the juridical structure) and a reconfiguration: "la pone en contacto con otras 'realidades'" [it puts her in contact with other "realities"] (793). This too is the case of Gaspar de Alba's characters, for it is only through the acceptance of this strange new subject position, that of the woman who has deliberately killed other human beings, that Mercedes can be pressured into the other reality: that of serving as host mother for the curandera's miracle conception.

Finally, this narrative twist has further consequences, ones that carry heavy implications for larger social structures. Ludmer concludes her lucid argument with the proposal that women who kill "son delincuentes de la verdad y de la legitimidad, los valores del estado: . . . se sitúan en el campo semántico de la duplicidad" [are delinquent from truth and legitimacy, the values of the state. . . . they are situated in the semantic field of duplicity] (795), and thus, curiously,

> Ese abrirse camino en las diferencias es el "delito": un instrumento que traza una línea de demarcación y transforma el estatus simbólico de una figura . . . y también un instrumento fundador de culturas. (793)
>
> [This opening of paths among differences is the "crime": an instrument that traces a line of demarcation and transforms the symbolic status of a figure . . . , and also an instrument that founds cultures.]

Mercedes' crime inescapably projects her into this founding role, and even in the confession of murder, and her husband's absolution for this act, she retains the secret of the price she was required to pay for her actions: agreeing to carry the child who will recuperate lost memories of the last five hundred years. In the curandera's words, "only by seeding the new world with the old names will the memories come back" (101). Estrella González's concrete reference in this passage is, of course, to the name "Xochitl" (Nahuatl for "flower") that she gives the baby; however, by a narrative twist, the memories that return are also the memories of previous crimes, or justifiable acts of rebellion against conquerors past and present: vomiting words in various tongues, piercing the conqueror's member with cactus spines, poisoning the abuser, aborting or eliminating the monstrous fruit of rape.

Significantly, Mercedes finds it easier to confess and expiate the old crime than to explain the—for her—even more tormenting secret of her daughter's conception. The narrative makes it clear that Mercedes sees this old crime as merely the prologue to the real story she has to tell and cannot confess. This unconfessed crime, more than anything else, seems to catalyze the crisis at the end of the story, in which Mercedes is simultaneously tormented by the wails of her ghostly son (her murdered husband causes no twinge of conscience) and the burden of her secret pregnancy. Throughout the collection, the folkloric/mythic figure of La Llorona, the weeping woman who murdered her children in a fit of madness, haunts such intimations of a mother's guilt for abandoning her child. Here, in this final story, the tale of murder and madness is once again given a twist. Xochitl María Espinosa (the prickly last name is entirely apropos) breaks open both the piñata and the Pandora's box, releasing all the messy complexities of memory and historical imaginings, but does so in the context of a feminocentric (if vaguely sinister) genealogy that ties recuperated memory to cultural destiny.

Anne McLeod describes the effects of feminism for women as a process of unhinging, of imagining "antithetical relations between the parts in such a way that the ontological framework within which they have been thought comes unhinged" (59). Likewise, Gaspar de Alba's inquiry into the twists and torsions of a Mexican American woman's narration of her doubled and duplicitous histories point toward an unhinging of both U.S.- and Mexican-based masculinist ontological frameworks. To take this step runs the risk of becoming unhinged in its second sense as well: thus the continual flirting with madness. Gaspar de Alba's literary practice challenges readers to rethink the category of the woman as discursive subject/object outside the essentialist frame into which she has so traditionally been cast, as she also forces us to return to a question relative to the field of literary study at large, that of the struggle with and against the power of words. In putting pressure on ignored and reinscribed histories of origins, she suggests not only a model for revitalizing national and cultural mythic structures, but also a method for dislocating the hinge between linguistic and extralinguistic binaries such as the one that has exercised us over the last few pages.

This, of course, brings us back to the original question of the canon and its theoretical twists and turns. The Gaspar de Alba who resists a nostalgia for a universalizing, utopic, abstract borderness is equally careful in her stories to resist cooption into another version of the North's hermeneutic map. In these powerful texts, it is through Gaspar de Alba's reinscription of concepts of gender right in an uncompromisingly bilingual context that she exposes the weakness and bias of much Mexican, Chicano/a, and mainstream U.S. theoretical meditations on borders. And that resistance, of course, makes her a problematic candidate for canonicity. At the same time, thinkers throughout the Americas have become disillusioned with canonical theoretical models that were created out of and for other cultural conditions.

Most important, the last few years have seen a widespread recognition of cultural basis and bias of a theoretical structure formerly imagined to be transparent and universal. While the power/knowledge relations remain severely unequal between theory talk and any kind of border-grounded work, the most pertinent question seems to us to be how to rethink issues derived from both Euro-American and Latin American theoretical discourses so as to recontextualize them for a reality that we all know is vastly distinct.

# 3. Displacement

*Rosario Sanmiguel*

Es difícil, en el lado mexicano, acudir al término cultura del modo habitu-
al: alta cultura, manifestaciones de la vida espiritual de un país, conexiones
con el corpus de Occidente . . . , etc. Pensada así, difícilmente se puede
hablar de cultura fronteriza.
                    —*Carlos Monsiváis, "Cultura de la frontera"*

Mexico's northern border has been perceived from the center of the
country as a space where the language, customs, and lifestyle of the
United States enjoy easy cultural penetration by virtue of immediacy
of contact with that country. In the best of cases, border culture has
always been understood "como 'diferente' a la que predomina en otras
regiones" [as "different" from that predominating in other regions] (Castellanos and López y Rivas, 68), where the "scare quotes" around the key
word point to whole vocabularies of loss. Many times border culture
is rejected as nonexistent, oxymoronic, or inexplicable, as Monsiváis
suggests in the epigraph to this chapter. Often in these types of discussions, the inhabitants of the northern border are pitied or despised as
uprooted, unpatriotic individualists with no proper sense of national
identity—"pochos" or "vendepatrias"—among other, even worse and
more pejorative, slanders.[1]

The border stereotype grounds itself, on the one hand, on the central Mexican need to express a single national identity, a concept inherited from nineteenth-century positivism and from the felt urgency of creating a strong and impenetrable sense of Mexicanness in the face of the national trauma of having lost half of its territory in the war with the United States.[2] These practices are reinforced by a tendency toward the "estudio de 'lo cultural' como algo folklórico [y no como] un aspecto fundamental de la práctica social y política de nuestros pueblos" [study of "culture" in the context of the folkloric (and not as) a fundamental aspect of the social and political practices of our people] (Valdés-Villalva, 251). On the other hand, this consolidation of the border stereotype derives from reference to exclusionary cultural practices, such as "interpretaciones subjetivas de ciertos datos, como el uso de palabras del inglés, castellanizadas para el uso coloquial" [subjective interpretations of specific data such as the use of English words and Spanish-English loan-blends in colloquial use] (Bustamante, "Frontera," 109).

In recent years, the popularity of border studies and the creation of binational research institutes on the Mexico-U.S. border has done much to ameliorate this situation.[3] A gradual demythification of old, derogatory stereotypes has taken place as the perspective on the border has slowly become more adequate to social reality, including, from a central Mexican perspective, a recognition of the undeniable economic attractions of the border area as the most prosperous and rapidly industrializing part of the country (albeit through emphasis on highly controversial maquiladora plants). At the same time, in the academic world the explosion of culture studies and the pervasiveness of postmodern philosophy have assured a privileged site for "the border," in which emphasis has rested not on studies of *the* national identity or on a single, abjected, countervailing border identity, but rather on the concept of multiple and fluid individual, regional, and national identities.

Within the reevaluation (and revalorization) of the border space, the problematics of identities and their expression or representation has been on the agenda in many disciplinary fields. Nevertheless, despite the boom in border studies, and the impression that border literature (or literature without borders) is a hot topic of discussion, there is still a good deal of inertia to overcome on the part of the general public, which mostly still subscribes to the view articulated (presumably ironically) by Monsiváis that there is no culture on the border. For those scholars who do border studies on the literature and culture of Mexico's northern border from within that space, it seems unbalanced and unhealthy that critics and thinkers of the stature of Carlos Monsiváis or writers like Carlos Fuentes achieve the bulk of national attention on border issues. Yet these writers, who are, perhaps, passionately drawn to the dynamic quality of the border cities, seem to have set themselves the goal of redeeming this region through their writing, while at the same time their written apologia necessarily stumbles and falls short in representational power. Thus, Fuentes' novel-in-stories, *La frontera de cristal* [The crystal frontier] reflects a life and a language very familiar to metropolitan readers of that author's other works, and very distant from the realities of daily life and language on the border. It is, nevertheless, widely touted in both central Mexico and the United States as an important work of border literature, to the exclusion of writers from the border area who are certainly less well connected to international publishing and distribution circuits.

Similarly, Monsiváis's statement of typical centrist sentiments could not be more clear. There is little knowledge or recognition in central Mexico of border artistic production, whether in painting, literature, or music, for which reason the definition of border culture self-limits to a kind of anthropological side note. We come back to this important Mexican essayist and chronicler at various points in this study since he represents for us one of the most powerful voices of dissent in central Mexican culture, while at the same time we can trace out how the hegemonic discourse underlies and penetrates the ideologies even of smart dissenting intellectuals like him despite efforts at resistance. Monsiváis, a shrewd and judicious observer of contemporary urban culture, perhaps unwittingly falls back into the structures of dominant discourse because even for him it is difficult to imagine the cultural products of the border under the rubric of Culture with a capital *C*. The effect of such inadvertent substructures is to marginalize these noncentrally produced artistic efforts both from the "vida espiritual" [spiritual life] of Mexico as well as from the larger discourse of Western thought.

Rosario Sanmiguel, unlike Fuentes and Monsiváis, has lived practically all her life in the area of Ciudad Juárez–El Paso, and her collection of short stories, *Callejón Sucre y otros relatos* [Sucre Street and other stories], has suffered from the intellectual colonialism we have traced out in the introduction to this book. While she is not well known in centrist circles, Rosario Sanmiguel's first texts began to circulate in and from

Mexico City in cultural supplements to newspapers five or six years before the "boom" in interest in literature from the northern border. In order to achieve this basic level of national circulation, Sanmiguel had to cross multiple borders. One such border was the distance between the northern provinces and Mexico City, which also meant making a transition from minor local publications with no particular reputation to newspapers that enjoy national distribution. This transition permitted her to "colarse en la literatura nacional" [infiltrate national literature]. Another important boundary she had to cross was that of gender, still a formidable barrier given the characteristic shape of Mexican culture and the very real gender limitations posed by the constitution of those groups holding literary power in that country. For a woman writer from the northern border of the country to see her work validated in black and white in the center signified a long, slow process and a silent presence that only gradually began to make itself visible on a national level.

In this day and age it is no longer news to talk about the historical silencing of women writers. Nor is it novel to celebrate the post-1980s surge in the recognition of women writers. The fact is, women authors, mostly from the center of the country and from Mexico City, have achieved not only visibility but also large-scale distribution on the international level. Rosario Sanmiguel is not one of these privileged few; although she has paid her dues and crossed the bridges to the national literary scene, her work has not become as well known as that of certain of her contemporaries, including, most obviously, Laura Esquivel, whose border-located *Como agua para chocolate* [Like water for chocolate] was not only an international bestselling novel and a megahit movie, but also inspired restaurants in the United States, Europe, and Mexico to reproduce that novel's meals on their tony menus. Perhaps this lag in the attention given to Sanmiguel's work is because presses prefer to gamble on new writers from the center of the country, perhaps because there is still an incomplete understanding of "la posición que ocupan las mujeres con respecto al lenguaje y a la tradición literaria de las que han sido excluidas, [ni se ha logrado] desenmascarar las ideologías de los textos y los supuestos sobre los que se basan las políticas editoriales" [the position that women occupy with respect to language and the literary tradition from which they have been excluded . . . (nor has it been possible) to unmask textual ideologies and suppositions upon which editorial policies are based] (Golubov, 123). Perhaps the problem is that, unlike authors such as Fuentes who speak in a familiar centrist idiom even when discussing exotica like the now-popular northern border, Sanmiguel speaks from the border in a language and with a perspective derived from that zone.

In this chapter we want to highlight first of all the way in which Rosario Sanmiguel uses language and the literary tradition as narrative strategies which she employs in a dialogic and self-conscious manner as a kind of springboard for her specific concerns. Consequently, these strategies permit her to locate herself on the borders of convention in order to rearticulate and to authorize her own writing. We understand by textual border those moments in the text when the writing subject manifests her preoccupation with the act of writing, or when we note an intertextual conversation that serves, in multiple instances, to authorize a marginal writing practice. In this analysis we have had recourse to the theoretical constructs developed by Iris Zavala and Myriam Díaz-Diocaretz; for both these critics, dialogism occurs through the exchanges of real voices and not exclusively through textual encounters. Such dialogic voices, in Zavala's terms, allow us

> releer y reescribir las formas genéricas hegemónicas mismas y sus códigos maestros, y mostrar las formas en que se han re-apropiado, neutralizado o coaptado los textos. Pero además . . . distingue entre la noción de *textualidad* y la de *práctica textual,* separándose así de la teoría feminista más difundida. Podríamos decir que es una práctica desde el *margen* y la *diferencia,* que sitúa la lectura interpretativa no sólo incorporando la diferencia, sino la polivalencia tácita de los discursos. (75)

> [to reread and rewrite the generic hegemonic terms themselves and their master codes, and to show the forms in which texts have been reappropriated, neutralized, or coopted. Furthermore, . . . it distinguishes between the notion of *textuality* and that of *textual practice,* separating itself thus from the most accepted feminist theory. We can say that it is a practice from the *margin* and from *difference,* that situates interpretative reading as not only incorporating difference, but also the tacit polyvalence of discourses.]

Díaz-Diocaretz and Zavala's project presupposes a reading in which the relation among the voices in the text presents itself through a "multiplicidad de elementos discursivos que pueden actuar con estrategias diferentes" [multiplicity of discursive elements that can act with different strategies] (Zavala, 75), without conceptualizing one discourse as oppressive and the other as oppressed. This is an essential concept in analyzing Sanmiguel's works, for while there is clearly a power differential in the dialogue between dominant and border cultures, Sanmiguel's stories stand out for the subtlety and nuance she provides in her intertextual exchanges.

In the same manner, Sanmiguel's texts problematize female discursive practices. The point of departure in this context is the plurality of social experiences through which female subjects have been/are being constructed in conventional literary practice; thus, "la escritura está determinada por el contexto histórico de producción y recepción: la escritora, el referente, las características formales del texto y la lectora" [writing is determined by the historical context of production and reception: the writer, the referent, the formal characteristics of the text and the reader] (Díaz-Diocaretz, 120). It is important to recall that Sanmiguel, as a writing subject, dialogues with certain norms and literary conventions implicit in her choice of expressive genre. These conventions are, of course, profoundly linked to the hierarchies of textual practices. In Latin America, such hierarchies can be most typically represented by key aesthetic moments like modernism, magic realism, and the New Novel. One important aspect of the analysis of Sanmiguel's work, then, would be to trace out the exchanges of social values that have left their mark on her work, and how these values have been internalized or subverted by their translation to the border space.

Thematically, *Callejón Sucre y otros relatos* immerses itself fully in the border problematic, with all the complexity, both positive and negative, such a commitment will necessarily imply: the author does not shy away from revealing ugly realities like the existence of ethnocentrism, marginalization, poverty, violence, and uneven industrialization. At the same time, Sanmiguel is careful not to fall into the easy recuperability of folkloric "costumbrismo" that would betray co-option by the too-simplistic centrist projection of border life and customs. Instead, in her stories she

aspira a una visión de mundo que incorpora . . . una preocupación mayor por detectar, en el interior de sus personajes las instancias fronterizas que enmarcan toda vida humana, y propone como frontera esos límites que todo individuo debe transgredir a fin de procurarse un destino más acorde a su condición. (Barquet, 85)

[aspires to a vision of the world that incorporates . . . a principal concern with detecting in the interiority of her characters the border instantiations that delimit all human life and she proposes as a border those limits that each individual must transgress in order to achieve a destiny more coherent with his or her nature.]

Consistently in these stories, the social and political imperatives of border life are played out with relation to a deep imbrication in internal processes relevant to individual characters and their personal conundrums.

Thus, Rosario Sanmiguel's literary project reflects an internal search for relevant models of modern life on the part of her mostly female characters. Her prose is not only reflexive but contestatory, although at the same time subversion tends to occur in subtle and almost unheard gestures, by way of which she hints at an extremely sharp social critique. Thus, Sanmiguel requires that her readers pay careful and nuanced attention to the messages she sends us since, in addition to dialoguing with her geographical space, the narrator constantly challenges assumptions about perspective and agency. Her narrative shifts and changes exist in a constant flux with respect to the reader's position. In addition, Sanmiguel plays with temporal structures so that just when the reader begins to believe that the narration is operating in a smooth linear process, she abruptly changes temporal and spatial referents, creating in this manner a fragmented border textuality.

The female characters in Sanmiguel's short texts exist in dialogic relation to, and transgressively displace, the image of border women (or at least of women from Ciudad Juárez) created by official discourse and insistently reaffirmed in recent years in the national and international press. This stereotypical image of women of Juárez is linked almost exclusively in the public mind to the continuing horrors of the unsolved murders of young women in the city and to the recent wave of violence associated with drug trafficking. In a comment typical of this yellow journalistic coverage, Charles Bowden presents Juárez as a city so frightening that "even the devil is scared of living there" (44). Sanmiguel, on the other hand, without ignoring the dangers of her city, shows her readers a vital urban space inhabited by people from different social classes and ages who live in their city day after day, in an ordinary way.

The only male protagonist in this collection appears in the title story, "Callejón Sucre." Since this is also the first story in the volume, it has considerable significance as the text that establishes the spatial image for the city in which the entire volume of stories will take place: the border between Juárez and El Paso. This story sets the scene for the book in other important ways as well; it underscores the realization that along with the geopolitical border, this author will be creating other interior borders that are perhaps less perceptible to the observer but equally important to the reader. "Callejón Sucre," for example, presents the border between life and death, between the urban exterior and what the character feels. We see the way in which the world as imagined by human beings transforms itself. In this story there is a twist in the articulation of the cityscape, as the city and its bars—spaces typically associated with the male city dweller—are recuperated through Sanmiguel's impeccable reconstruction:

> Recorremos la avenida Juárez colmada de bullicio, de vendedores de cigarros en las esquinas, de automóviles afuera de las discotecas, de trasnochadores. A ambos lados de la calle los anuncios luminosos se disputan la atención de los que deambulan en busca de un lugar donde consumir su tiempo. Yo me quedo en el Callejón Sucre, a la puerta del Monalis. (10)

> [We travel down an Avenida Juárez filled with noise, cigarette sellers on the corners, cars outside the discotheques, night owls. On both sides of the street the lighted signs fight for the attention of pedestrians searching for a place to kill time. I remain on Callejón Sucre until I reach the door of the Mona Lisa.]

In the Mona Lisa we find out that the protagonist was a former entertainer ("antiguo animador") (11) and Lucía, his girlfriend, is a dancer from the same nightclub. Sanmiguel describes the intimate moments (border instances) between the characters by describing each through the perception of the other. The perception of otherness on multiple occasions is not marked by binary oppositions, but rather with what Barquet calls a complex relation between the "you" and "otros tús con quienes pueden relacionarse y exteriorizar su intimidad" [other "you's" with whom the characters can interrelate and so exteriorize their intimacy] (Barquet, 86). Sanmiguel writes, for instance:

> Una mujer de ojos achinados baila sobre la pasarela que divide el salón en dos secciones.Un grupo de adolescentes celebra escandalosamente sus contorsiones. . . . Una hermosa madeja de cabello oscuro le cae hasta la

cintura, pero un repugnante lunar amplio y negruzco le mancha uno de los muslos. Mientras la oriental baila imagino a Lucía trepada en esa tarima. La veo danzar. Veo sus finos pies, sus tobillos esbeltos, pero también viene a mi memoria la enorme sutura que ahora marca el vientre, las sondas, sueros y drenes que invaden su carne. (10–11)

[A woman with almond-shaped eyes dances on the catwalk that divides the hall into two sections. A group of adolescents rowdily praise her contortions. . . . A lovely mop of dark hair falls to her waist, but a repugnant huge, blackish mole stains one of her thighs. While the oriental woman dances I imagine Lucía climbing up on that platform. I see her dancing. I see her delicate feet, her slender ankles, but at the same time the huge suture mark that now scars her belly, the probes, the saline and drain tubes that invade her flesh also come to my mind.]

The description of the oriental woman first takes cognizance of her sensuality, a not-unexpected gesture in descriptions of border life, which all too often tend to focus on the sleazy aspects of nighttime entertainment in the zone. Likewise the mole can be easily encoded in stereotypes about the border's miscellaneous crowd of fallen women. However, this is a narrator who speaks from inside this scene, with genuine knowledge and affection. At the same time, the combination of an appreciation for the exotic dancing, and the exaggerated description of the repugnant mole disrupts the reader's and the narrator's appreciation for the dance and brings the character into his immediate reality. It is precisely at this point that the protagonist projects his dying wife onto the dancer. The parallelism that exists between the oriental woman's pretty head of hair and the disgusting mole on the one hand and Lucia's lovely ankles and the huge suture mark on the other, place all the characters in a perfect border space. It is in a state of betweenness from which one can observe the moment of transition perfectly delineated: between beauty and ugliness, aesthetic appreciation and vulgar lust: in the final analysis, between Lucia's life and the death.

Furthermore, the world of the Mona Lisa allows the character to recognize himself in the other: "en su cara veo la mía" [in her face I see mine] (11), he muses, as well as to reencounter himself and come to terms with his past: "Nada vine a buscar; sin embargo, encuentro la imagen oculta del antiguo animador de un cabaret de segunda" [I didn't come here looking for anything; even so, I find the hidden image of the former second-rate cabaret entertainer] (11). The moment also forces him to imagine his own crossing into the future of imminent widowerhood: "Para distraer el ánimo enciendo un cigarrillo que sólo consigue amargarme el aliento. De regreso, [al hospital] . . . me tiendo a esperar que transcurra otra noche" [in order to distract myself I light a cigarette that only gives me a bitter taste. Back again, [in the hospital] . . . I lie down to await the passing of another night] (11–12).

Clearly, the nightclub/cabaret that Sanmiguel imagines in "Callejón Sucre" has little similarity to the sensationalized location referenced by so many colonizing discourses. Rather than merely a site of female exploitation, it becomes a historicized locale that allows the protagonist the opportunity for self-examination.[4] When Sanmiguel transforms this space of a sleazy performance into a space of "quiescent life," the hegemonic images of the nightclub and the border are subverted. In this sense, Sanmiguel's representation uses the image of the border and of the cabaret as given by metropolitan discourse, but she shifts it into an entirely different image clearly at odds with that located in the realm of dominant culture.

In "Un silencio muy largo" [A very long silence] Rosario Sanmiguel also recuperates this masculine space of the bar in another respect, although in this story the protagonist is a woman and it is the men who slip to the background as "un elemento más de la cotidianidad espacial" [one more aspect of everyday space] (Rodríguez Lozano, 239). The arrival of Francis, the protagonist, in the Las Dunas bar causes a considerable consternation among the regular clients in the place, since it is absolutely unexpected that a woman "de su categoría" [of her quality] would show up in place like that one. Once again, in this unexpected juxtaposition, the stereotypical chronotope of the nightclub is undermined. Francis invades a space that is associated with purely masculine efforts to drown their pain, and asserts her right to do the same. The writing subject (Sanmiguel) permits the subject of her narrative (Francis) to take possession of and operate freely in this space, which in quotidian reality is still reserved exclusively for men.

The title of the story comes from a sentence placed near the end of the story, after the request is put to Francis that she not return to this locale. In the final scene in the narration, from which the phrase is taken, the "long silence" refers to the lapse of time between the men's request and Francis's response; however, structurally, this silence can be parsed on three levels. On the first and most obvious level, it represents the clock time in which the narration is developing. This chronological tracing of the narrative would begin with the protagonist's arrival in Las Dunas in the middle of winter, and end with her departure when spring winds are beginning to make themselves felt. The second level references psychological time, the time that parallels the introspection of the main character and reflects her meeting with her lover, their breakup, and her recuperation. The third level subtly links the author to the sociocultural text, and the long silence broken in this respect would be that of Latin American women writers who have been excluded from or written out of the male cultural text and who have only recently begun to demand access to such jealously guarded male sanctums (Guerra-Cunningham, 39–40).

In this story Rosario Sanmiguel cedes the narrative voice to the different patrons of the bar and, through this shift in focalization, registers their distinct ideological positions. From the very moment of Francis's introduction to the reader, we know that she has broken with traditional values by accepting a relationship with a married man, that in taking the decision not to see him again she once again steps outside the expectations of female behavior, and that she cements her unorthodoxy by coming to Las Dunas in order to perform the eminently masculine task of forgetting the faithless lover with a dose of hard liquor. The cold and snow outside, the shadowy atmosphere of the bar, and her own intromission all help the reader to imagine the interior world of this character, and the contrast of the noisy surroundings and her own silence reinforces the protagonist's isolation.

This silence is, of course, a voluntary one, deriving from Francis's own decision with respect to her long-term lover that after ten years "estaba dispuesta a cualquier cosa con tal de sacárselo definitivamente del cuerpo y de la memoria" [she was prepared to do anything in order to shove him definitively out of her body and her memory] (52). This proposition, too, suggests a clear (if subtle) break with the conventional course of love affairs; it is Francis who has broken up with Alberto and wants to clean herself of their mutual past: first from the body, the symbol and source of her desire, and then from her memory, the guardian of the past. Briefly: the author transgresses the established order by proposing a flesh-and-blood woman as her main character, a woman capable of feeling and admitting her desire. Francis is a decisive woman as well. In order to make a complete break with her former lover, she changes both her home and her job to keep him from contacting her. In this manner, she completely rejects her previous behavior and retools herself as a dynamic subject searching for her autonomous identity. This is another marker of the new subject, a subject who, to use Rosario Castellanos's famous term, is open to "otro modo de ser" [another way of being]. At this point the protagonist is finally ready "para salir a la vida—a la *suya*—nuevamente" [to go out into life, *her* life, once again] (54) (emphasis added). She is no longer willing to pretend to play the patient Penelope role and wait for her boyfriend to get a divorce; she realizes that he never will do so, and so takes the initiative of leaving him. She opts for recuperating her life: "Estaba lista para partir. 'Primero pasar unos días con mi madre y buscar la reconciliación; luego, retomar el hilo de la vida'" [She was ready to leave. "First I'll spend a few days with my mother to reconcile with her and then I'll pick up the thread of my life"] (72).

Reconciliation with the mother is a constant theme in Sanmiguel's narrative.[5] Almost all of Sanmiguel's protagonists are in open conflict with their mothers, mostly because of generational differences. In Francis's case, the section entitled "La ventana" [The window] clearly defines these differences:

> Su madre la había educado en los principios de las buenas costumbres y la religión católica. No imaginó que su hija pudiera querer una vida diferente a la que ella le había impuesto: escuela de monjas, modales recatados y horarios restringidos para salir y llegar a casa.
>
> Francis quería ver el mundo, sentirse libre, por eso cuando se sintió con fuerzas para abandonar la casa familiar, lo había hecho. (62)

> [Her mother had educated her in the principles of good manners and the Catholic religion. She couldn't imagine that her daughter might want a different life from the one imposed on her: convent school, modest behavior, and restricted hours for leaving and returning home.
>
> Francis wanted to see the world, to feel free, that's why she left home as soon as she felt strong enough to do so.]

The most important function of this quote is precisely to delineate the shape of this generational divide. The mother—the standard-bearer of tradition—wants that familiar structure for her daughter, and this desire is in direct conflict with the daughter's wishes. Equally important, the reader is advised that the protagonist of Sanmiguel's stories is no longer inclined to blindly follow the dictates or the rules of dominant discourse, whether articulated by men or women, lovers or mothers.

Francis's actions are subversive on every level: with respect to her family, in her relations with Alberto, and in her invasion of a male public (private) space. Not only does she leave Alberto when dominant discourse would dictate that he abandon her, but she leaves him because she can no longer put up with his cowardice. His actions, she notes, "eran actos de cobardía disfrazados de cinismo. Así como no era capaz de dejar el trabajo que tanto le disgustaba, tampoco lo era para establecerse y vivir en pareja con ella" [were acts of cowardice disguised as cynicism. Just as he was unable to leave the job he hated so much, neither was he able to establish himself and live in relationship with her] (64). Furthermore, the relationship Francis envisions as the preferred partnership also remains outside traditional canons of behavior since "no se trataba de casarse, tener hijos y pagar las letras del refrigerador. La cuestión era vivir juntos, intentar ser felices, cualquier cosa que eso pudiera significar" [it wasn't about getting married, having children, and making refrigerator payments. The idea was to live together, try to be happy, whatever that might mean] (54). She refuses to accept the formula for a happy-ever-after story as homogenized by social convention and maternal mores.

Other women in the story serve as counterpoints to Francis, as they have interiorized the dominant discursive norms for women. These women include China and Morra, "las empleadas más antiguas en las Dunas" [the oldest employees in las Dunas] (52), along with Katia and Nely, two young prostitutes who regularly hang out there. At first, when Katia has an argument with Francis, she thinks the other woman has no place in the bar, given the obvious social class differences between them. The prostitute is concerned and jealous that Francis might steal away potential clients.[6] The tensions between Katia and Francis signal a problem of class expectations, along with pressures involved in the evolution of a new ethical model that gradually makes itself more apparent as the story develops. This new ethics has to do with the solidarity that eventually establishes itself between Francis and the prostitutes despite the fact that they belong to different social classes and constantly antagonize each other. Their ultimately supportive attitude opposes the generalized projection that a woman's worst enemy is another woman. The scenes with Katia and Nely also offer entry into a subaltern discourse related to relations between men and women in nightclubs that is quite distinct from dominant discourse. There is in this story no sexual or sensual exploitation of the prostitute's body, nor of the relationships established among Francis, China, and Morra. For instance, after a supposed robbery involving one of the clients we hear this exchange:

> "Cincuenta pesos no pagan un minuto de vejación."
>
> "No entiendo señora, pero pa' mí que usté tampoco entiende," respondió Morra fastidiada.
>
> "Quiero decir algo muy sencillo Morra," dijo Francis mirándola fijamente a los ojos, "aquí las robadas son ustedes."
>
> Las palabras de Francis crepitaron como la flor olvidada en un libro.
>
> . . . Ella también sentía eso, aunque nunca lo hubiera verbalizado. (58)

> ["Fifty pesos doesn't pay for one minute of humiliation."
>
> "I don't understand, ma'am, but I don't think you don't understand either," responded Morra, annoyed.
>
> "I want to say something very simple, Morra, "said Francis looking her straight in the eye, "here, you're the ones who get robbed."
>
> Francis's words crackled like the forgotten flower in a book.
>
> . . . She felt it too, though she had never said it.]

More than a judgment against the prostitutes or a reaffirmation of the stereotype of that aspect of northern border life, Rosario Sanmiguel criticizes the exploitation as well as the social discourse in which some of these women have been submerged. This exploitation of women along the lines of gender expectations on numerous occasions runs from generation to generation. Sanmiguel's story projects this fact through her characterization of China and Morra, who had worked in this bar since Old Varela's time, and brings it up to date with Nely and Katia, who work for Young Varela. But Sanmiguel also projects an alternative discourse. Francis's words and Morra's acknowledgment of the exploitation unveil a silenced voice of rejection against social practice of prostitution, deriving from the prostitutes themselves.

The story ends when Francis takes leave of China and gives her the ring that Alberto had given her the last night they spent together. This handing over of the ring, a standard symbol of union, is the most concrete evidence supporting Francis's determination to remake her life.

Winter has ended and spring is about to arrive. The change of season and the departure from the bar where she has buried her silence all support Francis's initiative. She leaves with her new vision of the world intact, and those who remain behind, at least during the period of her participation in the life of that place, also find themselves displaced. Morra's vision of her fellow women becomes one more piece of data that helps us to understand this change in episteme:

> Morra conocía a muchas mujeres, unas más hermosas o más feas; algunas desaliñadas o perezosas; otras inteligentes y sagaces. Nada las hacía imperfectas. ¿Qué era la perfección—creía ella—si no la luminosidad del alma en ciertos momentos de la vida? (73)

> [Morra knew many women, some more beautiful or uglier, some unkempt or lazy, others intelligent and wise. Nothing made them imperfect. What was perfection—she believed—if not the luminosity of the soul in certain moments in one's life?]

This final observation rearticulates the third level of silence noted above with respect to the feminine subject who writes and represents herself. In this story, Sanmiguel describes a handful of women, all of them perfectly within the considerations of this new ethics that is under construction throughout the story, leaving behind the old masculinist aesthetic models that no longer fit their feminine understandings of themselves or their border reality. Furthermore, she constructs this alternative ethics in the context of and with reference to border instances in the lives of each character. Most important, in Francis we discover "la reflexión sobre el pasado, indagación sobre el presente y, finalmente, el rescate de todo aquello (la madre y ella misma) que la ha de acompañar en su futura travesía por la orilla de su vida" [reflection on the past, inquiry into the present, and finally, a retrieval of all that (related to the mother and herself) which she will carry with her in her future travels on the riverbanks of her life] (Barquet, 86). Here, as in "Callejón Sucre," the exterior space of the bar provides a frame for an interior meditation by a character who crosses the border of depression and repression to pick up the pieces of her life and continue, now stronger, alone.

While "Un silencio muy largo" begins to analyze the parameters of topics once forbidden to earlier writers, "Paisaje en verano" [Landscape in summer] corroborates the rupture of this old silence. "Paisaje" tells the story of Cecilia, a young girl who experiences two important instances of border crossings: the transition from childhood to adolescence and her parents' separation. In addition, despite its brevity, "Paisaje en verano" also crosses several textual borders. Sanmiguel makes use of the old Cervantine technique of intercalating a second story alongside the main tale in this text—a technique the author deploys in other stories as well. "Paisaje en verano" tells us about Cecilia's fascination with reading by way of an omniscient narrator. Not only is the reader repeatedly reminded of this interest, but fragments of the novel Cecilia is reading are reproduced in the text. Added to this already rich mix, Sanmiguel also makes reference to biology texts and encyclopedias, as well as numerous mass culture materials, such as popular music, comic-book characters, and pop-culture figures.

"Paisaje en verano" revisits the literary tradition and subverts temporal structures, disarticulating linear and historical time as a coherent narrative thread. At the same time, this is not the kind of temporal dislocation of a Joycean stream of consciousness, a Rulfo-like deployment of fragmented vignettes of the dead, or Cortázar's or Asturias's temporal spirals. Sanmiguel in this story imprints the narrative surface with what Kristeva has called "women's time." Although time runs chronologically in "Paisaje en verano," the narrative voice measures it with respect to recurrence and biological cycles. This emphasis on a woman's time as marked by the cycles of her body is underlined in the opening of the story, when a young girl worries about what she considers the lateness of her first period. The story ends with an evocative metaphor: "Cecilia, montada en bicicleta, se alejaba hasta convertirse en una mancha rojiza y vibrante" [Cecilia, riding her bicycle, distances herself until she becomes a vibrant reddish spot] (88). In evoking the time of a woman's biological cycles as a frame for this story, Sanmiguel hints that the borders Cecilia is crossing include those related to both the biological as well as the cultural texts. In her anticipation of her menstrual period, Cecilia inhabits the border between childhood and puberty.

The young woman's appreciation and appropriation of space also represents a transgressive act, both in her infringement upon specific territories and in her sense of the freedom that her urban wanderings provide her. Young Cecilia makes into her own familiar space the streets, the library, or the café, the characteristic haunts of both middle-class and marginalized men. Throughout the story we see her walk from school to home, enjoy her solitary wanderings, go to the movies or the library, and take pleasure in the solitude of her room as she dedicates herself to reading. For example, after the Spanish teacher throws her out of class, instead of going to her next class Cecilia decides to "recorrer las calles del Centro, donde el mundo, el verdadero—según su percepción—, no estaba regido por ley o autoridad alguna que le impidiera sentirse libre, ir a todas partes para observarlo todo" [to wander up and down the streets downtown where what she perceived as the real world was not ruled by any law or authority that would prevent her from feeling free, from going wherever she wanted so as to observe everything] (80). In contrast with the nighttime city and the nightclub evoked in "Callejón Sucre," a site of transgressive actions that marks the border between Lucía's life and death, in "Paisaje en verano" the city is fully alive and replete with the daytime expectations that mark the separation between childhood and adolescence: "A medida que se alejaba las calles se tornaban más excitantes y ruidosas, pero fue hasta la de 5 de Mayo—punto donde en la ciudad se demarcaba el oriente del poniente—, cuando en verdad se sintió dueña de sus pasos" [The farther she went, the more noisy and exciting the streets became, but it was only when she arrived at 5 de Mayo—the exact point in the city that divided east from west—that she really felt in control of her wanderings] (80). In addition to reflecting the potentiality of a young girl on the threshold of adulthood, this description of a living, lively, livable city offers a contrasting view with typical border descriptions of crime and violence such as that we have already noted in writers like Charles Bowden.

This story places a special emphasis on the act of reading as an everyday practice, and it is through this habit of reading that the character is most forcefully constructed. Certainly, reading serves the young girl as an escape from family problems. At the same time Cecilia uses the books she reads in order to explore and understand her woman's body. Here, as in other Sanmiguel stories, we can discern the author's intention of restoring to narrative the body of the woman in all her different stages. Thus, the reinscription of the protagonist's body is doubly encoded in this text: by what she reads, and by how we read her.[7] Through Cecilia's eyes and her readings, we are also thrust into a preadolescent meditation on menstruation and on masturbation. At the same time, the reader also uncovers hints of a revalorization of a potentially lesbian body, partly suggested through the insinuation of incestuous desires for her mother:

Las sábanas eran blancas, limpias y frescas; a pesar de ello, sentía mucho calor y no lograba concentrarse en la lectura. . . . Entonces dejó la cama para ir en busca de su madre. La encontró en su recámara, dormida, vencida por el llanto; miró compasivamente su rostro sereno en el sueño y sintió un fuerte deseo por besar sus labios. Sólo el temor de despertarla impidió que lo hiciera. De vuelta en su dormitorio, Cecilia se quitó el camisón y se tendió sobre las sábanas. Estaba inquieta. Sus manos empezaban a recorrer el cuerpo, los brotes de los senos, el vientre, el pubis tierno. Sus dedos jugaron con el vello que le cubría el sexo infantil. Nadie creería que aún soy una niña, susurró perturbada. Su cuerpo, sus emociones no armonizaban; sintió náuseas; la tardanza de su primera regla la angustiaba. Bajó la mano un poco más, sus dedos presionaban la carne púber hasta que obtuvo una sensación agradable. A los pocos minutos también ella se quedó dormida. (83–84)

[The sheets were white, clean, and fresh, but despite that fact she felt very warm and was unable to concentrate on her reading. . . . So she left the bed to look for her mother. She found her sleeping in her bedroom, exhausted by her tears; she looked compassionately at her face smoothed out in sleep and felt a deep desire to kiss her on the lips. The only thing that stopped her was her fear that she might awaken. Back in her bedroom, Cecilia took off her nightgown and stretched out on the sheets. She was uncomfortable. Her hands began to explore her body, her budding breasts, her stomach, her tender pubis. Her fingers played in the hair that covered her child's sex. No one would believe that I'm still a child, she whispered, perturbed. Her body and her emotions were not in harmony; she felt nauseous; the lateness of her first period filled her with anxiety. She lowered her hand a bit more and her fingers pressed her fleshy pubis until she obtained an enjoyable sensation. A few minutes later she fell asleep.]

Sanmiguel reappropriates the female body confiscated and confined by tradition and demythifies it in describing the young woman's masturbatory moment. This scene is completely outside canons of good and evil, or as Amelia Valcárcel might say, the border narrator authorizes her character with "el derecho al mal" [the right to wickedness] (169). By reinscribing Cecilia's bodily manipulations as a textual strategy, the author begins to address a literary vacuum and to posit a different signification for the female body. As the same time, when Sanmiguel invents Cecilia's body, feelings, and desire, she also puts into question the sociohistorical and cultural terms defining the imaginary in patriarchal contexts. For Sanmiguel the representation of the young girl's exploration of her budding sexuality—whether encoded in her attraction to her mother or in her act of masturbation—is no longer a topic that should remain silenced. It is a phenomenon that exists and should therefore be articulated. This personal exploration of her body and her feelings is a natural part of Cecilia's search for her self, a search that takes her through byways different from those encoded in the novels and biology books she reads.

Rosario Sanmiguel is an able and subtle manipulator of intertextual reference in her stories, which often only fully reveal their palimpsestic quality only after several attentive readings. In "Paisaje en verano" the metaliterary reference to Quintela's novel is very obvious, as is the allusion to Kalimán, the protagonist of the comic book derived from the real-life story of "Kalimán, the escape artist," and likewise the brief mention of a puppet show. All of these references reverberate with Cecilia's own secret life, in that they centrally involve juggling, deception, and concealment. Perhaps such allusions are Sanmiguel's way of indicating her own concealment behind the text of her narrative, her ostensible disauthorization as the creator of this story. Or perhaps they are part of Sanmiguel's exploration of her own literary authority, or of Cecilia's independent self. The citation from Cecilia's novel speaks to both concerns, as it addresses the writing subject's manipulation of literary resources, while it also supports Cecilia in her exploration of the phenomena of her life through textual reference to a woman in childbirth: "Una mujer pálida y sudorosa que continuamente se humedecía con la lengua los labios resecos, acostada en un camastro de madera sentía que empezaba a derramar los fluidos del alumbramiento" [a pale and sweaty woman who continually licked her dry lips, she lay on her wooden bed feeling her uterine water break and begin to spill] (78).

In addition to all these popular texts, there is an intertextual reference to Sor Juana Inés de la Cruz which is almost imperceptible on first reading. This allusion can be located in the inquisitive nature of the young girl, her search for scientific knowledge about adolescence, and her use of certain phrases and gestures that recall the sixteenth-century nun's famous *Respuesta a Sor Filotea* [Response to Sor Filotea]. If in *Respuesta* Sor Juana constructs herself in the carefully parsed self-authorization/disauthorization with respect to her own knowledge and that of the ecclesiastical authorities, in "Paisaje en verano" Cecilia will construct herself in relation to her readings, her mother, and her relationship with Gorda Molinar. Josefina Ludmer's brilliant and seminal analysis in "Las tretas del debil" highlights in *Respuesta* the strategies of "no saber" [not knowing] and "no decir" [not speaking] as keys to the nun's practice and her deployment of the tactics of the weak when challenging the seemingly unbreachable structures of authority. For her part, Cecilia too begins from a basis of knowledge, in her case garnered from the Quintela novel and the biology texts she consults "afanada en desentrañar algunos misterios . . . que . . . la llevarían a esa comprensión de la vida que buscaba, de sus leyes y de su razón de ser" [eager to uncover the mysteries . . . that . . . will take her to the understanding of life that she sought, the knowledge of its laws and reason for being] (81).

The confrontation with the texts of the past in this story are mediated by the unnameable and the "no nombrado" [unnamed]. Just as Sor Juana has recourse to other knowledge bases to educate herself, Cecilia takes refuge in the erudite voices of biology books in order to learn from them the structural functions of life, supplementing this information with that derived from her novel in order to support her understanding and to anchor it in everyday practices. Like Sor Juana, who says she learned much from humble experiences such as cooking, Cecilia corroborates what she learns in books in her curiosity about watching a dog give birth to her puppies, in her experimentation with masturbation, and in her testing out of the truth of menstruation with reference to her own body. This constant search for self through books and bodies recapitulates the author's search for language and writing. In this way, by naming what has been unnameable—in this case Cecilia's body, feelings, and desires—the author uncovers traditional silences in the literary record, making visible the invisible and creating an alternative discourse with a different vision of the world than that available in dominant cultural representations.

Like Sor Juana in her consciousness of her marginality, Sanmiguel finds it necessary to deploy certain "tactics of the weak" in order to authorize her writing. The main character in "Paisaje en verano" recurs to the narrative strategies of her favorite readings in order to survive as an authority; that is, she takes from the narrative tradition those images she desires to possess. In a parallel manner, behind an ostensibly omniscient voice the narrator locates herself in a third, decentered space in which that voice is leached of authority. In this interstitial space, the dominant voice of the omniscient narrator slips into another kind of voice, one that constructs itself in relation to the armature of support provided by other literary, scientific, and cultural texts and anchored by relation to the insistent corporality of her protagonist. In a similar manner, the geographical space of Ciudad Juárez is reelaborated with respect to the clichés of dominant discourse that had constructed a particular, sensationalized image of the city for national consumption. Sanmiguel's literary practice—like Sor Juana's passionate defense of her hard-won search for knowledge four hundred years earlier—searches out, plays on, negotiates with, and rearticulates the space of the other, subverting in this manner the structures of power.

While in "Paisaje en verano" these textual crossings are examined as if in a microscope, in "La otra habitación" [The other room] textual borders are more obviously constructed. This story establishes an intertextual play with Virginia Woolf's *A Room of One's Own,* and also refers back to Uruguayan Juan Carlos Onetti's masterpiece, *La vida breve* [Brief life], and resonates as well with Argentine Sylvia Molloy's *En breve cárcel* [Certificate of absence] in its narrative structure. Sanmiguel learns the lessons of Woolf's *A Room of One's Own* and utilizes "las herramientas del amo" [the master's tools] (35), so that as a writer she is neither excluded from public discourse nor trapped within a narrow band of expectations.[8]

The title of the story already suggests that the text is in dialogue with Woolf, and it locates Anamaría, Sanmiguel's protagonist, not in Woolf's room, but in "otra habitación" [another room], analogous to but not identical with the space inhabited by the British writer.[9] Thus, numerous details of Sanmiguel's story offer direct references to Woolf: the details of the window, the movements of the character, the reference to noises from the contiguous room. At the same time, Sanmiguel wrenches this Woolfian room out of its familiar environment and resituates it in a very different space. No longer is the reader immersed in the world of a prestigious British university college's rooms, a space surrounded by trees, meadows, and a lake, nor do her neighbors belong to the British academic scene. Instead, the room in Sanmiguel's story is on the second floor of a cheap hotel, on a street known for its nightlife and its strip clubs; Anamaría's neighbors include a cabaret dancer and a contraband seller. In this manner the writing subject engages in an act of mimicry, she puts on a Woolfian mask and negotiates her own writing, a writing that will emerge not from a prestigious British room of one's own, but rather from a poor and peripheral "otra habitación." Sanmiguel's story evokes the gardens and landscapes that Woolf sees from her window, but these scenes are transposed onto the daily life of Avenida Juárez. It is from this perspective that Anamaría's intimacy will open out onto the collectivity and the border space will expand visually:

> La melodía del acordeón se mezclaba con el fragor del mundo. Algunas monedas caían en el sombrero a los pies del músico. Hacia el poniente la catedral soltaba las campanas. Los fieles a misa. Atrás del campanario devoraba una naranja en llamas. El templo metodista abría sus puertas. Los cholos buscaban sus guaridas, cercanas a las vías del tren. Las indígenas recogían sus tendidos de yerbas y de dulces. Los gringos cruzaban los puentes para beber toda la noche. (37)

> [The melody of the accordion mixed with the fragrance of the world. A few coins fell into the hat at the musician's feet. Toward the west, the cathedral's bells began to chime, calling the faithful to mass. Behind the bell tower an orange in flames was devoured. The Methodist temple opened its doors. The cholos looked for shelter near the train tracks. The Indians picked up their offerings of herbs and sweets. The gringos crossed the bridges in order to drink all night.]

In parsing out the particulars of Anamaría's story, Rosario Sanmiguel offers one specific answer to the question: what do women write? Because Anamaría enjoys the benefits of the five hundred pounds and a room that Woolf proposes as the minimal conditions for such activity, the protagonist of this story can boast of both economic and emotional stability. She has a formal education, reads local and national newspapers, and, like Woolf, is interested in writing, although in a somewhat indirect manner since she dedicates her free time "para las horas muertas de la tarde" [in the dead hours of the afternoon] to translation (27).

   In addition to the obvious homage to Woolf in this story, and Sanmiguel's rewriting and relocation of the Woolfian room of one's own, this story also resonates with Juan Carlos Onetti's *La vida breve* by placing her protagonist is a setting similar to the one that Onetti uses in the famous opening of his novel.[10] Rosario Sanmiguel's story takes as its point of departure Anamaría's inadvertent eavesdropping on the voice of Cony, who lives in the contiguous room. Here, once again, Sanmiguel borrows an authorized and canonical voice in order to articulate, as does Onetti, a voice from the margins, and to legitimate herself from the perspective of difference, as Zavala would have it. Like Onetti, the writer in this story hides behind the voice of Anamaría, who tells us of her daily life.

Sanmiguel as the writing subject thus locates herself in the interstices between creator and created, occupying the in-between, from which perspective Anamaría takes possession of the narrative voice, and with this power escapes from the dominant voice of Sanmiguel to the extent that in addition to telling us her own story, she also imagines and narrates that of Cony. While this kind of doubled narrative displacement is typical of Onetti and the direct relation between "La otra habitación" and *La vida breve* is obvious,[11] in Sanmiguel's story the narrator is careful to elaborate on the construction of the subject in her writing, which is a quite different enterprise from the misogynist appropriation of/ seduction by the unseen woman on the part of Onetti's male narrator/ blocked scriptwriter in his earlier novel. In the case of the Mexican woman writer, the female protagonist also locates herself in the same margin as her counterpart on the other side of the wall, writing from a position of difference with respect to the dominant culture.

This subtle border crossing among texts, and this ability to splice together works as different as Woolf and Onetti, suggests to us the possibilities of a decolonized border writing, which takes into account— without allowing itself to be overburdened by—existing master codes from several traditions, both European and Latin American. In this story one of the elements that stands out is the story's willingness to negotiate with the hegemonic forms of textualization, without falling into binary us-them divisions, pointing toward a textual theory and practice in which a multiplicity of discursive elements appears simultaneously. These discursive principles allow the author to refer, at one and the same time, to Virginia Woolf and to Juan Carlos Onetti and to remind us that even the bare information given by the title, "La otra habitación," dialogues with the literary tradition and uses it to establish the frame of her narration. At the same time in the context of the narrative itself, this allusion refers as well to another writing, one that has been absent or marginalized from the dominant text. It is a writing that reevaluates the conventional forms by taking on the self-same image of that which it wants to possess and in the process submits the desired and appropriated other to a process of both appropriation and critique (see Barthes, *El grado cero,* 88).

Finally, Sylvia Molloy's *En breve cárcel* is the literary text with which Sanmiguel's story seems most closely allied on the level of plot. In both works, the protagonists arrive from a trip in which the action of the story takes place; they move into a rented room, and this space serves as the site of self-knowledge and sexual experimentation. Likewise, both protagonists choose to return to the hotel where they have shared relations with their lovers rather than opting for some other, alternative space. "La otra habitación" and *En breve cárcel* also share a revaluation of the lesbian body.[12] While in Molloy's novel the protagonist manages a double identity throughout as a writer and as a lesbian, in Sanmiguel's story the main character is a translator and her lesbian identity is only revealed on the last page. At the same time *En breve cárcel* constructs a narrative around an exploration of the protagonist's relationship with two women, both former lovers, and the text is so claustrophobic that it is difficult to imagine a heterosexual world outside the novel. In a similar gesture, in the story "La otra habitación" Anamaría articulates her text with respect to her sister-in-law and to Cony, the next-door neighbor. Nevertheless, Sanmiguel's story is less claustrophobic in tone, though also restricted to the space of a single room, and there is a bisexual underpinning, since the narrator's memories also include her ex-husband, and Cony shares her room with Tejera, the contraband seller. Both texts share an emphasis on the importance of memories of the past associated with the family, and in both there is a discussion of the art of narration that refers specifically to writing as exorcism (see Kaminsky, 104).

Finally, the titles of all three of these Latin American works themselves firmly underline their intertextuality and their dialogue with the literary tradition. Kaminsky reminds us that in the English translation of Molloy's title, there is a shift from one literary tradition to another, evoking different aspects of the narrative. The title *En breve cárcel* comes from a line of Quevedo's poetry and underscores the claustrophobic quality of the novel. The phrase "certificate of absence" is borrowed from Emily Dickinson and refers to the freedom that one obtains through anonymity. Ironically, of course, in the English title this anonymity itself comes into being thanks to operations of the "certificate" that permits the official documentation for persons and things. Sylvia Molloy, thus, authorizes her lesbian writer through Quevedo's canonical poetry and certifies or makes visible the silencing of these marginal topics with her English-language allusion to Dickinson. Likewise, Onetti's novel explicitly reminds the reader of its intertextual allusiveness; most obviously, the title translates a French song cited in the text at a key moment: "la vie est brève/un peu d'amour/un peu de rêve" [life is short/a little love/a little dream] (148).

Molloy's novel is the only one of the texts mentioned above that Rosario Sanmiguel has not read (or, at least, had not read at the time of this writing).[13] This fact forces us to engage with the arbitrary nature of elaborate theorizations about "women's writing" or "feminine writing," which, as Golubov reminds us "no es más que un constructor útil y arbitrario pero a la vez riesgoso, porque parte del supuesto de que existe una identidad genérica estable que subyace a toda literatura escrita por mujeres" [is no more than a useful and arbitrary, but also risky, construction, because it relies in part on the assumption that there exists a stable generic identity underlying all literature written by women] (Golubov, 116). Furthermore, as Spivak has taught us, what can become a too-facile association of all products of women's minds and pens may also run the risk of reducing the richness of texts and not taking into account important sociocultural differences that mark the writing/reading subject.[14]

It would be quite erroneous to pretend to compare Sanmiguel with Molloy from a simplistic, essentializing feminism that would note the similarities in the texts as "proof" of a posited distinctive feminine consciousness. Such a project would reduce the richness of the texts and would condemn the writers to a sort of biological determinism. At the same time a rich conversation can be established between Molloy and Sanmiguel, taking into account the "herencia de textos recibida como legado histórico-cultural" [received inheritance of texts as a historical-cultural legacy] (Richard, "¿Tiene sexo la escritura?" 135) and pointing out the selection strategies that affect the choice of materials and their two writers' parallel textual manifestations.

As has been noted above, "La otra habitación" takes place almost entirely within the confines of a hotel room. Anamaría returns to Ciudad Juárez for a business matter; she has been named the executor of her ex-husband's will and her sister-in-law Alicia is contesting the will. Anamaría's return to the city implies confronting her past, evaluating her present, and taking responsibility for her future. Within this structure of the return home, Sanmiguel again enters into dialogue with a deeply rooted occidental tradition that is more often associated with epic poetry or long narrations. This story, predictably, will subvert the reader's expectations about the mythic trip home so amply documented in canonical narratives. Anamaría returns because she has been requested to do so, and so her voyage has nothing of the mythic overtones of an initiating impulse in the search for self or for the origins so well established in the Latin American and occidental tradition through novels like Alejo Carpentier's *Los pasos perdidos* [The lost steps], Juan Rulfo's *Pedro Páramo,* Julio Cortázar's *Rayuela,* or James Joyce's *Ulysses* (or even, perhaps, the Homeric *Odyssey* itself), to mention only a few of the most salient examples.

The masculine characters who dominate these canonical texts tend to have heroic or sentimental objectives for taking on the exigencies of difficult travels: the search for the father, the search for self, the return to a lost love. Frequently, this is a trip that submits the protagonist to a series of trials and frequently ends in tragedy. The father-city-country has been forever lost (as in Rulfo's novel) or, as in Carpentier and Homer, water erases the road that will bring the protagonist to a potential reencounter with his beloved. In Sanmiguel's story, by contrast, the voyage is far less overdetermined with mythic resonances. The protagonist has a simple objective: to solve the legal problem that brought her to Juárez and to return in the most expeditious manner possible to her home in Monterrey. And yet, of course, whispers of this long tradition will shape the substructure of the story and will enrich the intertextual dialogue. Succinctly, concisely, Rosario Sanmiguel reevaluates and reelaborates a homey feminine take on a mythic structure too overladen with accrued meaning to serve a useful function in this border space.

"La otra habitación" is narrated in the first person, a seldom-used point of view in *Callejón Sucre,* and all the more significant for that reason. This first-person point of view allows the narrator to be self-reflexive while at the same time indulging in a kind of "voyeurism," though this usually condemned curiosity is ameliorated by virtue of the protagonist's sympathy for Cony and thus less violent than the masculinist musings of Onetti's misogynist first-person narrator. By the same token, the reduced space of the room restricts the narrative and the readerly perspective, making even more patent Anamaría's desires, thoughts, and sensations. Since the narrator in "La otra habitación" cannot write Cony, instead she listens to and imagines her. And even her creative vision fails, for when she meets the "real" Cony she realizes that her imaginary perception was entirely erroneous. In this respect the apparently authoritative narrative voice disarticulates itself when the imagined figure and the real woman come into conflict. Through this gesture the author activates what Homi Bhabha calls "mimicry," by which means the reader is made to recognize the faultlines in Anamaría's re-creation of Cony, the subject/object of her desire, which only succeeds in producing a distorted image that must later be reanalyzed and reinscribed.

Within the textual borders and outside its relation to other texts, "La otra habitación" references a concern with the writing process itself. There is a constant questioning of the role of writing as a discursive practice and an awareness that narrative reconstruction will always be a second-hand communication, based on translating and reconstructing the voice of the other. It is in this respect extremely important that Anamaría explicitly does not "create" with her own writing; her task as translator is to interpret and re-represent another's voice and story. Thus, the writing subject is perfectly conditioned and primed to speak to us of her practice:

> Había llevado conmigo . . . un largo poema para traducir. Era un placentero ejercicio que yo misma me había impuesto como una calistenia escritural *mientras me llegaba mi momento,* me decía. Sólo que *ya parecía* que me conformaba con traducir, con buscar la palabra más cercana, buscar el ritmo . . . todo lo que implicaba trasladar el mundo que encierran las palabras—el mundo de otros—a mi propia circunstancia. Era una delicada, cobarde manera de revelarme. (27, emphasis added)

> [I had brought with me . . . a long poem to translate. It was a pleasant exercise that I had imposed on myself as a writing calisthenics *while I was waiting for my moment to arrive,* so I told myself. Only it *now appeared* that I was resigned to translation, to look for the closest word, to seek the rhythm . . . everything that was implied in transferring the world enclosed in words—other people's world—to my own situation. It was a delicate, cowardly way of revealing myself.]

Sanmiguel, as writing subject, takes up the word and makes the space of writing her own, albeit in a masked and displaced manner. Through counterpoint with her character, she presents herself as a person who orders worlds, knows the right word, and ably manipulates languages. And yet a distance is always maintained between the writing subject and the enunciation. Sanmiguel's character avoids calling herself a writer. Her words slip away from her in two directions: on the one hand, she posits writing as a method for transforming the world through language; on the other hand, she reveals that her potential work is unfinished, that her writing talent is untapped, still held in abeyance: "mientras [le] llegaba [su] momento." Rosario Sanmiguel takes advantage of this in-between state and writes into the text this undetermined moment of authorization and deauthorization. The narrator assumes her role as a translator most fully when she comes to understand that her moment to create independently will never arrive. And yet, the act of writing in this text exists nowhere but in the in-between space of a failed narration and an unfinished translation, as a potentiality in flux and subject to constant rearticulation. It is perhaps relevant in this context to note that "La otra habitación," before its publication in *Callejón Sucre y otros relatos* was first printed in *Entorno* in an incomplete form. Sanmiguel revised her own text and as a parenthesis to it added the subtitle "segunda mirada" [second view].[15] In these two versions the author gives the reader two alternative variations on the stories of Anamaría and Cony, where the second version is more mature and polished, and thus articulates a different view of the world. Nevertheless, for the informed border reader, this already internally doubled text is in this manner ironically submitted to further doubling through a publication history that makes the second version a retake on the first.

Reminders of this constant process of rearticulation include not only the direct discussions of the process of translation or interpretation in the narrative, but also in the constant use of second-hand (i.e., translated) information to build the story. While the story is told in the first person, we learn about other characters through other voices, heard through the walls, or recreated in memory rather than through direct, first-hand accounts. Much of what we know about Anamaría's life is filtered through her sister-in-law Alicia's perceptions, and vice-versa. We learn about Cony through what Anamaría hears through the wall of the other room. This constant filtering of material through other voices recalls Walter Benjamin's observation: "Translation passes through continua of transformation, not abstract ideas of identity and similarity" ("On language," 86). From another point of view, the strategy addresses not only questions of the transformative quality of identity, but also, if we follow Montes' line of argument, has a particular ideological weight as well: "La constante fluctuación de la posición del lector es una de las estrategias mejor logradas en el cuento para promover un cuestionamiento ideológico" [the constant shifting in the reader's position is one of the most well-achieved strategies in the story for promoting an ideological questioning] (Montes, 95).

This story plays with a series of intersecting voices, including the voices of the characters, as we have already seen, but also taking into account the varying and complexly interwoven voices of the cultural context. Sanmiguel positions her main character at the heart of a nexus that includes Cony, who is the subject/object of her desire, and Alicia, who represents dominant discourse. Both Cony and Alicia serve the protagonist-translator as points of departure for her to construct/ translate her story along with her discussion/translation of the stories of the other two women. By this means the narrator develops an awareness of a particular feminine consciousness, that of Anamaría, propped upon the support of the other two women's tales. At the same time, these other two characters are articulated and disarticulated through Anamaría's construction of them. Alicia represents the mores of the given social context, condemning her sister-in-law for her explorations of lesbian relationships even during her husband's lifetime. Cony seduces the narrator and helps her rediscover her body. In this triangulation of voices, Anamaría questions the root values of a society based on heterosexual relations and ownership of property as the accepted guarantees for social acceptance.

This rediscovery of the body through exploration of the lesbian subtext clearly challenges the official cultural text that defines a woman (or a woman's body) as socially significant only insofar as she responds to male needs and desires. In "La otra habitación," the corporeal is most signally placed with relation to the writing subject, and in any case the bodies in question in the story are marginal to the heterosexual economy which, necessarily, continues to surround Anamaría outside the walls of her room. Anamaría's exploration of her body's aging process is intimately tied to these other cultural histories:

> De cualquier manera no me estaba permitido el autoengaño. Conocía de
> sobra mis altibajos emocionales como para dejarme sorprender por esa
> tristeza que ya me cundía por todas las ramas del cuerpo. La proximidad

de la regla, los síntomas prematuros de la menopausia, la migraña que me martillaba los recuerdos. Todo se amalgamaba en la historia de los abandonos. (26)

[In any case, I couldn't allow self-deceit. I was far too familiar with my emotional swings to be surprised by that sadness that was seeping into every crack of my body. The closeness of my period, the premature symptoms of menopause, the migraine that hammered memory. All this came together in the story of abandonment.]

Experience and the knowledge of her body disarticulates the heritage that has prevented her from speaking of taboo topics such as menstruation, menopause, or masturbation. Like the young girl in "Paisaje en verano," the older woman in this story expresses the physiological functions of her body without censorship. In addition, her references to her impending menopause, when taken in the context of the sexual relation between Anamaría and Cony that closes the story, combat the myth about older women that "cuando dejamos de menstruar somos ángeles o sirenas" [when we cease menstruating we are angels or mermaids].[16] The women in this text are mature adults who give themselves to each other, entirely ignoring the traditional cultural distaste for sensual menopausal women or for lesbian relations. In this manner, the author shifts the ground from under the cultural codes, replacing the woman as object of passion with the woman's own expression of her passion (Kaminsky, 98). As in "Paisaje en verano," in this story Rosario Sanmiguel is able to suggest a resignifying praxis for women in a concise manner, through a minimalist sketch of the women's reappropriation of their own bodies and feelings. Both Anamaría and Cecilia have recourse to the search for a language of their own, one that allows them to express the truths of their bodies, irrespective of the demands of dominant cultural codes. The body, then, for Sanmiguel becomes a primary space for the reinvention of an alternative way of positioning oneself in the world. It is also a mechanism in a search for fuller and more complex form of expression, and while writing offers one possibility for such a project, it is not the only means of achieving it. The search can also engage in such activities as travel, reading literature, translation, subversion of familiar and exotic spaces, crossing geographical and sexual borders.

Most basically, Sanmiguel's story transgresses the old tale of domesticity and reinvents the home (here transgressively displaced in the more transient context of the hotel) as a space of cultural rearticulation. The limited confines of the hotel room allow Anamaría—in her own terms and in those of Cony—to look for the possibilities of her own voice, outside of and against the mere translation of a male text. This closed space opens up onto self-affirmation. At the same time, the use of the hotel room (rather than a middle-class home) and the expression of sexual desire between women both recalls and subverts the most typical border stereotype that associates sleazy hotels as exclusively the site of heterosexual relations between prostitutes and their clients.

Rosario Sanmiguel knows the literary and cultural traditions to which she is alluding, and which she is transgressing. Her story rearticulates both cultural mores and canonical textual expectations, with a textual economy that places the writer, the narrator, and the reader in a proximity that may become uncomfortable. There is a tight imbrication that we could trace, following upon Kaminsky, as "women writing/women loving women/beings with women's bodies" (Kaminsky, 112). The feedback relation between local space and self-construction takes into account in a very precise manner the complex cultural and social conditions obtaining on the Mexican border and interacting with the border inhabitant.

In this story the narrator mediates between the writing subject who lives in the world outside the text and the translator-protagonist evoked in the pages of the story. The woman who confirms and affirms herself in "La otra habitación" is not an isolated individual, but rather a fully adult person whose growth of consciousness comes about through her interaction with other persons and other voices. In this sense there is no rigid self/other separation, but rather a fluid interweaving of a subject in process. This experience, for Anamaría as a character, for Sanmiguel as writing subject, for us as readers, is a liberatory one: for Anamaría in the sense that she is freed from the obligation to stand in as an authoritarian eye that sees and judges; for Sanmiguel, in her play of entering and leaving literary tradition through textualized conversations and reevaluations of the cultural text; for the reader, who translates all of this through her own experience and is permitted to imagine alternate spaces. Furthermore, through situating her story in Ciudad Juárez, Sanmiguel also evokes the tension between and affirmation of the other that results from a constant awareness of the proximity of the United States and from a deep questioning of the stereotypes deriving from both sides of the border and inflecting this cultural space. Sanmiguel does not reduce the scene of recognition to a clichéd encounter of "la identidad individual del habitante de la frontera a su obligada confrontación con dicho 'otro'" [the individual identity of the border inhabitant in its obligatory confrontation with that "other"] (Barquet, 88), but rather creates the possibility of self-exploration that both takes into account and operates outside reflection on gringo otherness.

It is important to clarify that the sexual relation between Cony and Anamaría occurs only at the end of the story. Throughout the text, both heterosexual and lesbian desires are represented indiscriminately, without any textual confusion. The final scenes of the story refer twice to "la otra habitación" and these scenes are far more ambiguous than the rest of the text. The first scene is introduced with the following: "[d]esde la ventana, alto minarete, escuchaba los silencios de la otra habitación" [from the window, a high minaret, I listened to the silences from the other room] (37). From the context, we can infer that the other room here is Anamaría's interior life, since the space of the silences is punctuated textually by a colon (:) followed by three short paragraphs describing Anamaría's childhood, adolescence, and adulthood. In the first, a child seeks her mother on a muddy path, then a young girl runs through the woods to arrive at

> la hora madura de la noche, [cuando] la entraña de una mujer amada rezumaba su deseo. La entrega perpetua era un juramento. Las palabras amantes tejían la enredadera, su aliento perfumaba el aire de la habitación sellada.
>
> Abrí la ventana. En la otra habitación, Cony me esperaba. La vida se renovaba. (37)
>
> [the darkest hour of the night, when the innermost recesses of a beloved woman exude her desire. Perpetual surrender was a solemn oath. The loving words wove the net; their breath perfumed the air of the locked room.
>
> I opened the window. In the other room, Cony awaited me. Life renewed itself.]

After this scene, the narration ends with the typical Sanmiguel gesture of opening out onto the surrounding reality. This last room evoked in this narrative is not the space of memory, but the ordinary room, where Anamaría has consummated the seduction and where her travels come to an end. The narrator steps out of her introspection and into an encounter with that other voice/character that had been filtering into her consciousness since her arrival in the room and, on finally meeting her, reaffirms her own existence. The description of the space outside this charmed enclosure reminds us that this private and intimate room is part of a public space and a border life that must be taken into consideration in Anamaría's story as well. The private lives of Cony and Tejera already project the reality of relations between the two cities and two countries when, for instance, Cony tells Anamaría that she went to El Paso to get an abortion. Here, too, we are asked to think about the complex web of legal/illegal relations in the two countries and in the activities associated with each side of the border in this dynamic exchange, while at the same time the story firmly inserts itself in its Mexican reality and in the power of Mexican laws and customs over a woman's body. Most significantly, the counterposition of these two nations with their respective cultural understandings and typical blind spots reminds the reader to take into account the cultural baggage that underwrites and authorizes any text. Through the play of ambiguities, the double voicing, the insistence on a practice of translation, Sanmiguel offers a contestatory response to the voices of centrist prejudice that insist upon seeing the border area as a cultural desert.

In the texts by Rosario Sanmiguel that we have chosen for this particular analysis, we have highlighted the author's rearticulation of a writing practice operating in full consciousness of a complex cultural nexus that interweaves with and crosses her own, that sometimes displaces the border text, and equally frequently is displaced by it. In any case, the textual strategies deployed by Sanmiguel allow her to authorize her own marginalized literary production, avoiding simplistic reinscriptions of the obvious binaries of dominator/dominated, and asserting her own dynamic space of multiple exchanges among many different female subjectivities. Other critics agree. *Callejón Sucre y otros relatos,* despite the disadvantages of its border location and lack of centrist recognition, has in fact already "logrado ya un papel importante en el amplio corpus literario de fin de siglo" [achieved an important place in the ample literary corpus of the end of the century] (Rodríguez Lozano, 219). Montes praises the work for its destabilization of cultural (and especially gender) codes (94), and Barquet calls it a work with both local and continental interest (92). This final evaluation is perhaps the most telling; Rosario

Sanmiguel's work is insistently and specifically located in the streets and locales of her home city, Juárez, and addresses itself to a peculiarly border sensibility. At the same time, along with the dialogic relation to this specific geographical area, her characters develop in contexts that overcome geographical limits and pose a larger interrogation to often-unquestioned parochial and patriarchal social norms, especially those governing gender relations.

# 4. Snapshots

*Norma Cantú, Sheila Ortiz Taylor,*

*and Sandra Ortiz Taylor*

Mama raised me without language,
I'm orphaned from my Spanish name.
                    —*Lorna Dee Cervantes*

Confessional practices and (auto)biographical gestures are popular these days: witness the success of the celebrity biography on E!, the proliferation of analogous programming on the History Channel, *Time* magazine's and *Biography's* countdown to the greatest person of the millennium (a list, which, unsurprisingly, highlights such millennially essential figures as Elvis and Jackie O), the perennial bestseller-dom of tell-all memoirs, and the amazing popularity of mockudramas and feature films based on historical characters and famous, scandalous, or inspiring contemporary individuals. Likewise, indubitably, the appeal to some irreducible core of "truth" gives weight and power to a host of mediocre made-for-television movies about ordinary people caught in tragic circumstances. In all of these popular forms, the use of artistic license in the service of the creation of a more dramatic story is understood; yet, the tag "based on a true story" presumably speaks to the public in compelling and highly saleable ways.

In academic circles, spring 1999 brought us the raging academic controversy around David Stoll's exposé of beloved Guatemalan activist Rigoberta Menchú in his book, *I Rigoberta Menchú, and the Story of All Poor Guatemalans.* The fall 1999 official biography of Ronald Reagan, *Dutch,* sparked a highly critical reception to Edmund Morris's interjection of a fictional alter ego into his tale, by which device he speaks in first person and recalls details of imaginary meetings and conversations with the former president. Robin Wilson captures the heart of this debate succinctly when he suggests that, with respect to the Guatemalan woman, "the criticisms are particularly damning because even Ms. Menchú's advocates don't regard her book as a literary masterpiece; its value has been its claims to authenticity" (A15). Similar critiques abound, focusing on the destabilizing effect of Morris's postmodernly overt blurring of fiction and fact, pinpointing the readers' uneasiness about their reading experience in a genre that usually highlights transparency and authenticity as its most preeminent values. For very different reasons, and at opposite ends of all possible spectrums of politics, gender, race, and power, in both cases, those who object to *Dutch,* like the detractors of Rigoberta Menchú, presume that narratives such as Morris's and Menchú's respond to similar underlying generic requirements. The most virulent critique suggests that in these retellings/testimonios root values of truth-telling and authenticity are unacceptably put into question. The implicit or explicit response to such concerns (whether in TV docudrama or printed biography/testimonio) often takes the form of arguing that a judicious adaptation of unrevealing fact more accurately depicts "truth" with a greater degree of authenticity than more narrowly defined, pedestrian tales.

These debates, in a more abstract sense, go to the heart of contemporary theorizing about the autobiographical form and can serve as a point of departure as well for our discussion of two border narratives that implicitly insert themselves into this ongoing discussion. Both Norma Cantú's *Canícula* and Sheila Ortiz Taylor and Sandra Ortiz Taylor's *Imaginary Parents* adapt the form of the autobiographical genre to fit their playful, fragmentary adaptations of this form. Cantú, for example, says in her introduction: "life in la frontera is raw truth, and stories of such life, fictitious as they may be, are even truer than true." Thus having established a certain, ambiguous claim on the essential truth of her work, even as she edges toward fiction, she goes on to stake out its equally ambiguous generic definition: "I was calling the work fictional autobiography, until a friend suggested that they really are ethnographic and so if it must fit a genre, I guess it is fictional autobioethnography" (xi). Similarly, novelist Sheila Ortiz Taylor, in her introduction to the volume she created with her graphic-artist sister, radically confuses genre limits: "Call this book autobiography. Or memoir. Call it poetry. Call it nonfiction. Or creative nonfiction. Call it purest fiction. Call it a codex. Give it a call number" (xiii). Sandra Ortiz Taylor adds a second introduction in which she writes of her parents' mythic self-invention as their fundamental truth, and hints at the slippery boundaries between truth and myth that have given shape to the family's understanding of itself: "it was as if they invented themselves. It is no wonder that we are participants in their myth" (xv).

It may be a cliché at this point to summarize the typical presumptions about the autobiographical genre, but it serves perhaps as a necessary reminder in the context of reading Cantú and the Ortiz Taylor sisters, whose prefatory remarks to their respective works suggest that they are keenly aware of readerly expectations about this kind of book and propose to subvert or contest such generic rules. Thus, their comments, like the negatively valenced critiques about Menchú and Morris, suggest a common underlying presumption that this kind of narrative is a cultural document that derives its value, and makes a certain ethical claim to authenticity, through rigorously exact truth-telling. In autobiography, one assumes, one must tell the truth, the whole truth, and nothing but the truth. Attractive literary qualities associated with fictional works—poetic devices, creativity, plot manipulation, character development—may be viewed with suspicion, if not straightforwardly and universally condemned.

Traditional studies of the genre have also reminded us that autobiography is specifically associated with the West and, in Georges Gusdorf's classic discussion of the genre, "expresses a concern peculiar to Western man" (48). Recent feminist and postcolonial scholars have underlined both elements in Gusdorf's definition: that is, that autobiography is, in its most established form, a peculiarly European and Eurocentric genre, and that it is overwhelmingly associated with the Great White Man's recapitulation of his personal successes and failures. Thus, whiteness is the unmarked racial category, just as maleness is the unmarked gender that delimits the proper subject of traditional autobiography and also sets up the terms against which contestatory autobiographical models create their dialogical response: not Eurocentric, not white, not male.

Says Lionnet of the typical autobiography described by the Gusdorfian model:

> [T]his individualistic approach to the genre contrasts sharply with the one used by most postcolonial writers, male and female . . . [and] is based on a view of autobiography that is rather reductive and narrow, since it does not take into account the culturally diverse forms of self-consciousness, or the necessarily devious and circuitous modes of self-expression that colonized peoples have always had to adopt. (321)

Postcolonial writers bear the weight of—and frequently write against—this structural and stylistic heritage, deriving from their cultural circumstances complexly negotiated modalities for puzzling out the question of self-definition in a format that is both individually based and communitarian in reach.

Furthermore, the canonical autobiographical tale poses itself traditionally as a single, coherent narrative that starts at the individual life's beginning and continues without significant gaps to the moment in which the writer lays down his pen. As Foucault notes, "Continuous history is the indispensable correlative of the founding function of the subject: the guarantee that everything that has eluded him may be restored to him; the certainty that time will disperse nothing without restoring it in a reconstituted unity" (*Archeology of Knowledge*, 12). Recent autobiographies, like the border narratives under discussion in this chapter, tend to take the form of discontinuous and fragmentary narratives, as if the grounding (and no longer *founding*) function has gone radically astray in the contemporary certainty that no unity can ever be fully reconstituted from the bits and pieces of these bicultural pasts that serve most signally as sites of cultural mediation.

Even the presumably irreducible quality of truth-telling is put into doubt—more overtly in the contestatory forms of autobiography—but, as canonical theorists on the genre have commented, to some degree in traditional forms as well. Gusdorf describes the narrative subject as "the effort of a creator to give the meaning of his own mythic tale" (48). Philippe Lejeune comments wryly, "Most autobiographers use a narrative model that has only a remote relationship to what they are living, at least we hope so for them" (235–36). The genre as it is typically perceived and practiced, Lejeune suggests, is hopelessly antiquated and needs to be renewed through a profound reevaluation of the rules of the game and the meaning of the genre. He gives the example of the trite narrative beginning "I was born . . .":

> I admire all those people who believe they are born, who seem to know what it is to be born, and who do not ask themselves more questions than this. We have the impression while reading their autobiographies, that their birth is like a piece of property that they would own in the country, or like a diploma. This grounds their whole narrative on an irrefutable beginning, a kind of cornerstone like the ones used in unveilings. Would it only be for this, the model of biography seems to me unstable for autobiography. . . . My birth will become a historical event only when I'm dead . . . Not that autobiography should give up narrative; but it must be put back in its place. (235–36)

Both Lejeune and Gusdorf thus put pressure on the most fundamental quality associated with the genre, its association with truth, by highlighting its teleological quality (Gusdorf) or its clichéd structural dynamics (Lejeune). It is precisely at these already somewhat slippery points of entry that current contestatory autobiographers stake their more disambiguous claims to novel styles of meaning creation and alternative narrative structures. The two works under analysis here seem to respond directly to such concerns. These border autobiographies are tales that in both cases frustrate expectations of beginning at the origin and instead cohere around a common image more typically associated with the end of life: Sheila Ortiz Taylor's first words are: "this book is made of bones. *La Huesera,* Bone Woman, crouching over the bones of the dead coyote, sings them back to life. I crouch over the bones of my parents" (xiii). In a parallel fashion, Norma Cantú gives a prominent role to the "huesario," the pile of disinterred and unclaimed bones lying beyond Don Viviano's yard, that serve as one of the dominant metaphors for her fragmentary narrative (71), as do the photographs through which "the dead return" (xii).

Cantú and the Ortiz Taylors are writing against the clichéd understanding of this genre, of course, but they are also anchored in another, already well-grounded tradition of self-narration, one that includes such texts as Rigoberta Menchú's testimonio and other ethnographic accounts of women's lives, as well as the well-known works of Chicana autoethnographers such as Cherríe Moraga's 1983 *Loving in the War Years* or Gloria Anzaldúa's 1987 *Borderlands/La Frontera.* In these works, the

Chicana writers take on the challenge proffered by scholars and critics and readers of the autobiographical genre in recognizing the ways in which the idea of autobiography itself limits how the author can tell her life story to those forms with which readers are familiar and will accept—that is, strictly tied to "what is true" and "what is unambiguously one's own experience." Works that describe themselves as "creative nonfiction" or "fictional autobioethnography" defy the boundaries of generic preconceptions and resist the established constructs of reliability, validity, and truth-telling. To use a metaphor that lies persistently on the edge of consciousness for both these writers, they are border crossers, testing the limits and frontiers of genre so as to find a form of self-representation to structure and organize a specifically fronteriza feminine discourse. Thus, for Cantú crossing the bridge (or, alternatively, crossing the river) is a permanent referent not only for her family's binational life but also for the structural integrity of her tale. For the Ortiz Taylors, it is the "For Sale" sign on their house and the periodically repeated promise/threat of moving the family to Mexico. In both cases, these metaphors of crossing into the other country serve both as one of the crucial organizing images for the text and as a structuring device.

Furthermore, following upon the insights offered by testimonios, these writers define their work less as a reconstruction of an individual self, and more as a patchwork collection of fragmentary units that help flesh out comprehension of a collective identity. These self-sustained fragments—interrupted in both texts by family photographs and, in the Ortiz Taylors' case, by photographs of Sandra's artistic boxes organized around the found objects that help her rethink her family history in plastic form—hint at the multidimensionality of women's lives and the controlled chaos that seems naturally to follow upon the task of making sense of discontinuously apprehended events and influences. In defining their own autobiographies as ethnographic/aesthetic works or as literary (creative) texts, Cantú, Anzaldúa, Moraga, and the Ortiz Taylors all speak to the critical project of reconstituting and resituating textual authority and appeals to generic demands for authentic narratives about (marginalized) women's lives. For Mary Louise Pratt, this kind of self-writing can be best described as an individual's autoethnographic expression. This term

> refer[s] to instances in which colonized subjects undertake to represent themselves in ways that *engage with* the colonizer's own terms. . . . Auto-

ethnographic texts are those the others construct in response to or in dialogue with those metropolitan representations. . . . [They] are not, then, what are usually thought of as "authentic" or autochthonous forms of self-representation. . . . Rather, authoethnography involves partial collaboration with and appropriation of the idioms of the conqueror. (7)

Cantú uses a box of photographs as the organizing point of departure for her narrative and plays with the reader's expectations that in the photographic record there may always be found some irreducible residue of fact. And yet, at each moment, Cantú warns her reader not to be fooled by appearances. In her introduction to the book, she says, for instance, "in *Canícula,* the story is told through photographs, and so what may appear to be autobiographical is not always so. On the other hand, many of the events are completely fictional, although they may be true in a historical context" (xi). A little later she adds, "[I]t is a collection of stories gleaned from photographs randomly picked, not from a photo album chronologically arranged, but haphazardly pulled from a box of photos where time is blurred" (xii). In the first of these comments, then, Cantú reminds her reader that the visual image is no reliable test of veracity, and that, in fact, people can use photographs to tell an amazing range of authentic-sounding personal inventions. The only assurance she gives her reader is that the historical context for her photographic series is, in general terms, quite possibly realistic, if not verifiably factual. In the second comment, Cantú abstracts yet another quality of the photographic series—the expectation that if the tales are not entirely true, readers can at least imagine a progression that relates one picture to the next in a chronological sequence, mimicking the ordering process we expect from photograph albums. Instead, Cantú frustrates these linear dreams of a temporally defined order with the promise of a discontinuous, randomly organized set of unreliable narrative fragments.

These warnings are amazingly easy to forget; the sequence of short tales looks roughly chronological, the photos have all the amateur qualities of family snapshots, and it is nearly impossible not to associate—for example—the image of an old woman with the story of the abuelita that follows and to draw conclusions about the authenticity of the tale as verified by the evidence of the image.

Furthermore, Cantú's narration gives us the impression of following a linear sequence despite its fragmentary quality. Here, too, she is subtly nonspecific. In her introduction she emphasizes that *Canícula* is the second book in a trilogy, thus setting the book into one kind of temporal order. She also makes reference to another in emphasizing the relation of the book's title to the time period in which it was written: "[T]he *canícula* of the title refers both to the time when I wrote the bulk of the material—the dog days of 1993—and to the idea of a particularly intense part of the summer . . . in South Texas . . . the time between July 14 and August 24, according to my father" (xi–xii). Thus, Cantú allows us to imagine that the text was written between the very specific days of July 14 to August 24, 1993, while also inserting those dates within the time of custom and legend ("according to my father"). This rupture in linear, historical, chronological time disarticulates the suggestion of an autobiographical pact with the norms of historical process that pretend to give foundation to a narrative sense of "reality" in writing. Here, in these introductory words, Cantú validates the structures of a personal memory as the mechanism for recuperating her community's past.

In the text as a whole this discontinuity between historical records and personal recall remains a constant. The text makes reference to a sequence of such events that have marked not only border relations between Mexico and the United States, but also other parts of the world: the Texas War, the Mexican American War, World Wars I and II, the Mexican Revolution, the Spanish Civil War, the Vietnam War. These conflicts are contextualized in Cantú's work not as the great and necessary historical processes, but rather as lived experiences that have caused great pain to specific individuals. This style of presentation points toward the destabilization of the concept of Nation itself.

Cantú gives us at least one additional hint of how to read this textual/photographic montage. In addition to her set of negative proscriptions (these images are not autobiographical, not historical, not chronological), Cantú explicitly evokes Roland Barthes's famous discussion of photography in *Camera Lucida* as her narrative's theoretical pre-text (1). It is Barthes, then, that Eurocentric commentator on and brilliant deconstructor of European culture, who serves as the site for a crucial theoretical and methodological encounter in Cantú's Mexican American counterautobiographical text. She does not follow up on the implications of this reference, leaving that further step to her reader/spectator, even though, we might argue, Barthes's intensely psychoanalytic and semiotic analysis of photography pervades the Chicana's narrative, her "random" collection of family fictions. In this respect, as in others, Cantú echoes

Barthes's earlier recognition of the power and duplicity of the photographic image that creates and structures memories, even to echoing his famous description of what a photograph is *not:* "Not only is the photograph never, in essence, a memory . . . but it actually blocks memory, quickly becomes a counter-memory" (Barthes, *Camera Lucida,* 91).

In *Camera Lucida,* Barthes describes two effects of photographs; the first, the *studium,* he defines as the average effect of a photograph on a viewer. The studium derives from taste, and from liking; it is "a kind of education (knowledge and civility, 'politeness') which allows me to discover the Operator, to experience the intentions which establish and animate his practices" (28). The second quality of the photograph, says Barthes, is the *punctum,* or that which "will break (or punctuate) the studium. . . . It is this element which rises from the scene, shoots out of it like an arrow, and pierces me" (26). While the first element allows for the spectator to exercise aesthetic appreciation for a well-composed scene, it is the second element that most concerns Barthes in this analysis; the pricking, penetrating quality of the photographic punctum has an implicit double charge of aggressive sexuality and murderous violence. Strikingly enough, in Barthes's study this violence continually comes home to his own autobiographical recollections, and most specifically rests on his contemplation of photographs of his mother, for whose loss he is still clearly grieving:

> By giving me the absolute past of the pose (aorist), the photograph tells me death in the future. What pricks me is the discovery of this equivalence. In front of the photograph of my mother as a child, I tell myself: she is going to die: I shudder . . . over a catastrophe which has already occurred. Whether or not the subject is already dead, every photograph is this catastrophe. (96)

Here, in another register, is the quality that Cantú also intuits in her *Canícula:* the association of the photograph with real or anticipated death; the metaphoric leap between the box of pictures and the tumbled bones of the huesario that underlies and undergirds the meaning structure of this narrative. While Cantú's evocation of these losses is tinged more with the Mexican acceptance of death that makes the Day of the Dead an important holiday than with the European male's absolute devastation in the face of his loss, the two writers meet in their shared interest in photographic effects and functions, and in their nicely tuned analysis of the way photographs mean. For Barthes, this meaning structure is ultimately tied to the realization of death and the European's shuddering fear/delight in that ultimate, violent punctum, which must be distanced in order to be apprehended. "Society, it seems, mistrusts pure meaning," says Barthes. "It wants meaning, but at the same time it wants this meaning to be surrounded by a noise (as is said in cybernetics) which will make it less acute. . . . [A]t the limit, no meaning at all is safer" (36, 38). Thus, for Barthes, meaning is the uncontestable ground but must be softened and surrounded by noise to make the punctum less severely penetrating; mourning for the loss of his mother, in this sense, can be blunted in the protective noise that surrounds this shuddering catastrophe. In Cantú's case, the question is a U.S. border woman's concern with how to adduce meaning at all in a social space defined by meaning's lack or loss: "For Bueli the move brought back memories, mental photographs gone now. . . . And in 1948 crossing meant coming home, but not quite" (5). In contrast with Barthes, then, who uses noise to make meaning less acute, the Mexican American woman struggles not to let her fragments of meaning dissolve in the overwhelming presence of a background dissonance.

One of the ways Cantú actualizes this loss of meaning for her reader/spectator is to periodically foreground the lack of fit between the fragmentary tale and the photograph that ostensibly sparks this memory (or countermemory). Thus, for instance, the photograph on page 47 shows two couples, one partially cropped, inside what looks like a church. The women are dressed in dark clothes. The man in the center of the photograph looks gravely out of the corner of his eye at the camera; on first glance, he seems to be wearing a mourning band on his right sleeve.

This, in Barthesian terms, would be the studium of the photograph; the punctum, its evocative power encrypted in the steady gaze of the man into the camera, the woman's straightforward posture and movement at a slight angle to the photographer. The title of the narrative section immediately below this photograph is "Lola's Wedding," and the text begins with a cheery note: "It's a wedding—the photo taken as we stand on the front steps of Sagrado Corazón Church in Monterrey. . . . I think Lola is beautiful with her alabaster skin, just like the Virgin Mary's statue, her color-of-amber hair and her laughing gray eyes" (47).

The reader is immediately struck by a cognitive dissonance: wedding—or funeral?, front steps—or inside the church? Joyous occasion—or sorrowful one? The uncomfortable distance between image and text is

Figure 1. Norma Cantú, *Lola's Wedding*, 1995. Reprinted with permission of the artist.

eventually resolved in a throwaway description set in the middle of a paragraph, referring to the parents' exit from the church and the mother's black velvet dress (48). In rereading the photograph in light of this description, the mourning band becomes the mother's gloved hand, the dark dress is wedding-day elegant and not an expression of sadness for a recent loss, the couples' grave faces represent the solemnity of the holy vows of matrimony they have just witnessed and not the expression of deep sorrow at a funeral mass. And yet, of course, Cantú has directly informed us that her photographs evoke fictions, and Barthes reminds us that photographs penetrate us most deeply in that they define a future catastrophe made present in contemporary recall. What if our first impression was real? What is real? In a sense, both the wedding joy and the funeral mourning are accurately doubled in this photograph, for the textual description of happy, laughing Lola on her wedding day is almost immediately overlaid with more recent memories: "thirty years later, when Pepe died, a distraught Lola came to visit me in Madrid to forget her pain" (48). In this canny juxtaposition of image and text, Cantú recreates in the reader this double apprehension. In this sense, the first reading of the photograph, more accurately than the "real" reading, depicts this anticipatory mourning for a future catastrophe that cannot even be imagined in the moment of the snapshot, but the encoding of which defines the photographic punctum for the spectator.

If in Cantú the autoethnographic tale is given richness though the doubling of fact and fiction in textual and photographic form, in the book by Sandra Ortiz Taylor and Sheila Ortiz Taylor the richness is compounded through the collaborative efforts of the sisters who created this project. According to *Imaginary Parents,* the roles of the two sisters were defined early: Sheila tells stories. Sandra paints. In the book they have created together, Sandra's memory boxes and the "descriptive annotations" she writes for them serve as complement and counterpoint for her sister's narrative; Sheila's written descriptions of nine "photographs" are interspersed among the narrative fragments, without any reproductions of their ostensible visual referents. In this manner, the two artistic forms mimic each other so that at the same time that Sheila's writing tends toward visual image, Sandra's art appropriates the qualities of text. Sandra notes, "When I work with boxes as found objects they may be containers for pieces. As such, I frequently regard them as books" (xvi). In a complementary gesture, Sheila gives her text a visual art referent pertinent to the style of her sister's work: "Reader, This book is made of bones. . . . I say it is an altar, an *ofrenda*" (xiii).

Appropriately enough, the dominant metaphors for this project created out of a deep collaboration between a creative writer/altar maker and a visual artist/bookmaker are books and boxes, both of which are hinged and need to be opened:

> This book you hold, this ofrenda, like all altar art and most rescue work, was not realized in solitude. My sister and I collaborated in this piece. She created the visual art and I wrote the text, though much of my writing was inspired by our conversations and re-collections as we cooked together or dreamed our way through boxes of family photographs. (xiv)

Like Cantú, the sisters find in the figurative and real exercise of sorting or "dreaming" the way through boxes (rather than albums) of photographs a point of departure. It is important to underline this apparently random conjunction. In both books, the work of reconstruction begins with the box of photographs rather than the album, suggesting that the process of sorting through randomly shuffled bits of the past has a creatively inspirational quality that cannot be achieved through the book-form emulated in the photograph album (although the readers of both books might find an ironic disjunction between the creative possibilities of the randomly organized box and the chronological format of the resulting books). It is the struggle among images that provokes the subtle reconstructive processes for both books' authors, but also and at the same time reminds the reader that these autobiographies are taking a twist away from authentic reproduction of fact. At the core of each of these projects is a displacement from history into reverie, from fact to dream, studium to punctum.

As in Cantú's work, the book-box-photograph has an explicitly evoked association with the huesario and, like the South Texan writer, the Californians trace the poetic etymology of this image back through the figure of their grandmother: "The elder daughter lies on her bed, the bed resting on the same floor boards as the bed of her grandmother. A book is open on her bed. The book lies open like a secret revealed; the book lying open over the bones of her grandmother" (232). In *Imaginary Parents*, as in *Canícula*, the grandmother serves as the embodiment of the Californians' hard-won wisdom. In their case, this slippery rooted/ migrant knowledge is best captured in what they call the "que será será" philosophy of the Ortiz y Cabares branch of the family. The maternal grandmother, Della Caroline Ortiz y Cabares Shrode, called "Mymama" throughout this text, serves as the best single resource for this philosophy. She is at the same time the repository of minimalist memories (her "pocadillas," for example) and of vaguely defined losses (for instance, the fading memory of "this territory that the Mexican government granted my great grandfather Miguel Ortiz for an obscure favor performed long ago, land subsequently lost to the family out of certain characteristic vagueness about property and ownership" [52]). Thus, the book constructed over the grandmother's bones hints at a deeply felt sense of attachment to place and family, while at the same time the operative family philosophy was more typically associated with an urge toward detachment, ignoring of the past, and personal reinvention.

It is no wonder that the Ortiz Taylors' narrative is a bit unsettled/unsettling, especially if we add to the Ortiz y Cabares mix the Texan father's wanderlust and continual urge for change. In the father's case, this need manifests itself in a beautiful but idiosyncratically constructed and always-in-process home and in his frequent pronouncements about selling the house and sailing around the world before moving to Mexico. These two family traditions (one unsettled, the other unsettling) fit together uneasily and at the same time are met with a third destabilizing element—the nature of the text itself. The sisters are aware that their collaborative work has a sui generis bifocality: "In our working we did not try to make art and text replicate each other, but rather to refract, casting new shadows, throwing new angles of light" (xiv).

Not surprisingly, the sisters have a strong affinity for doors of all sorts—boxtops and book covers that hold things in and organize experience—and many of Sandra's pieces take the form of boxes or suitcases or retablos with hinges that allow them to open and close, at least theoretically. Many of the illustrations in the volume show both open and closed views of the same artistic pieces. In general, the closed boxes appear in the black and white interspersed images of "la vía" and the opened boxes are grouped together in the color photographs of "la galería." One such particularly charged image is that of Aunt Winifred, and the box dedicated to her is reproduced in both interior and exterior views. In "la vía" Sheila notes, "This narrative concerns the suicide on Christmas day of our favorite 'in-law' aunt. The attached book has my sister's text from which I created an artist book" (viii). The inscription on the book/box itself clearly reads: "L.A. Snapshots—Her story," where the photographic referent of "snapshot" is shifted both in Sheila's and Sandra's texts into a memory of a gunshot.

Figure 2. Sandra Ortiz Taylor, *Winifred: Her Story, Exterior.* Photograph by
Philip Cohen. Reprinted with permission of the artist.

In "la galería" Sheila comes back to this book/box and adds a commentary on the interior: "Winifred lived and died before our feminist movement. Part of our motivation for telling her story comes from the lack of perspective we had, being children, at the time of her death. . . . All the family snapshots in which Winifred appeared were torn to eliminate her visage. I hope in some small way we are restoring her image." Here, signally, the lack of photographs in the box of family memorabilia serves as an even more powerful spur to a reconstruction of this ruined life than the more banal memories evoked through reviewing old snapshots. In this case, the hole in the sisters' imagined family album generates the memory of something excessive, and hence purposefully misplaced: a punctum without a supporting image.

Sandra's version of this story—the version Sheila mentions in her annotation?—is called "Street Map" and goes back and forth between the grandmother's household as the family awaits the arrival of Winifred and her family for Christmas dinner, and Winifred's thought processes as she meticulously prepares for her suicide (96–101). Graphically and textually, in these doubled accounts of the death of a favorite relative, the Ortiz Taylors describe how the family "closed the book" on a traumatic event. The recuperation of Winifred's tragedy requires opening up these books and peeking behind the doors: of the two houses, of Winifred's room, of her mental state at the time she decides to take her life. At the same time, the book/door marks the limit space into Otherness, the forbidden territory, the threshold that—even now—the creators of this text cross at their peril.

This artistic pressure brought to bear on images of the threshold space is a hallmark of the text as a whole. In one of Sheila's most compact and richly evocative metaphors, the mother's door tempts and repulses her young daughters: "The door to the heart of this off-limits world was my mother's dressing room, a sanctuary guarded appropriately enough by a mirrored door. From the doorknob radiated a single crack crossing the width of the door like the faultline traversing the California coast. Or like a strand of barbed wire" (6). What is particularly striking about this image is the way it so efficiently pulls together and sets at the heart of the children's home the mystery that defines their narrative and artistic project: the vexed relationship between the beautiful mother and her gawky half-grown daughters; the off-limits sanctuary, like the forbidden

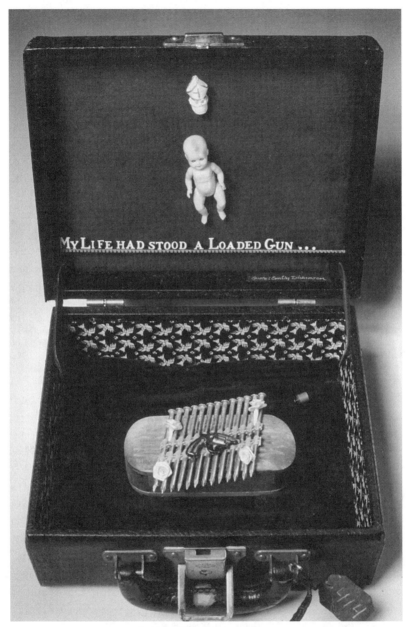

Figure 3. Sandra Ortiz Taylor, *Winifred: Her Story, Interior.* Photograph by Philip Cohen. Reprinted with permission of the artist.

door in Bluebeard's castle that attracts and horrorizes; the mirror that reflects back the girls' images of themselves in a metaphor perfectly chosen for this refractive, doubled tale; the crack in the glass that at the same time evokes the permanent menace of California's unstable geology and the barbed-wire fence that impinges inevitably on the Californians' border consciousness.

"Artistic creation," says Georges Gusdorf, "is a struggle with the angel, in which the creator . . . wrestles with his shadow" (48). The Ortiz Taylors take this struggle out of the arena of white male privilege that makes public life a measuring stick for meaningfulness and reinsert the drama into the domestic space. Winifred's partially comprehended tragedy is one such moral tale; the concrete representation in the mother's mirrored door is another. For if the door to the mother's room will open into revelations and terrors that are also inevitably self-perceptions, then the ground of the self-fashioning has slipped from public performance to a psychodrama. Here, for instance, Sheila describes another door, and the potentiality it represents:

> The beam outlines the edge of the closet door and I see that it hangs open.
>
> Open. She has forgotten, and when she has forgotten things can come out. Things.
>
> It seems like my mother would remember something like that, as dangerous as a closet door. A mother would. (42)

The role of the mother as guardian of the secret spaces (of the heart, of the house) is underlined in this passage; at the same time, the reader, of course, knows that the "things" that come out of this closet door have both visual and textual representation in the closed and opened boxes of the narrative and visual art pieces. Like Cantú's photographs, these represented or found objects have both the qualities of studium and punctum. Thus, for example, we can analyze Sandra's boxes as artistic/ aesthetic objects, can read Sheila's narrative as poetry. At the same time we are forced into the direct apprehension of a faultline that is all the more terrifying because it is nonspecific and tagged to our deepest, most abstract nightmares.

The narrative, however, continually pulls the reader back from nightmare into loving banality, and in its overall aesthetic gently pokes fun at such dark thoughts. In the chapter entitled "In the Closet," Sheila hints gently at some of the innocuous Things hidden behind closet doors, their own as well as their mother's doors (homemade stuffed animals, banana cream pie, mother-and-daughter dresses), and Sandra's "Night Closet" (167) dispels nighttime terrors in a serene landscape of green forest behind "my sister's Robin Hood hat and vest" (ix). These scary and comforting Things in the closet also condense narrative moments, in a way that is wholly appropriate for the maternal tradition.

The mother's family holds out the promise of an intergenerational transmission of stories and cultural knowledge among a network of women, but at the same time the mother's background is working-class Mexican American, which she is determined not to duplicate in the next generation, dedicating herself instead to a life of Hollywood elegance and measured beauty. Both parents, but especially the mother, "managed, together, to live out the American Dream, Southern California style. It was as if they invented themselves" (xv). Such self-invention is difficult and ambiguous at times, full of dreamlike qualities and fragile awkwardnesses, especially insofar as it requires determination and discipline that run against the core of her family's "que será será" style and her own mother, Mymama's powerful presence. The Southern California American Dream requires continual maintenance. For the mother, this delicate balancing act occurs primarily in the subtly ideologically charged spaces of the family home, in her dream of the perfect U.S. family. It is no surprise that her artistic talent displays itself in sophisticated hats and identically styled mother-and-daughter dresses; the mother lavishly directs her talent into the creation of a feminine style that she dreams of reproducing in her children, filling their closets and hers with the products of her art.

The always impeccably beautiful mother looks at her tomboy daughters with incomprehension. Why don't they play with dolls? Why do the girls' lovely dresses always remain in the back of the closet? Despite the girls' denials—the dolls, subjects of scientific experiment, look well used; the dresses are dutifully taken out for occasions they hate and the mother loves—the mother is not fooled. She knows there are other Things in her daughters' closet as well, Things that jar with her wistful expectations and her American Dream hopes:

> Now, when she stares into our closet, she maybe has the feeling her plan
> to be the mother of little girls has not quite worked out the way she

always thought it would. . . . My mother stares in astonishment, like she has given birth to Tom Mix and Will Rogers instead of to Shirley Temple and Elizabeth Taylor, the way she had planned. (84–85)

Ironically, despite her ostensible rejection of her roots, it is the Ortiz y Cabares philosophy that "makes resignation and perhaps even love possible" (84) in the face of her bewilderment with such unfeminine little girls. The mother herself is, of course, a self-made work of art in the American Dream school.

Appropriately enough, the mother's artistic qualities are first and most fully revealed in her decision to leave school and go to work in a toy factory, painting delicate flowers on yo-yos. In the reconstruction of this moment, the mother is described as a potential Georgia O'Keeffe (32), and yet, of course, no art critic will discover her or appreciate the artist talent lavishly spent on an inexpensive children's toy. The mother, it seems, is doomed to such evanescent displays. And then, too, the Ortiz Taylors' repeated reference to the mother's past as yo-yo artist invites a teasing out of the metaphor with respect to her most insistent personal qualities: her love of art, expended on small, domestic items for lack of a larger canvas, her own yo-yo-like nature: going forth a short distance into the world, always tethered, and always returning to her home. The girls' own obsession with holding funerals for brightly colored but short-lived butterflies, burying them in decorated matchboxes after elaborate ceremonies, can be seen as an extension of their mother's grasping after the permanence and beauty of fleeting things, pulling them back from flight and planting them in her own backyard.

While the mother is associated with delicate beauty and a fragile, unstable Ortiz y Cabares rootedness to place, the father's Texan heritage is one of movement and continual change, albeit inexplicably stymied in the context of this narrative. The most persistent metaphor of his yearning for flight is the "For Sale" sign on the house that serves as one of the markers of the father's shifting moods:

When we round the horseshoe, there it is again, the sign saying: For Sale by Owner.

"You moving?" asks Pig Nose.

Our father does this all the time. Puts up the sign. Takes it down. We never know when.

"We're moving to Mexico," I tell Pig Nose. "Or maybe we're going
to sail around the world."

"How come?" says Pig Nose, reasonably.

"We're not," says my sister. (156)

Ironically enough, the father's "For Sale" sign also has a yo-yo quality
to it: it goes up and down upon being taken out irregularly. The exchange
among the three schoolgirls suggests as well the different readings of
this action. Are they going to throw themselves wholeheartedly into the
father's dream? Are they going to understand it as just one more passing
fad, destabilizing at the moment, but not definitive? The sisters are split
on this question, though they remain, as always, "in relationship" (138),
their own shifting loves and allegiances defined by the wholehearted acceptance of, or resistance to, the father's never-to-be-realized dreams.
After the father's death, the mother, whose Californian rootedness has
always exercised a counterforce to the father's restless dreams, puts the
house on the market one last time. This woman who has never conduct-
ed a business transaction in her life, even so small as writing a check,
sells the house within a week, belying the father's lifetime of failed attempts, and moves to Mexico with her daughters. This "inscrutable"
action on the mother's part serves not only as the epilogue to the bulk of
the text, but also its condition of possibility (244). It is, in essence, the
other side of the faultline/barbed wire inscribed on the mirrored door
to the mother's room, the necessary distance vouchsafed by the mother's
agency and by which all the Things in the closet—from Aunt Winifred's
death to the awful mother-and-daughter dresses—can be shaken out and
given order and ordinariness.

For Norma Cantú, the promise of mother-daughter cultural transmission through women's stories is more explicitly carried out: "In 1985,
back in that safe space, between two countries, the woman Nena and
her mother bring out the boxes, untie the white-turned-yellow shoelaces,
and begin going through the memories" (2). Like the Ortiz Taylors,
Cantú uses a kind of yo-yo metaphor: going away, coming back, achieving the distance that permits reflection, returning to the home space
that contains the memory boxes that need to be opened in order for
this narrative to take shape. For Cantú, the space of narration is located between the two countries, in the ambivalent and ambiguous "safe
space" where she was brought up. This safe space is, nonetheless, fraught

with legal complications, and concerns of legal identity continually sift their way into the stories she tells. Cantú's narration insistently marks nationality, describing family members as U.S.-born, Mexican-born, or, that best of all worlds: Texas-born ("her land lies beyond borders," 42). Thus, for example, Comadre Fina "was U.S. born and married to a real Mexican macho who wooed her back to Mexico with promises of wealth." When she realized the promises were never going to become reality, Fina moved her family back to the United States, eventually followed by her Mexican husband. This family, in some ways so typical of the border-crossing experience, seems foreign to the narrator by reason of a central versus northern Mexico cultural difference that is entirely blurred in U.S. dominant culture: "they have corn tortilla tacos with beans for breakfast—so unlike our own flour tortillas filled with papas con huevo" (18). The narrator's mother was not born in Mexico but was sent there at age ten, and she moved back to the United States after marriage (40). Her father's older brother, a typical border crosser, left two widows: one Texan, one Mexican, both of whom showed up for the funeral (16). Such complications hint both at the artificiality of the political border for families who have members and allegiances on both sides, while at the same time the insistent reminder of the somewhat vexed nature of border crossing is underlined by compulsive references to official citizenship and national location.

For the narrator, border crossing is both an everyday event and a passage into an available alternative definition of self and space. She describes a photograph of herself—"Azucena Cantú"—at one year old, an image attached to her U.S. immigration papers, and alongside this photograph she sets another, of herself at age twelve, in which she is identified as a Mexican citizen (the two photographs reproduced in the text typically suggest the opposite: the one-year-old's card describes her as "nacionalidad mexicana"; the twelve-year-old's paperwork implies her U.S. affiliation by the home address in Laredo, Texas, 21–22). In either case, when she spends the summer in Mexico, she is "Mamagrande's spoiled pocha granddaughter" (27), tainted by her U.S. cultural affiliation; in her imagination in the present tense of the narration, she can dream of another life, "a life as a Mexican" (129). Cantú's narrator, thus, can try on and simultaneously retain and discard two potential identities, each of them fraught with bicultural complications.

Lorna Dee Cervantes' poem, "Refugee Ship," cited in the epigraph to this chapter, describes a community of women—grandmother, mother, daughter—and the faultlines that interrupt cultural transmission in this female-defined community: "Mama raised me without language./ I'm orphaned from my Spanish name" (41). For both Cantú and the Ortiz Taylors, the mother figures in the autoethnographic tale as an important force in defining their immediate sense of self, but the focus of Mexican-related cultural transmission skips a generation and adheres most powerfully to the mother's mother: "Bueli" in *Canícula*, "Mymama" in *Imaginary Parents*. The photographs and narrative fragments about Bueli always describe her as surrounded by children (4, 24), and she is a permanent presence in many other fragments as well: as caretaker and storyteller, she is the glue that holds the family together. Analogously, for the Ortiz Taylor girls, Mymama's house holds infinite small treasures; three long shelves of what the grandmother calls "pocadillas," small items she has collected or others have given her, each of which has its own story to tell (48).

For these writers, the ethnographic, as opposed to simply (or complexly), autobiographical promise of these narratives has a good deal to do with the way in which the subject of narration is delimited. For them, reframing the genre of autobiography implies exploring alternative genealogies of life-story telling that do not privilege the individual "I" as the epistemological ground of narration, but rather evoke a multiplicity of times, places, memories and countermemories, resonant metaphors, and internationally embedded networks of relationships. In so doing, both texts not only name their founding memories in other cultural contexts (huesario, ofrenda), but also insist on naming them in another language (untranslatable) and not just another style or a twist on genre. In both these texts, that other language (Spanish) and the other culture (Mexican) serve as central metaphorical referents and continually impinge themselves upon the mostly English, mostly U.S.-based narration:

> The "mother" tongue is at work within the other tongue. There is a permanent movement of translation from one to the other, a dialogue as with a mirror, extremely hard to elucidate. . . . The violence of the text takes shape precisely in this chiasmus, this intersection, this irreconcilable difference. (Abdelkebir Khatibi, trans. Lionnet, 332)

This second language runs under the first and gives it a richer quality; it also erupts into the English text at key moments, and it is precisely this richness and this irreconcilability that both texts seek to achieve.

At the same time as we mark and appreciate this counterpractice, we assume that the writers are publishing in English in a U.S. publishing house because they also want dissemination among dominant culture readers in the United States. Spanish, then, serves as a sign of difference that strains at the tolerances of a resolutely monolingual culture. Society, says Barthes, "mistrusts pure meaning" (*Camera Lucida,* 36), but it mistrusts impure or duplicitously framed meaning systems even more. Françoise Lionnet eloquently summarizes the predicament of the author who writes against dominant culture practices in terms of either language or style. To disrupt or resist established norms, she says, runs the risk of incomprehensibility for certain readers, of "having his or her message mistaken for meaningless noise" (332). For writers like Cantú and the Ortiz Taylors, there is no reasonable alternative to the double menace of exoticization on one side and incomprehensibility on the other.

Norma Cantú's narrative, more so than the Ortiz Taylors', textually marks the eruption of Spanish into English in the multiple crossings of the borderlands. Cantú describes this book as the second part of a trilogy, the first book of which is written entirely in Spanish. This book is set at mid-century and halfway between the two nations; of the third volume, *Cabañuelas,* we know only that it will take the story to the end of the twentieth century. Befitting its in-between nature, this narrative straddles the two languages as well as the two countries, at times uncomfortably:

> On a hot, hot, hot August day, the chicharras' drone forces me to the present; they madly hum incessantly, insistently. A long row of cotton to be picked, capullos de algodón, nothing moves; the dust has settled on the green leaves and on my skin. El olor a sudor, mi sudor, the heavy odor of sweat I wear with the blue plaid flannel shirt. (3)

While Cantú later tells the now-clichéd story of being punished for speaking Spanish (88), a circumstance often blamed for what Lorna Dee Cervantes calls being "orphaned" from her mothertongue (41), what is occurring in this fragment is not exactly a representation of the breaking of a childhood language across the back of U.S. dominant culture practices. Rather, Cantú wants to have it both ways here: to evoke the sense of a life lived in Spanish while providing sufficient markers for the English-only reader to follow the text without background dissonance or meaningless noise.

Thus, in each sentence, one key image is described in Spanish: "chicharra," "capullo de algodón," "olor a sudor," and the reference is made in plain type, with no exoticizing scare quotes or italics to set it off as a foreign element. In the first case, the context suggests the translation, and while a monolingual reader might confuse cicadas with bees or some other humming insect, the general description of the scene is clear. In the second sentence, the English "cotton" is followed by the Spanish translation "algodón"; the "capullos," or bolls, are an added element, there to be appreciated or missed, but not crucial to the meaning. Likewise, Cantú follows the Spanish "olor a sudor" with its precise English translation, this time adding an adjective to the English variation: "heavy odor of sweat." While not all of Cantú's text makes use of Spanish to this degree, there is a continual undertow of the other language's presence in this mostly English text, which to the monolingual reader offers a biting reminder of the cultural otherness of this lived experience.

At the same time, for the bilingual reader, Cantú's text may at times fall into irritating redundancy as translation inevitably accompanies insertion of words and phrases that mark a fronteriza's reality. And yet, of course, how else is Cantú to negotiate the difficult territory of two monolingualisms that rub up against each other and fall back into a middle generation's bilingual stutterings? There is, of course, no facile solution to this oft-identified problem in biculturally sensitive texts. At one level, these "foreign" phrases and cultural markers reflect once again the quality of background noise that Barthes signals as essential to buffering meaning and making it both more palatable and less acute (36). On another, what for Eurocentric ears can be heard as noise is, in fact, as Lionnet reminds us, too often the very core of meaning in the marginalized woman's text. And the reverse. Thus, for example, Cantú reminds us that English, for much of her family, is the frustrating noise in the background of comprehensible language: "Everywhere the English sounds, like the sounds of an unfamiliar engine that he couldn't decipher" (28–29).

The Ortiz Taylors take a somewhat different approach to the same problem, using Spanish even more sparsely than Cantú, but casting key metaphors and textual leitmotivs in relation to a Mexican American– flavored reality, often to humorous result, so that the overall effect is one of a continual flow between the different cultural models. Here, for example, are the Ortiz Taylors on a banal topic, using a specific metaphor that is both evocative and immediately graspable, while also tied tightly to a fronterizo cultural environment. The girls describe the father's impeccably (if futilely) well-organized closet, with its "socks tucked into burrito-shaped bundles" (8). This apparently throwaway metaphor works perfectly to underscore a certain biculturally flavored perception of ordinary life. The same effect holds true even when the metaphorical bias runs the other way, toward dominant culture. Thus, the girls contemplate "an authentic replica of a Mexican hearth, though to us it looks like an igloo"; by the necessary slippage of narrative logic this hearth becomes forever after in the text the "Mexican igloo" (20–21).

Promiscuous and comic blendings of culture happen at all levels but are most forcefully and effectively centered on representations of the home and of domestic life. In one of the most lyric evocations of the mother in this book, the narrative describes her in the kitchen, one of her most profoundly creative artistic sites, in the aftermath of her own mother's death. The mother prepares dinner, recalling the image of her mother in the casket surrounded by votive candles, and the tears in her eyes come both from a memory of that loss and from the acrid smell of the chiles as she toasts them over the range, the gas flame echoing the flickering of the candles in the church. Her lost mother, suggests the narrative, lives on in the delicate dance of the girls' mother in the kitchen, carrying on the family traditions: "This woman knows the rhythm of chiles. . . . She moves back and forth . . . cooking en un acento puro, this woman who says she cannot speak one word of Spanish, cooking only en la lengua, moving with a ritmo that is her own. Is her mother's" (231). In this lovely passage, the judicious use of Spanish defines the rhythm of the text as well as the cultural context. And yet, of course, how different is this passage from another, which describes more precisely one of the mother's delicious creations: "Hormel's chili con carne with fresh chopped onions, plates of tortillas with melted jack cheese" (23). Continually, the Ortiz Taylors bring the readers back from the lyric to the banal, making of the dissonance between and unexpected blendings of cultures the very core of their tale.

In their family, the Texan-Anglo father speaks perfect Spanish; the Californian mother admits to no such bilingual contaminations, although her own mother, Mymama, prefers Spanish over her broken English. The girls' mother, like her siblings, at times has recourse to comically broken Spanish: "ay dos mío" (109) is one of her favored expressions; along similar lines, "that's a lot of cangada" is her brother's (110). Whenever she employs one of these phrases, the father, who is much more worried than she about losing the language, "steers her gently in the direction of the dining room where he keeps his Spanish books for just such emergencies" (110). The father also tries to insist on using Spanish with their daughters, seeing in the language an important link to their cultural heritage. In a typical exchange described in one of Sheila's family "photographs," he tries to get his daughters to ask for the rice in Spanish while the three of them are eating dinner at Mymama's house: *"Dígame en español,"* he insists as Mymama hands around the bowl and spoons on sugar. The girls' mother, passing through the room, complains: "Padie, she doesn't need that," at which comment the grandmother "withdraws her hand as if she's been scalded. . . . '*Arroz,*' he says" (160–61). This exchange, paired to the loving description of the mother's unconscious cultural ties in the kitchen scene, suggests both a surface pragmatism about a land and a language the mother associates with second-class citizenship, and a deeply felt and rooted connection to a culture she overtly disavows.

The mother's particular resistance to learning Spanish—a considerable and repeatedly referenced bone of contention between husband and wife—is never fully explored, although it obviously stands in for unexplained tensions within the family. Nonetheless, this refusal or inability to speak Spanish serves as a point of reference to define the magnitude of other accomplishments; for example: "My mother, who has not learned to conjugate either form of the verb *to be* in Spanish during two years of intense lessons with my father, will learn to drive expertly in three afternoons" (145). An incommensurable disjunction between the two experiences ("has not learned . . . will learn") only solidifies their unlikely pairing. Much later, in an inexplicable turn of events, it is the mother who decides to fulfill the father's dream by moving her family to Mexico. Once she is committed on this course: "My mother, who never could remember how to pronounce *hay* during my father's nightly Spanish lessons, now understood *cada palabra*" (247). The other language, thus, like the "Things" in the closet, loses all its nightmare qualities when taken out and brushed off for use in the service of some other vision than the American Dream of a Hollywood family life.

One of the most beautifully nuanced leitmotivs of this narrative involves the slow and subtle shift from the mother's "ay dos mío" to the shocked "Ay, dios mío" of a surely apocryphal Amalia Jerez, sweeping out the Cine Real in Tepoztlán on a rainy day in the second to last fragment of the book. This fragment, entitled "Moving Pictures," contrasts with the explicitly still images of the "photographs" narrated throughout the text and focuses on Amalia Jerez's astonishment as the Ortiz Taylor women drive by in their overloaded Buick Century: "she sees them. Sticking out of the window, the boots of a dead man! Slowly and in wonder she crosses herself twice, murmurs 'Ay, dios mío,' watches as the car carries the man to the next level, then disappears down into the rain" (255). The Mexican cleaning woman's shocked exclamation brings the text full circle from the mother's earlier idiosyncratic variation on the familiar Spanish phrase. Likewise, the reader knows, as the accidental witness does not, the full history of the boots sticking out the window. The sisters have capped off their lives in Mexico with a variation on their grandmother's pocadillas, but writ large. Very large. Instead of tiny miniatures, they have accumulated, among other items, a six-foot-tall straw Pancho Villa (luckily passing on the opportunity to purchase Villa's equally life-size horse), and despite all the rearranging of the luggage, somehow the famous Revolutionary hero suffers the indignity of only partially fitting into the already overloaded car (252–55). There is something both monumental and silly about this straw man and the unfinished tale of his travels.

The reason that Pancho Villa seems "necessary" refers directly back to other Ortiz y Cabares stories that intricately interconnect the legendary figure with the Californian family. Mypapa is the proud owner of a Colt pistol given to him by Pancho Villa (130), and it is this gun (or another, Sheila does not clarify, although Sandra's comments on the complementary artistic piece say that it was a shotgun [x]) that Mypapa uses to kill himself after Mymama's death, when he realizes he cannot go on without her. Sandra sees this suicide as the crucial moment defining the final dissolution of the family; the thrust of the narrative, however, belies this dark reading, and the six-foot Pancho Villa seems an appropriate—if fragile—token for the family's endurance and continuing respect for its heritage.

From another point of view, Pancho Villa's Colt is, in objective terms, as likely to be apocryphal as the cleaning woman's reaction to the supposed corpse in the car, since presumably it derives from the same source and the same time period as Pancho Villa's whip, proudly displayed in the Ortiz Taylors' dining room. Family lore tells of the famous Revolutionary general sweeping down on the family's California ranch for unspecified reasons, waiting around only long enough to receive enthusiastic greetings and to leave behind the treasured artifacts (but wait! Didn't Sheila tell us the ranch had been lost an indefinitely long time ago? And when did Pancho Villa invade California, anyway?). The whip has at least two important stories associated with it. The first, the mother's story, tells of personally being scooped up into Pancho Villa's saddle during his brief visit and enjoying the great man's embrace: "and when Pancho Villa sets down my mother he lifts a long coil of braided leather from his saddle horn and hands it to my grandfather, who accepts it in all honor." The other story, the grandmother's story, tells of the day her son, Uncle Jimmy Doll, came home crying from school after being whipped by the principal, at which point: "my grandmother took that whip down from the wall, carried it coiled in her hand, walking all the way to Allesandro Street School, the school built on the land of her own people, carried the whip into the main office, called out the principal, whipped him as he had whipped her son" (92). The various Pancho Villa stories reflect an important and permanent aspect of the otherwise easygoing Ortiz y Cabares family besides the more obvious pride in their Mexican heritage: their old-fashioned sense of honor, their finely honed sense of how to balance justice against necessity.

The last scene of the Ortiz Taylors' text is set in Tepoztlán, in a Mexican house that belongs to their father's niece, Dolores. The final words of the narrative make explicit the technique that has been followed throughout this narrative: "In this house under the stars we will fall asleep, dreaming the past into tropes and signs and symbols, beginning the dangerous art of fitting it all back inside the heart of a child" (257). It is through such highly charged symbols that the sisters are best able to convey this imaginary autobiography, this homage/ofrenda to their parents, and it is only in that other space, in their cousin's Mexican house, that they can recapture and reinvent the childhood in California.

For Norma Cantú as well, the autoethnography requires the estranging distance of another country as its condition of composition. In the very first pages of her narrative, Cantú writes, "In 1980 on the squeaky iron bed in a seventh-floor piso in Madrid two lovers intently go over photographs kept in an old cigar box." These photographs are not the narrator's, however, but pictures of the lover's family taken both before and after the Spanish Civil War. In contrast with her lover's loquacity, the narrator is mute: her land is unknown and unfathomable for her lover, whose Spanish experience gives him nothing to grasp and no images to cement a connection to an imaginary U.S./Mexico fronterizo world. It is in the context of his family stories that she realizes that her own experience cannot be told: "she has no photographs to offer" (1). Nevertheless, it is this first, nonreciprocal moment with her lover that provokes the narrator into the second sharing, back in the borderlands, with her mother in 1985, where they in turn open old boxes and release long-forgotten memories (2). Here too, as in the Ortiz Taylors' case, it is only in the physical displacement of the narrators to another land that the recuperation can begin, only in the evoked presence of a fleeting and potentially apocryphal catalyst (the Mexican cleaning woman, the Spanish lover) that the narrative begins to take shape. And in both cases, it is only in the imagined presence of that uncomprehending other that the self-refashioning can occur fruitfully, so that the impossibility of understanding becomes the challenge and the point of entry into a nuanced tale. The reader, then, like the unnamed Spaniard, like Amalia Jerez, is invited into the text exactly at this originary point of incomprehension, and that background noise gives shape both to the "autobiographical" and the "ethnographic" aspects of the texts.

This question of "noise," and the concomitant recognition that a consciousness of noise depends on positionality, and that positionality in the borderlands always involves a destabilizing in-betweenness, may be played out on structural (generic) or textual (linguistic) grounds. In either (both) cases, the narrative always comes back to the tensions between traditional conceptions of autobiography and the particular circumstances defining an interstitial or fronterizo cultural space. It is telling that both of these autoethnographies require physical displacement from, and return to, the borderlands in order to open a free space for creation, and that one of the most crucial defining characteristics of these two fronterizo texts are their encoding of border life as constant movement, either realized (as in the multiple border crossings of Cantú's family), or potential (the periodic "For Sale" sign on the Ortiz Taylors' California house). Finally, as must be clear by now, alternative life-story projects like these two fronterizo autoethnographies also enter seriously into the theoretical debates about revisionary autobiographical projects, and implicitly as well as explicitly stake out a theoretical claim to a different kind of narrative project. Valéry famously said that "there is no theory that is not a fragment, carefully prepared, of an autobiography" (cited in Eakin, vii). These projects, in their explicitly contestatory narrative stance, as well as in the fulfillment of the promise of these alternative ethnographic projects through the body of the text and accompanying images, also remind us that autobiography, carefully prepared, is a fragment of a theoretical position.

# 5. Unredeemed

*Rosina Conde*

They wanted to turn us into pseudo-Chicanos/as.
—*Rosina Conde, interview*

A few years ago Carlos Monsiváis published an article in a volume on the North American Free Trade Agreement (NAFTA) in which he under-lines the political, social, and cultural cost of the traditional division be-tween Mexico City and the rest of the country:

> Se sanctificó el juego de los opuestos: civilización y barbarie, capital y provincia, cultura y desolación. Desde principios de siglo . . . cunde una idea: la provincia es "irredimible," quedarse es condenarse. (197)

> [A play of opposites was sanctified: civilization and barbarism, capital and provinces, culture and desolation. Since the beginning of the centu-ry . . . the idea has propagated that the province is "unredeemable," that to stay is to be condemned.]

From Mexico City's point of view, the northern border is imagined as perhaps the most "unredeemable" of all the provincial representations. From a centrist perspective it is the region most affected by the cultural, linguistic, and moral corruption of Mexico's unfortunately proximate and powerful neighbor, the United States. Rosina Conde, a product and chronicler of the Californian border, has been, we suspect, one of the victims of this centrist snobbery about the northern border region. Her numerous volumes of fiction and poetry have been published by a variety of small, provincial presses, have received very little attention from the Mexico City mainstream cultural critics, and have been unfortunately understudied in Hispanist circles in the United States as well.[1] Both Chicano and mainstream Mexican writers have tended to ignore contributions of Mexican border writers like Conde, who do not fit well into either group's cultural agenda; for Chicano/a literature the border tends to serve as a utopic abstract reference. In Mexican border literature the topic of the border occupies an ordinary space, a place that is infrequently represented in writing.

Conde asks us to move away from a world imagined in terms of Mexico City versus the provinces or Mexico versus the United States; likewise, her works demand that we rethink a notion of human motivations based on gender stereotypes of passive women and aggressive men (cf. Paz's influential dichotomy of men and women in Mexico according to the Chingón/Chingada binary in his *El laberinto de la soledad* [Labyrinth of solitude]). This border writer often focuses on what Trujillo Muñoz describes as a region "beyond taboos" in his brief note on this author, and he continues with a lapidary phrase that has become the most quoted comment on Conde's work: "Rosina Conde fue la primera escritora bajacaliforniana en explorar, sin ninguna clase de cortapisas, la relación amorosa en un mundo de dominados y dominadores" [Rosina Conde was the first Baja Californian writer to explore, without any restraints, the amorous relationship in a world of dominators and dominateds] ("La literatura bajacaliforniana contemporánea," 181). We would go somewhat further than Trujillo Muñoz in this characterization and say that Conde's work not only thematically insists upon representing the familiar, border-inflected worlds of assembly plants, prostitution, and striptease—the still-largely taboo topics—but that her particular take on this world forcefully inserts itself into a larger dynamic, such as the one ironically underlined by Monsiváis, and requires the reader to rethink old stereotypes about national identity.

This is most strikingly true when Conde brings her reader, as she often does, into the liminal world of abusive relationships, or of female sexuality bought and sold in Tijuana's many nightclubs. In these stories Conde's interrogation of the tight imbrication of (provincial) identity and (deviant) female sexuality is particularly pronounced. In a manuscript on female prostitution in Tijuana, María Gudelia Rangel Gómez writes a concise summary of the working of this stereotype:

> Como puede observarse en el proceso histórico de Tijuana, tanto su crecimiento poblacional como su desarrollo económico han ido de la mano de actividades estimatizadas o consideradas prohibidas en otros lugares, esto ha provocado que la concepción generalizada de la ciudad haya sido un proceso de feminización de Tijuana; identificada primero con una "dama generosa" que permitió mejores niveles de vida a su población, posteriormente una "joven coqueta" que atraía hombres para "perderlos" y finalmente la visión que se tuvo de una "prostituta decadente y grotesca" que utilizaban aquellos que pasaban por Tijuana. (30)

> [As one may observe in the historical process of Tijuana, its population growth as well as its economic development have gone hand-in-hand with activities that are stigmatized or prohibited in other places. This has resulted in a generalized conception of the city in terms of a process of feminization of Tijuana; identified first as a "generous lady" who allowed a better standard of living to her inhabitants, later as a "frivolous young woman" who attracted men who "got lost" and finally, the vision of a "decadent and grotesque prostitute" who takes advantage of those who pass through Tijuana.]

Rangel Gómez's reading of Tijuana's infamous international image as a meat market for the United States—U.S. men cross the border to purchase sex from Mexican women, while Mexican men cross the border to sell their labor in U.S. fields—is a potent one, suggesting that from both central Mexico as well as the United States there arises a tendency to feminize Tijuana in a particularly marginalizing and stigmatized manner. Tijuana, in this respect, confirms the primacy of centrist notions about the provinces by antinomy. By setting Tijuana and its inhabitants outside the traditional construction of the motherland *(madre patria)* as a domestic space writ large, those Tijuanan generous ladies, frivolous women, and decayed prostitutes help define the normalized space, holding up a distorting mirror to central Mexico's sense of itself as a nation of decent women and hardworking men. Even more curiously, in view of Tijuana's notorious representation through an image of undomestic femininity, until very recently, whether because of or despite the stereotype, writers and social scientists have tended to avoid analysis of the actual women who work in the nightclubs as waitresses, dancers for pay, stripteasers, and prostitutes. As Patricia Barrón Salido acutely comments, even in respected studies of marginal figures from Tijuana, "parecería que la prostitución queda entre puntos suspensivos" [it seems that prostitution remains in the ellipsis] (9).[2] It is this slipperiness of a term which is both essential and elided that Conde explores, and that requires further analysis.

This slipperiness is patent in one of Conde's most polished stories, narrated from the point of view of a suicidal ex-prostitute called Sonatina currently involved in an intermittently oppressive relationship with Pilar, the lesbian lover who took her out of the life on the streets. "Nunca se esperan que una reaccione" [They never expect one to react], says the lover to Sonatina at one point when two men threaten them silently and Pilar responds with an aggressive gesture. Sonatina tells the reader that Pilar specifically emphasizes the feminine form of the word "one": "porque siempre se refirió a sí misma como *una,* recalcando la *a* para reafirmar su condición femenina. Pilar es ingeniera agrónoma, y estudió en la UNAM porque, dice, es la única universidad en América Latina que te da el título en femenino" [because she always referred to herself as *one* (feminine gender marker) stressing the *a* in order to reaffirm her female condition. Pilar is an agricultural engineer, and she says she studied in the UNAM because it is the only university in Latin America that gives you a degree in feminine] (*Embotellado,* 25). Pilar's gesture and her insistence upon finding an equal space for the feminine in language is an important one. Likewise, her consistent ideological stand on the issue of all degrees and levels of gender oppression is admirable, ranging from her attention to biases built into the language to a concern for women's right to hold fulfilling professional careers. For Sonatina, however, her lover's familiar response is at the same time appropriate and excessive. The ex-prostitute initially applauds her lover's liberating feminist gesture, while later she comes to believe that men need such mostly harmless displays of symbolic violence in order to reaffirm their oft-threatened and insecure masculinity. Extrapolating from Sonatina's perspective, the reader is led to understand that the aggressively butch attitude of the lover only inverts an unjust gender-based hierarchy without seriously questioning it.

On another level, there is in this text a clear desire to reappropriate and reimagine canonical discursive practices. The title of the story echoes that of one of the most well-known poems by the great Latin American modernist poet, Rubén Darío, and also reminds the reader of Virginia Woolf's *Room of One's Own,* with its famous injunction that in order to think and write a woman needs five hundred pounds and a room of her own. Although Conde's "Sonatina" is neither educated nor independent, thanks to Pilar she does have the space and leisure Woolf enjoins as necessary to reflection. A bisexual ex-prostitute with only the most rudimentary schooling, the protagonist of this story has no interest—*pace* Woolf—in the exigencies of writing as process or a discursive practice, but she is willing to tell her story. And, after all, telling stories is as much a successful prostitute's stock-in-trade as selling sex—sometimes even more so. At the same time, this unfolding tale of the psychological processes of a woman who finds herself imprisoned by the banalities of everyday life situates the character firmly in Woolfian territory. In this manner, Conde mocks the authorizing voice of Virginia Woolf at the same time as she takes from the celebrated English writer a model for her own story.

"Sonatina" not only poses a challenge to the classist basis of Woolf's theory, but also projects a transgressive response to Darío's now-exhausted late-nineteenth-century aesthetics modeled on the quintessence of beauty: a bored, hyperfeminine princess imprisoned by the pomp of her role. Conde's story begins with a shocking response to the famous question that opens Darío's poem, "¿Qué tendrá la princesa?" [What's wrong with the princess?] (Castillo, *Antología,* 157). Here the contrast between the two texts could not be more striking. The melancholy that afflicts the Darian princess is part and parcel of the aesthetic tendency of the modernist movement in general and reflects the poet's depression on his isolation from a society that has displaced writing as a profession. Conde's protagonist, on the other hand, resoundingly underscores her banality of both vision and expression, her marginality to a cultural formation that has made ideals of such rarefied inventions as golden princesses.

One of the most obvious ways in which Conde's story responds to Darío is by allowing the protagonist to express herself in her own voice. In the famous poem, the princess is envisioned from afar and remains subject to the impositions of the lyrical poetic voice. In Condé's version, the roles are inverted; in this later "Sonatina," the woman speaks brusquely and unlyrically to an interlocutor who remains silent. In contrast with Darío's poem—in which "el feliz caballero que te adora sin verte, / y que llega de lejos, vencedor de la Muerte, / a encenderte los labios con su beso de amor" [the happy knight who loves you without seeing you / and who arrives from afar, defeating death / to burn your lips with an adoring kiss] (158)—in Condé's story the role of knight errant is handed over to the protagonist's lesbian lover. But even here Condé's reinscription is equivocal. Although Pilar serves as a liberating figure in the early sections of the story, because "me pasaba muy buena lana y me llevaba a restaurantes muy elegantes. . . . Me trataba de 'mami' y luego hasta empezó a comprarme ropa y zapatos" [she gave me a lot of money and took me to elegant restaurants. . . . She called me "sweetie" and even began to buy me clothes and shoes] (105), as time goes on she metamorphoses into something like the evil dragon of the modernist poem. In her dragon mode, Pilar keeps Sonatina's activities under close watch and her jealousy makes Sonatina feel imprisoned.

An important element of the story, and one that plays no role in the poem, is that through her monologue Sonatina comes to a personal questioning of her situation. Darío's princess has a primarily decorative function and is melancholy despite her beauty and privilege; Condé's ex-prostitute is fed up with Pilar's restrictions and bored with her life. However, her function, too, because of her lack of skills, has devolved into a decorative one. She notes:

De lo que sí me di cuenta fue de que no sirvo para nada: no sé escribir a máquina, no sé taquigrafía, ni tengo buena ortografía; así que de secretaria no la hago. Tampoco sé coser. . . . El caso es que de lo único que podría buscar trabajo sería de recepcionista o de obrera y, sin embargo, me daría miedo o hueva salir a buscar en un ambiente desconocido. (111–12)

[What I have realized is that I'm not good for anything. I don't know how to type, I don't know shorthand, I don't spell well, so I can't make it as a secretary. I don't know how to sew either. The thing is that the only kind of job I could look for would be receptionist or factory work, and yet, I'm scared or bugged out about the idea of looking for a job in an unknown place.]

The narrator here meditates on her situation and also reveals to what extent she has interiorized the cultural presuppositions about a woman's options for gainful employment. Despite her partner's untraditional education and position, when she contemplates her own prospects beyond returning to prostitution, Sonatina's imagination is limited to the traditional women's jobs: secretary, receptionist, garment worker, factory employee. At the same time, and despite—or perhaps because of her previous experience—Sonatina projects a cultural mindset that advises women to stay at home and not venture outside for employment, as there are unknown dangers in the public space.

Sonatina's self-reflection takes a surprising turn at this point. What looks like indolence, or an inability to decide and to act, resolves in a coming to consciousness of her true capacities. But this transformation does not take either a traditional shape or one that feminist culture critics might expect. After a profound crisis and various suicide attempts, the protagonist decides to stay in Pilar's house and in this way affirm herself as an independent human being. She remains, she says, "porque tengo ganas de chingarla; de cobrarme todas las que me ha hecho y sigue haciéndome; porque ni siquiera tendría adonde ir y finalmente, ésta es mi casa" [because I feel like fucking her over, like making her pay for everything she's done to me and continues doing to me; because anyway I don't have anywhere else to go and after all, this is my house] (120). We may not agree with her methods, but the end result is that Sonatina transforms the space where she had felt herself held prisoner.

The woman in this story is not, finally, the same Darian princess who needs a prince (or a lesbian lover) to rescue her. She is a woman who little by little comes to consciousness of her own fragmentary condition, accepts herself, and rearticulates her position as an independent being outside Pilar's authoritative sphere of influence. In the same manner, the prison-house is transformed and Sonatina chooses to remain—under her own conditions. Conde's "Sonatina" does not, however, represent simply the voice of the Other with respect to the monological voice of a patriarchy conceived in either Woolfian or Darian terms. Conde focuses on the woman as the site of a resistant enunciation, deconstructing and rearticulating various discourses. First, Conde confronts the masculinist system with the social text of womanhood, and she deals with feminist expectations of sympathetic readers by handing us a marginalized woman's challenge. With respect to the literary canon, she reevaluates,

repeats, and reinscribes a different text, one that opposes a highly educated and refined aesthetic position with a defiantly lower-class perspective and voice. Finally Conde's text takes upon itself the prerogative of
naming. Pilar, Sonatina's lover, inverts the masculine tradition of reliance
on the name of the father; arrogating to herself the authority to name
Sonatina, hence establishing an apparent feminine genealogy—albeit
one from which both the author and the protagonist eventually decide
to distance themselves.

Thus, the most nuanced commentary on gender performativity in
this story comes from an unexpected source, as filtered through an insistently female-gendered perspective, but one that is referred to the readers through the counterpointed perceptions of that most unreliable of
storytellers, a prostitute, and the most marginalized of women: a butch
lesbian defiantly out of the closet. Conde's overall project in this story
offers a point of view similar to that espoused by Monique Wittig. In
her 1984 essay, "The Mark of Gender," Wittig reminds us that in French
(as in Spanish, and unlike English),

> Sex, under the name of gender, permeates the whole body of language
> and forces every locutor, if she belongs to the oppressed sex, to proclaim
> it in her speech, that is, to appear in language under her proper physi-
> cal form and not under the abstract form, which every male locutor has
> unquestioned right to use. The abstract form, the general, the universal,
> this is what the so-called masculine gender means. (6)

What Conde does in her story is to disturb this assumed universality of
the masculine gender in foregrounding gender itself as a problematic social and ontological category. "Sonatina" privileges the point of view of
a feminine "they," who provide its basic narrative grounding. Yet there
is no attempt to counterpose "ellas" to "ellos" in a universalizing gesture.
Instead Conde opens up the discourse to a multiplicity of distinctly positioned "ellas" whose streams of voice combine to create the narrative
point of view.

It is this technique, more than any other, that marks Conde's literary practice and makes it a welcome addition to modern Mexican literature. This same estranging technique makes her stories seem so unfamiliar, difficult to read, and so ineluctably part of a border reality. This edgy
quality, it seems to us, is exactly what will make Conde's stories attractive
to the U.S. literary establishment, which has a long-time connection to a

certain professional understanding of border-ness. María Rosa Menocal points to the significance of the community of exile scholars in the United States in shaping the discipline of comparative literature, which she argues is structured along the lines set out by "the legacy of exilic Romance philology . . . [having] no set languages or texts, no necessary borders, no temporal constraints or narrative shape" (137). Likewise, Emily Apter picks up on the importance of remembering the degree to which the personal experience of displacement has come to shape the theoretical concerns of literary study: "From Spitzer to Bhabha (despite their being worlds apart) one discerns a recalcitrant homelessness of the critical voice." Apter goes on to characterize "this unhomely voice, together with the restless, migratory thought patterns of the discipline's theory and methods" as the grounding of comparative literature as a discipline,[3] concluding, "I would tend to frame the issue as a border war, an academic version of the legal battles and political disputes over the status of 'undocumented workers,' 'illegal aliens,' and 'permanent residents'" (94). Apter's description of elite theory in terms of a metaphorical border crosser may make some border scholars uneasy, yet her point about the freshness of this emerging, "unhomely" theory is well taken. According to this argument, U.S. elite literary theory returns ineluctably to the shock of recognition born from these cultural displacements; thus, crossing the border offers an occasion for theoretical production precisely because of necessary personal accommodations involving a doubled cultural location.

Conde's contribution to U.S. theoretical discussions may well have something to do with an insistently gendered awareness of these border issues, as well as with sharpening our consciousness of the many regional differences among these writers and of the sometimes uncomfortable spaces they portray. Her characters, however, often operate in a translational hermeneutic space and tend consistently to function in an implicitly contestatory relationship to the everyday operation of the basic premises that underlie centrist political structures on the one hand and patriarchal authority on the other. In this doubly displaced cultural and social location, Conde's women (her point-of-view characters tend to be female, or marginalized males) engage in activities and exchanges that frame this limit space while at the same time demonstrating how sexist thinking distorts the relationships of women to each other.

The longest section of her chapbook collection *En la tarima* is a series of nine short prose pieces (eight numbered fragments and an epilogue) entitled "Viñetas revolucionarias" [Revolutionary scenes] and carrying the dedication: "Para Gilberto, hermano de armas" [For Gilberto, brother at arms] (11). Given the traditional obsession of Mexican writers with the 1910 Revolution, the reader newly come to Conde's work might forgivably expect to find in this section of the book a contribution to the well-nourished subgenre of postrevolutionary fiction. Conde's *En la tarima,* however, is specifically Tijuanan, referring not to the Mexican Revolution, but its namesake: "Revolución," the main avenue in Tijuana, the center of that international city's tourist industry and site of such notorious delights as the world's longest bar and some of Tijuana's toniest striptease and prostitution establishments. Each brief vignette in the sequence of "viñetas revolucionarias" gives the reader a glimpse into this Revolution: either through introduction to a half-dozen of its warriors: initiate stripteaser "Virgen, aún virgen" [Virgin, still a virgin] (15); Lyn, "la reina de la rumba" [the rumba queen] (16); Zoraída, immaculate in white (18); Mariela, the cocaine addict (20); Darling, the transvestite (22); and Zarina, who buries her pain in gluttony (24); or through evocation of the sounds of its battles: the songs "Granada" (17) or "Rumba-rumbera" (21), and the eager solicitations of sidewalk callers: "¡Camin, sir! ¡Camin, sir! ¡Chou taim nau, sir . . . !" (29).

In each of these brief sketches, the excessiveness of performance belies a narrative of lack. Thus, for example, the poignancy of the first vignette comes from the performative qualities of an unexpected display of virginity poised on the imminence of its loss. This young woman, still technically a virgin, performs a masculinist stereotype of virginity as a titillating spectacle in a striptease club. The performative innocence evoked through Virgen's appearance on the stage is, however, framed by two references to her sensuality which offset it and raise questions about the traditional Mexican society's obsession with a bit of hidden female flesh. The first reference to sensuality also involves a performance of sorts and is called into being by (presumably) her boyfriend: "Pablo vendría a verla y habría que ser sensualmente bella, sobre todo después de las flores" [Pablo would come to see her and she'd have to be sensually beautiful, especially because of the flowers], indicating a quid pro quo in which the man's gifts require a certain payment of a sensual—if not necessarily sexual—nature on her part. The second of the two men, the Master of Ceremonies, constructs her along similar grounds and demands an on- and off-stage performance aligned with that image: "A él le gustaba así: *sexy* e ingenua" [he liked her that way: *sexy* and naive] (15). Notably, it is very clear that what the men like in and desire from her is the staging of sexuality rather than the fact of it; as Virgen recalls to herself, her entire performance consists of simultaneously projecting sexuality and convincing the audience of her innocence—a double bind requiring an intense awareness of a denied presence. The central section of the sketch precisely delineates this dilemma: "Habría que bajar lentamente la escalera, apretando las piernas sin ver el público . . . cruzando las rodillas para esconder *aquello* con los muslos" [She had to come down the stairs slowly, squeezing her legs together without looking at the audience . . . crossing her knees to hide *that thing* with her thighs] (15). Virgen's performative focus on her physical virginity estranges her sexuality and makes it unhomely: a contortionist's trick. Furthermore, the display of virginity on the stage points to its fungibility; when the narrator tells us that she is "aún virgen" [still a virgin] Conde signals the appropriateness of the stage name to the physical woman, and also marks a temporal moment, that of the time just before virginity's loss, a moment of transit between physical states and identities.[4]

Conde's careful choice in verb and tense—"vendría," "habría que ser," "habría que bajar"—underlines this ambiguity. On the one hand, the conditional tense infers a possibility in the future that perhaps will not arrive. On the other, it signals an action that has been taking place repeatedly and that locates itself in well-transited territory. The last words of the vignette, after the introductions by the Master of Ceremonies, speak to another moment of decision. Virgen has the option of not going out on the stage, of not showing herself, of no longer staging a performance of virginity every night for the delectation of the club's spectators. Nevertheless, this night, once again, she assumes the risk and "se asoma por la escalera" [she appears on the stairs]. The very repetitiveness of this act assures the reader/spectator that she will once again cross this border.

This strategy of emphasizing contortions and concealment borrows heavily from the old border image of the striptease. Using this concept of the brief and revealing performance, Conde describes an intimate moment in the lives of each of these characters. It is by definition a transitory moment, of movement and crossing. There is no attempt to "redeem" Tijuana or to provide a revisionist understanding of the sex workers' lives, as is often the case in feminocentric texts by other authors.

The focus on something hidden is common to other sketches as well and tends to arise in situations that emphasize the estranging qualities of the stripteasers' lives. Zarina eats potatoes compulsively until they provoke nausea in order to hide from herself her possible pregnancy. Despite her efforts to deny it, her pregnancy is, nevertheless, narratively acknowledged and makes itself seen and salable in the short run: "subió a la tarima en biquini sacundiendo las nalgas y las chichis aumentadas de tamaño por el posible embarazo" [she stepped up to the platform in her bikini, shaking her ass and her tits, enlarged by the possible pregnancy] (25). In the stuttering syntax of this phrase the "possible" pregnancy becomes the proximate cause of the dancer's enlarged breasts, shifting the reader's perception between a fearful potential and a concrete actuality.

Darling, too, has a secret that must be hidden and displayed. A transvestite dancer, Darling has created an act that consists of convincing the audience of her realness, to the point of inciting a sexually aggressive gesture on the part of males eager to "prove" their masculinity (here satisfied when a young man leaps on the stage and kisses her), then revealing the secret that she is really a he: "Darling avienta penacho y lentejuelas y, sonriente, triunfante, muestra de lleno el *flet up* y un pecho plano y brillante ante los ¡ohes! estupefactos de los admiradores. Un hombre vomita" [Darling throws aside feathers and sequins and smiling, triumphant, shows off flat top and smooth, flat chest for the stupefied Ohs! of the admirers. A man vomits] (23). Darling's act is staged as much in the carefully chosen syntax of the sketch, which scrupulously avoids revelatory male gender markers until the reader and the audience are hit with the punchline at the same time. Curiously, both Zarina and the hapless overeager audience member in Darling's performance respond to the unhomely intrusion (the presence of the unwanted fetus, the unwanted—or unacknowledged—desire for the touch of male lips) with an identical gesture of physical rejection: the nausea that symbolically expels the forbidden/undesirable object.

The fifth sketch opens when Mariela applies makeup to her eyes to hide the traces of her disappointment with a man as she prepares for her act. The word choice in the meticulous description, however, once again calls attention to itself by a minute strangeness in the syntax: "Mariela *optó* por abrir el estuche de malaquita" [Mariela *opted* for opening the malachite box] (19). The importance of this odd phrasing, with its implication of options not taken, becomes clear only at the end of the sketch in which Mariela hesitates before going onstage, and picks up the malachite box again: "y lo abrió por el fondo; tocó con cuidado el talco—ahora blanco—con la yema del anular, lo acercó a la nariz, e inhaló" [and she opened the bottom, touched the talcum powder—white now—with the tip of the ring finger, held it up to her nose, and inhaled] (20). Economically, Conde turns the familiar scene of a woman's betrayal by her man into something quite different. The familiar and the estranged touch each other in the two sides of the malachite box, which holds facial powder to cover up bags under the eyes on the one side, and on the other, secret, side hides cocaine. At all times then, Mariela has two choices when opening the box, and the sinister weight of that unusual verb "optar" becomes clear in retrospect. Here two very different but equally stereotypical performances of the feminine touch in counterpoint. Yet, that very knife edge of contact between contrasting stereotypes points to the particular issue problematized in this sketch. In the contact between the two sides of the box, Conde once again addresses the contrapuntal force of the edgily marginalized border reality.

Strikingly, the "revolutionary vignettes" serve as a performative act by which the theme of the border as a brothel takes shape, yet the name of the city "Tijuana" never appears in the collection, and the main street, "Revolución," is only mentioned in passing. This technique of omitting the name of the city and referencing only a single street suggests that we could locate this trip through striptease clubs in any city anywhere in the world. For those readers who do not take cognizance of the significance of the brief reference to Avenida Revolución in Tijuana, these scenes could be equally easily extracted from Mariscal Street in Juárez or the show windows in Amsterdam. And yet, the epilogue to the vignettes once again insists upon the specificity of locale and discursive reality. In this last segment, the narrator leaves the clubs and turns to an observation of the spectacle on the street outside. Here Ave. Revolución itself becomes the stage for the performances of marines, tourists, soldiers back from Vietnam, Tijuana adolescents, and the professional cripples, beggars, and club barkers who make the street into a showplace. Conde's Revolución, and her revolution, thus is to focus on this border life occurring just on the limit, between light and shadow, in the sometimes indistinguishable borders of performances on the stage and on the street.

The title of Conde's later volume of short stories, *Arrieras somos* [Women on the road] emphasizes these edgily self-aware displacements once again, in a different key. From the very title of the collection readers know that we are dealing with a moment of transit, and, indeed, the book as a whole interrogates the boundaries of contemporary Mexican society through the active forgetting of the stereotypical domestic life. In a study of aporia, Derrida makes an apposite comment in his discussion of what we might call the border trauma induced by such transitional actions:

> The crossing of borders always announces itself according to the movement of a certain step *[pas]*—and of the step that crosses a line. . . . There is a problem as soon as the edge-line is threatened. . . . There is a problem as soon as this intrinsic division divides the relation to itself of the border and therefore divides the being-oneself of anything. (11)

For Derrida, the play on "pas," the French word for "step" and for "not," serves to clarify and delimit this problematic defining and dividing of the self. At the same time, the action of "crossing the line" evokes both literal movement across a boundary and the ontological and ethical decision to step outside traditional moral judgments.

Thus, for example, the narrator in "Barbarella," following a trajectory exactly the opposite of—and in implicit dialogue with—actress Jane Fonda's famous roles on film and in life, was once a perfect little lady according to her own self-description, but now wears 1980s Madonna-style, aggressively sexy clothes. In this story, then, female self-presentation has everything to do with a nuanced understanding and manipulation of implicit dress codes from at least two cultural contexts: middle-class Mexican and Hollywood American. Each context offers its own stereotypical coding of proper and improper dress, and each offers an implied narrative of the woman's destiny as ciphered in her choice of clothes. In "Barbarella," the two narratives play off against each other, each opening a space for commentary on the vagaries of female dress and on the shared affinity in both Mexican and U.S. cultural settings for encouraging girls to play with dolls, and to play with themselves as if they were just life-size Barbies. Thus, an exaggerated Shirley Temple mode of dress provides the young girl with the rewards of familial approval while allowing her to retain an ironic distance from her own style of presentation. Likewise, the aggressively rebellious implications of rock-singer clothing become part of a code tacitly understood by the narrator and the reader, and intentionally incomprehensible to the mainstream manifestations of either Mexican or U.S. culture, where Madonna(s) are always blonde Barbies and Barbarellas.

In this manner Conde's protagonist demonstrates how an exaggerated performance of femininity—whether through childlike bows or tight bustiers—points to a deplorable internationalization of pop-culture bad taste in which the worst of U.S. cultural models serve as visual signs of a Mexican woman's "stepping across the line" in both senses of the phrase, and with all the double charge of negativity and forward action that Derrida uncovers in his discussion. At the same time, and more important, Barbarella also reminds us how a performative attitude infuses clothing style with ideological content. She says of her clothes: "They intimidate whoever looks at me and they force him to swallow his thoughts because the sensual intimidates and attacks" (73–74). This perception of an edgily violent dimension of sensuality, one that women can manipulate to attack men rather than the reverse, gives overt form to a conflict that elsewhere in the collection is more often expressed in barbed comments, suggestive silences, and subtle rebellions against the status quo.

Frequently, though, for these women on the road, powerlessness and empowerment equally turn on questions of self-presentation and on the aggressive rereading and reinterpretation of a specific style. One of the most dazzlingly accomplished stories in the collection, "Rice and Chains," utilizes the metaphor of knitting, and mimics a woman's thoughts as she knits a sweater for her unborn child. As Sergio Elizondo notes in his introduction to the collection, the narrative technique in this story has a deliberate—and deliberative—monotony about it that simulates the placid activity it describes. At the same time, "we come to realize that the stitch that goes 'backwards,' the purling stitch, reveals that the protagonist also takes steps backwards; then, by knitting a few more stitches, she advances" (17). Knitting, then, is not just a typically female task, but also serves as a way of silently coming to a greater understanding of the narrative of a human life as well as a concrete embodiment for that activity. It too, then, concerns itself with a metaphorical "stepping across the line." In this complementary and counterpunctual activity of knitting and purling, Conde not only signals the strange shape of an embodied language, but also continually foregrounds its gendered quality.

Knitting can stand for gender oppression. The lulling process of setting stitches smoothes over the unhappy circumstances described, until at last we are pulled up short with a telling metaphor: "Isn't your knitting like your mother's life? Everything's made up of rice stitches and chains; stitches to the right, back stitches, loops, knots. Rice when she got married, chains in her marriage, knots in her throat" (28). Rice, chains, and knots symbolize a woman's life and her entrapment in the repressive discourse that harms her. In evoking her mother's story, the narrator, a single mother-to-be, signals the deep spiritual wounding of a Mexican woman living with repressive customs. Trinh T. Minh-ha comments, in words that seem equally applicable to Conde's aesthetic and also capture the back-and-forth motion of a woman's painful unlearning of institutionalized tropes as she works toward a more liberating language: "In trying to tell something, a woman is told, shredding herself into opaque words while her voice dissolves on the walls of silence. . . . And often [she] cannot say it. You try and keep on trying to unsay it, for if you don't, they will not fail to fill in the blanks on your behalf, and you will be said" (79–80).

Conde, however, differs from Trinh, for while she impresses upon us the potent image of the marriage chains and the knotted throat, her work also imagines an alternative to the mother's silencing. Silent herself, the daughter recognizes the fact of her mother's oppression and, through her own coming to terms with her knitting, allows us to see in this womanly task an unlikely process for working through a liberating discourse. It is, in fact, through the elegantly developed linguistic play on "basta" ("enough," but also a knitting term for loops) and "puntos a revés" (referencing a thinking back, but also purling stitches) that Conde most effectively makes the tight connection between textual expression and the knitted fabric growing under her protagonist's hands.

In this way, the words that wound and silence women, and that women use to wound and silence themselves, have an ambiguously empowering outlet by which the young woman is able to reevaluate her own life in the light of her mother's and to move toward a more conscious and empowered position. The young woman in this story, thus, imagines herself in the context of a textured, knitted language and in the projected embodiment of the next child in this knotted text, her own baby. While retaining from her mother's repressed world the silent and seemingly inoffensive practice of knitting, the younger woman uses that occupation as a strategy to situate herself on the borders of a different way of imagining that knitted text of a woman's life.

Still further: through the powerful image of a marriage characterized by "knots in her throat" of a woman who finds refuge in what hurt her, and of another, unmarried mother-to-be who uses the knotting threads as a silent reproach to masculinist constructions of narrative, Conde implicitly questions the Enlightenment heritage of a mind-body split and also outlines the far more radical question about the nature of representation itself. As Judith Butler says of Irigaray, in words roughly applicable to the Mexican border writer, "Irigaray would maintain, however, that the feminine 'sex' is a point of linguistic absence, the impossibility of a grammatically denoted substance, and, hence the point of view that exposes that substance as an abiding and foundational illusion of a masculinist discourse" (*Aporias,* 10). Substance, in these stories, is an abiding illusion, one ideologically charged by an unexpected performative, just as illusion offers a foundational reality for self-reinvention. Both alternatives involve a conscious self-presentation that may be deeply estranged from the home (as in the sketches from *En la tarima,* and in Barbarella's hip rebellion against her family mores) or, in "Rice and Chains," the coming to awareness of a practice of repression from within that repressive structure, and of a careful and strategically gauged narrative structure alert to the need to avoid appropriative gestures.

"My Birthday Gift" revolves around a busy husband, who leaves his wife a check and a note "in which he wished me a happy birthday and assured me, 'not without a certain perverse pleasure,' that the check was to be used to buy myself 'some lingerie'" (43). The wife takes umbrage, seeing the ostensible gift to her as in fact a gift to him, intended for his pleasure. The sister, on the other hand, reinterprets the gift as a way for the husband to show his appreciation of his wife, to enhance her pleasure (45). Each of these alternative interpretations is plausible, and each fits into a certain, well-traveled domestic economy. Conde once again takes a further step, one that crosses the line. The story ends not with a resolution of this counterpoint between these two homey alternatives but with an ambiguity that suggests a third, more "perverse" interpretation. The wife arrives home, strips, and steps into the shower, only to discover her husband already there. Here is the last sentence of the story: "Finally, I threw my stockings on the bed and stepped into the shower naked, surprising Gustavo, who smiled, delighted, with my lace panties in his hands" (47). Is Gustavo delighted because his wife is, as he imagines, offering herself for his pleasure? Or is the sister's interpretation more accurate? Or, equally likely, does Conde's delicate initial suggestion of a streak of perversity in the husband hint that his pleasure is found not in his wife, but in his wife's lingerie, which he enjoys as fetish objects or as the core of a transvestite wardrobe? The point is not to decide among these alternatives, though the body of Conde's work convincingly demands of its readers unhomely readings of unhomely situations, but rather to open out the ideological spaces by virtue of which dislocation and border-ness themselves become interpretative categories.

Other stories also turn on a conscious manipulation of stereotypical expectations about male-female relationships. In "Do You Work or Go to School," both Miguel Angel, the sales manager at the narrator's job, and her boyfriend, Antonio, manipulate the rhetoric of feminism in the service of ends that support male privilege. Miguel Angel "laid on a line about women's liberation: that I was intelligent, self-confident, and super sexy. . . . He lays it all on me and proposes that I go take modeling classes in San Diego" (31). When she tells Antonio about this suggestion, the boyfriend "starts on his women's liberation line, the exact opposite of Miguel Angel's. He started telling me how women become objects, things to be used, and how models are the worst thing about the capitalist system" (32). In each case, the men's motive is exploitation; reading the one against the other tells us exactly in which mode. Antonio, who tells the narrator that women become objects through modeling, is concerned because he does not want to lose the comfortable woman-object he has been enjoying for his sexual pleasure. Miguel Angel, who tells her that she is sexy and independent, eventually exploits her as the company prostitute to soften up potential investors. In this respect, the warnings of both men are very much on the mark. The narrator's eventual conclusion, however, once again shifts the discussion to surprising grounds. The rhetoric of liberation does not serve her, she finds, as the world is controlled by men, "and look! while guys don't come to some agreement as to what liberation is, well, we'll be going to hell, because they fix things to their advantage." Her decision is to play the system astutely, if controversially from a feminist perspective, against itself, refusing to participate any longer in this self-serving rhetoric. Instead, with a gesture typical of Conde's characters throughout her body of work, the narrator here uses a particular performative enunciation of her femininity to her own material gain:

> That's why now, when I meet a guy and he asks me, "Do you work or go to school?" I answer, like some bimbo, "Oh, gee, I don't work or go to school!" because that's what they want, idiotic little women who won't think and aren't economically self-sufficient.
>
> They're finally paying for everything. (36)

Once again in this story, as in "Barbarella," sensuality attacks, creating an unfamiliar, dislocated space for a feminist intervention in the unlikely staging of a helpless femininity. In each case, awareness of the undercurrents of language and of the shifting ideological frames allows the women in these stories to use men's strategies and expectations against them, even though in highly problematic terms.

"Do You Work or Go to School" is also one of the few stories in which Conde directly addresses the concerns and dangers of border migration. In typical Conde fashion, she displaces the moral lesson from the banal to the unfamiliar by beginning the story with the narrator's anecdote about how Tijuana came to be known as the "Perfume City." According to the story, people came to Tijuana not just to have a good time in the nightclubs, but also to buy expensive French perfumes at cut-rate prices. The narrator's anecdote is about a Spaniard who figured out a way to produce perfumes at home and had a factory behind his house in Tijuana. Eventually the police caught him and dumped out all his perfume vats in the backyard of his house, giving the trademark "embotellado de origen" ("bottled at the source," awkwardly translated in the English version as "bottled in the places they're from" [19]) an entirely literal twist. After this incident, rumors make it impossible for the Spaniard to remain in the city:

> The word got around that he molested little girls. . . . Then [they] went around saying that he was a sorcerer and had all kinds of test tubes and beakers, like an alchemist, and that in the middle of his room there was a circle for invoking the devil. . . . Then they concocted the tale that he performed abortions and offered up the fetuses to the devil during his

magical rituals, and who knows what other nonsense. The fact is that the poor man had to leave Mexico. . . . He left for the United States and we never heard of him again. (30)

This anecdote can be read on various levels. First of all, the rejection of the Spaniard can be seen as the reaction of a puritanical and intransigent society that expels one of its members for transgressing the law. The nuance here is that although Tijuana society is itself largely an immigrant population made up of people from all over central and southern Mexico, this particular individual stands out as a foreigner. The Spaniard in Mexico is by stereotypical definition associated with conquerors and opportunists; he is the archetypal image of that person who corrupted the pristine innocence of the country. What better foreigner, thus, to be sacrificed? What better Other to disarticulate national discourse?

Rosina Conde employs and defies this old and clichéd representation of the Spaniard in Mexico. Her challenge, however, requires a careful reading, since Conde very delicately writes a doubly coded story that dialogues from within Mexican dominant society and at the same time from the margins of this discourse and its concomitant historical understandings. Official Mexican history has tended to decenter the story of the conquest and the colonial Spanish heritage, creating an image of the Spaniard as the barbaric Other. This symbolic, malevolent father has been blamed for the past, present, and future problems of the country, and the Mexican national self-image has reconstructed itself after the Mexican Revolution largely, if ambiguously, through idealizing the indigenous past and deploring the colonial influence. In "Do You Work or Go to School," the narrator in part takes up these concepts of falseness and corruption associated with the colonial heritage and displaces them onto border society, where they immediately take on a different valence. The critique here is directed at any hypocritical society that, while harshly judging the outsider for breaking one of its rules, utilizes even more perverse methods of falsification to justify the punishment.

The anecdote of the Spaniard in Tijuana would seem to suggest the pervasiveness of anti-Spanish discourse perpetuated in the national self-representation. The perfume man is not only forced to leave the city of Tijuana because of foolish gossip and unfair persecution but is also forced out of the country itself, thus becoming doubly exiled: from Spain first, from Mexico later. And yet the reader of the story never loses sight of the triviality of the offense or of the way in which the locals all too eagerly displace guilt onto an easy target. Conde's implicit interrogation of a fragile pillar in the national imaginary has an important ideological charge for a context in which there is still a tendency to insinuate that all corruption comes from Spain. Even more important, and on a second level, in the context of Conde's story this anti-Spanish sentiment is linked to a masked anti-immigrant prejudice, although there is a considerable effort expended to hide that prejudice's racist underpinnings. On the one hand, thus, Conde points to anti-immigrant frictions frequently obscured by the language of class problems and class divisions; on the other, she explores how immigrants can be scapegoated as responsible for larger social constructions. Tijuana, a city of immigrants, which in the national imaginary figures as a city of excess and perversions, can, with this ritual cleansing, imagine itself as the "perfume city," the guardian of good conduct.

This story is not the only one of Conde's texts to deal with the question of border crossing and the myths and stereotypes of cultural cross-contamination. In "De infancia y adolescencia" [Of infancy and adolescence], Conde creates a first-person narrative divided into ten diary-like fragments, each introduced with a fragment of a jazz or blues song in English. The young girl who ostensibly authors this journal is a member of a highly mobile middle-class Mexican family, various members of which, in the course of this long short story, move from the center of the country to the border, cross over to the other side, and return to Mexico City. She listens to the Beatles as well as Duke Ellington, reads Sartre alongside Corín Tellado and the social pages of the local Tijuana paper, and watches soap operas from both sides of the border. Her boyfriend, Rogelio, plays American football, and the young girl writes, with a typical use of code switching: "llegué a ir a dos campeonatos de futbol americano en los que participó. Era right half back, y cuando entré al equipo de soccer en la high school de La Jolla escogí la misma posición" [I ended up going to two football championships in which he participated. He was a right halfback and when I joined the soccer team in High School in La Jolla I chose the same position] (22). In this manner, subtly, Conde evokes a site and rite of passage that involves playing American football in Mexico and soccer in the United States, and a way of life that includes the economic resources to send children to study in La Jolla.

In this same text, the author disconnects the idea of crossing into the

United States from an end in itself or from an impassioned search for the American Way of Life. In this story, border crossings are part of a local reality that does not preclude a strong sense of national identity in which, nevertheless, code switching is a natural form of speech. While this mixing of Spanish and English is common in some Chicano/a writers as well, it would be incorrect to interpret Conde's use of English words and concepts in her writing as an influence of Chicano literary models, just as it would be incorrect to evaluate her character's speech as evidence of the weight of the oppressor's language on the colonized border dwellers in this contact zone between two cultures. Unlike her Chicana counterparts from the other side of the border, the protagonist of this story does not conceive of herself as belonging to a minority culture, much less a racially distinguished or discriminated one. She is quite comfortable with the biculturality of her upbringing and, upon finishing high school in the United States, decides to attend university in Mexico City: a freely made decision given the family's economic possibilities. There is, likewise, in this text no urgency to seek or define herself with respect to a national identity, because the narrator gives no hint that she feels any anxiety about losing contact with her mexicanidad. Neither are there any suggestions that she feels she is being compelled to leave the hinterlands of barbarism (Tijuana) for the center of civilization (Mexico City); on the contrary, it is in Mexico City where she lives the kinds of experiences that hegemonic culture would see as barbaric: taking up a bohemian lifestyle, having relationships with several different men, and deciding to abort when she becomes pregnant.

In "De infancia," thus, the movements and exchanges serve to combine identities and borders in a manner much more complex than allowed in the monolithic concept of fixed identities constructed within the discourses of nationalism from either side of the border. In this fragmentary narrative that rhetoric defining the border space as a site of passage or a no-man's land is deterritorialized and reconfigured through a glimpse into the lives of middle-class Tijuanans with all their cultural and geographic specificities, their intimate interactions with and distanced perspective on centrist/dominant Mexican culture, their equally intimate and distanced relationship with U.S. popular culture forms.

Clearly, within this context of intimate migrations there is also a questioning of gender relationships that go hand in hand with relations of power; yet the gendered understanding is also bifocally located. Thus, in the context of expectations arising from a traditional patriarchially organized family, the narrator complains about the horrors of living in a society in which

> el apellido no te pertenece, que dependes del padre o del marido y que cuando haces algo que no vaya de acuerdo con sus principios estás piso-teando su nombre, como si a propósito hicieras las cosas para zapatear sobre ellos y no sobre ti misma. (14)

> [your name doesn't belong to you, you are a dependent of your father or your husband and when you do something that isn't in agreement with their principles you're stepping on their name, as if you intentionally did things to put them down and not yourself.]

While the narrator quite rightly chafes against the paternalism of a deeply hierarchical social structure, at the same time, unlike other young women from protected Latino/Latin American backgrounds, she attends high school across the border on her own, and, in a telling if minimal gesture, chooses her boyfriend's football position when she plays soccer—a game that is still not fully accepted as appropriate for well-behaved Mexican girls.

Conde puts us all, puts herself as well, in the position of observers upon these strange and familiar scenes. To some degree her stories rely for their effect upon an implicit bond between the reader and the narrator involving a shared understanding and a shared quirky humor about social representations, a reader-narrator complicity that requires the exclusion of each society's typical self-imaginings. Conde's intimate exploration of the Tijuana underworld, for example, is not a knowledge she can expect all her readers to share; however, we as readers are aligned with the liminal characters in her stories. More broadly, as a border writer, she is displaced by definition with respect to mainstream Mexican concepts of themselves. Monsiváis, in an ambiguously tongue-in-cheek taxonomy of Mexico's self-definition, lists eight different variations on how to imagine the "provinces" in central Mexican thought, among which he includes the northern border states as a provincial entity characterized by international cultural shock and the commercialization of nationalism: "en la frontera norte la mexicanidad es, a un tiempo, selección de lo entrañable, coraza defensiva y disfraz esporádico" [on the northern border Mexicanness is, at the same time, the choice of the essential, a defensive shell, and a sporadic disguise] (201–2). While Monsiváis's descriptions are meant to be provocative, and can be read as condescending, it is precisely this corrosive attention to marginality as essence, shell, or disguise that is one of the hallmarks of Conde's prose, whether in her oddly inflected domestic scenes or her nuanced portraits of women from the border underworld. On the surface, very little happens in these tales of delicate rebalancings and readjustments; nevertheless, enormous realignments of position take place in the subtext. Our illusion of complicity with her—of a joke or a delicately phrased insight shared—is undercut by the shifting positionalities of characters and narrators in the borderlands she limns.

We might be tempted to end our discussion at precisely this point. However, that would be to ignore the central problem haunting this reading of Conde's work. Strikingly enough, while it seems to us that it is this distancing element that is most likely to earn Conde additional readers in the United States, that appropriation of her work, like this chapter's discussion of it, tends to organize itself neatly around theoretical concerns Conde—unfortunately—might well reject. Her border is not, finally, contained in or defined by Derrida's or Apter's border metaphor, nor by Bhabha's academic homelessness. If indeed the theoretical structure of U.S. literary theory has a long historical connection to thought elaborated through the crucible of displacement and exile (the same could perhaps be said of the most influential variants of French theory as well: thinkers like Derrida, Kristeva, Todorov, and Cixous all carry with them impressive border-crossing credentials as displaced intellectuals), then those elements are precisely the ones that allow us to naturalize Conde within that literary-theoretical establishment without questioning its boundaries. Like Carlos Monsiváis, whose meditations on the central Mexican–northern border axis served as the frame for this chapter, Eduardo Barrera has commented on the strangely circular construction of much theorizing on border issues in his discussion of what he calls the "quasi-incestuous relationship" among Guillermo Gómez-Peña, Néstor García Canclini, and Homi Bhabha (152) by which their postmodern border theory and performative practice mutually inform and reinforce each other.

Conde and Barrera put their finger on precisely the problem that exercises us here, and to which we confess to having no solution. While imaginatively we can shift our positions, aligning ourselves with Conde's characters and, with a complicitous wink, pretend to step outside both the U.S. and the Mexican mainstream cultural establishments, in fact the presuppositions we bring to our readings inexorably shape our understanding of them. Neil Larsen poses the conundrum eloquently in his recent book tracing the intersection of North American Latin Americanist critical thought and Latin American writing:

> [W]riting and reading "North by South" has had continually to pose the question of its own authority. Even the most exoticist of gazes presupposes the exotic as an object whose legitimacy must be at least equal to the domestic. Thus, in directing its attention elsewhere, the North necessarily concedes something about its own sense of identity and authority, its own position on the hermeneutic map. The question of the object's legitimacy—why read this and not something else?—cannot finally be detached from the question of self-legitimation: what, at the outset, authorizes or justifies the subject as the reader/writer of this object? (3)

Larsen's question brings us directly into the realm of the ideological and cultural biases encrypted in the literary canon. He suggests, for example, that the Boom writers of the 1960s and 1970s became an international academic phenomenon partly because non–Latin American Latin Americanists found the Boom amenable to readings in which a European high modernist aesthetic coincided fortuitously with a sensibility made acute in opposition to the U.S. involvement in the Vietnam War.

We suspect that the Rosina Conde, who resisted being turned into a Gómez-Peña/Homi Bhabha pseudo-Chicana nostalgic for a universalizing, utopic, abstract borderness, is equally careful in her stories to resist cooption into another version of the North's hermeneutic map. The unsettling edginess of her stories, the slipperiness of terms and positionalities represent the first place to search for such traces of resistance. In these powerful texts, it is through Conde's reinscription of concepts of gender right that she exposes the weakness and bias of much Mexican, Chicano, and mainstream U.S. theoretical meditations on borders.

# 6. Homely

*Helena María Viramontes*

Sometimes she wishes she weren't born with such adhesiveness.
—*Helena María Viramontes, "Paris Rats in East L.A."*

Helena María Viramontes' collection of short stories, "Paris Rats in East L.A." (still unavailable in a single volume as of this writing)[1] returns to the barrio and to the mid-1960s time period familiar to us from several of the stories in her earlier collection, *The Moths.* Champ, the young girl who provides the narrative point-of-view for most of the stories in "Paris Rats," bears a kinship to the lost and bewildered Sonya of "Cariboo Cafe" in *The Moths.* Sonya, like many of the other characters in those earlier stories, is a living example of the anguish of displacement and the stress of homelessness. She has lost the key to her apartment, she cannot find her way back to her babysitter's house, she cannot orient herself in the maze of backstreets of the ghetto, and she wanders around helplessly with her younger brother until she ends up in the Cariboo Cafe, "the zero zero place," a greasy spoon refuge for drug addicts and illegal aliens. "Paris Rats"'s Champ is an altogether feistier and more self-confident protagonist, at home with herself and with her East L.A. streets, able to juggle poodle skirts, rock songs, and Miss Clairol hair colors along with La Llorona and other cultural markers of her Mexican heritage.

In an article focusing mostly on readings of Toni Morrison and Nadine Gordimer, Homi Bhabha revisits Freud's classic concept of the "uncanny" and revises it from a postcolonial's perspective as the "unhomely." For while the "uncanny" carries with it some element of the supernatural, of something hidden and mysterious that is ambiguously brought home, in Bhabha's account the postcolonial critic/writer's experience of the unhomely follows from "the estranging sense of the relocation of the home and the world in an unhallowed place" and he describes it as a common feature in border culture, in exile literature, and in Third World literature in general. Bhabha continues:

> In the stirrings of the unhomely, another world becomes visible. It has less to do with forcible eviction and more to do with the uncanny literary and social effects of enforced social accommodation, or historical migrations and cultural relocations. The home does not remain the domain of domestic life, nor does the world simply become its social or historical counterpart. The unhomely is the shock of recognition of the world-in-the-home, the home-in-the-world. (141)

Bhabha, of course, writes as a man who has lived in his own body the shock of recognition born from these cultural relocations; thus, in the unhomely, if not the uncanny, he constructs a kind of home. Likewise, Viramontes' readers may simultaneously occupy many spaces, some of them unhomely. Yet, while we are much indebted to Bhabha for the thinking that helped us start this chapter, and indeed Bhabha's concept serves as one of the running subtexts in this book as a whole, again and again we found the characters in Viramontes' "Paris Rats" resisting an unhomely reading. Eventually, we were forced to the realization that the East L.A. dwellers that she evokes no longer limit themselves to that confused and disorienting place of relocation and enforced accommodation. If the rich cultural substratum to the stories indicates that Champ's *amá* almost certainly formed her character in reaction to her parents' unhomely experience of cultural dislocation, that experience is no longer the reality lived by Champ and her brother Gregorio (Spider), or even by their larger-than-life and all-too-real amá, Arlene. They are quite unreflectively comfortable, thank you, with their mixed bag of strategies for survival.

These are *homely* stories. Sad and funny, plain and intimate, they deal with everyday life in the barrio. The streets and houses of East L.A. are all the home Arlene, Champ, and Gregorio know or can imagine, and the characters deal comfortably with their stridencies, since those streets and those interiors are their intimate domestic spaces. These stories are "homely" in a second sense as well, for they speak lovingly about ordinary, unlovely people and situations. In fact, we believe that the power of Viramontes' interconnected sequence of stories depends to a great degree on the double meaning of "homely"—both homelike and unattractive. This slippery border term helps also to define the boundaries of Viramontes' own implicit theoretical practice as an activist-writer. The ten-year-old budding "home girl" of 1963 is today's Chicana feminist, and in delving into the roots of Champ's story Viramontes reconstructs the historical and cultural conjuncture that led to today's Chicana's sense of cultural and political agency.

Viramontes' "homely" is a border-straddling word, and one that introduces a reading of a culturally diverse (some might say impoverished or contaminated) social reality quite different from the meditations usually evoked by the dominant culture's sense of the aesthetic process. Each of the stories in this collection focuses on a moment, shocking for the readers, in which two homelike/unlovely readings of cultures that the reader is bound to see as conflicting clash and absorb each other. The conflict posed in the title story—"Paris" (abstract image of civilization, high culture) versus "Rats" (concrete reality of ugly, vicious rodents)—is only the most obvious of these homely confrontations. "Miss Clairol" starts this way:

> Arlene and Champ walk to K-Mart. The store is full of bins mounted with bargain buys from T-shirts to rubber sandals. They go to aisle 23, Cosmetics. Arlene, wearing bell bottom jeans two sizes too small, can't bend down to the Miss Clairol boxes, asks Champ.
>
> "Which one amá?," asks Champ, chewing her thumb nail.
>
> "Shit, mija, I dunno." Arlene smacks her gum, contemplating the decision. "Maybe I need a change, tú sabes. What do you think?" . . .
>
> "I dunno," responds Champ . . . She is too busy thinking of things people otherwise dismiss like parentheses, but sticks to her like gum, . . . and sometimes she wishes she weren't born with such adhesiveness. (101–2)

Arlene's moment of uncertainty is also our clue to an intimate and liminal cultural identity. Neither Champ nor Arlene adjudicates between the cultural realities represented by K-mart, too-tight bell-bottom jeans, and chewing gum—stereotypical markers of a young working-class woman from U.S. dominant culture—and those very different cultural realities hinted at by the interjection of working-class Mexican Spanish—"amá," "mija," "tú sabes." Champ chews her fingernails and Arlene chews her gum, neatly framing a contingent position, one that negotiates a plurality of practices occupying the same homely space. This space is signaled through such markers as a linguistic practice taking advantage of code-switching, an aesthetic practice defined by a pop cultural understanding of the mainstream beauty system, and a narrative practice cannily aware of the more than metaphorical uses of such conventions of punctuation as the parenthesis. Viramontes hints that the contemporary Chicana herself can be seen as a product of the strategies developed, unconsciously or consciously, to deal with these constant shocks, these continual conflations of strange and disparate cultural borders that stick to her like glue, like used bubble gum.

Champ is well positioned for her protagonic role in this homely tale. Her fictive character is perfectly delineated in that lovely word, "adhesiveness," and if she sometimes feels herself to be the victim of circumstance (things stick to her), she is likewise compelled by her inborn nature to stick to things (and people) until she can puzzle them out. In a constantly shifting borderline world, Champ fights to keep the homely qualities of her existence from slipping away into the evasive margins of ghetto life. She cannily weighs, and Viramontes plays back for us, the potentialities and resistances of people and things in her world.

One of these homely interplays takes place precisely in the non-conversation between mother and daughter in the K-mart aisle. With Arlene, Viramontes deftly outlines a specific version of 1960s Chicana motherhood that implicitly decries the established literary tradition limiting Mexican women over the age of eighteen to saintly motherhood in all its stereotypical glory of tortilla-rolling, homebody self-abnegation. Despite Arlene's unlovely features, her brash and vital character points toward a reclaiming of female subjectivity too often denied the well-bred (or even the politically committed) woman of Mexican heritage. This is neither that familiar figure of the Madre Santa nor the Chicana Socialist Feminist who is an Honor to Her Raza; in her homely way, Arlene points to the necessity for a more nuanced reading of femininity that requires a reexamination of social intersections, a reexploration of Chicana sexuality, and a revised theory of representation. While it is beyond the scope of this chapter to explore all the modes and methods of this narrative practice, we would like to focus on three strategies employed in these stories: (1) speaking the acculturated Chicana presence, (2) unspeaking macho Chicano representations, and (3) spiking language.

SPEAKING THE ACCULTURATED CHICANA PRESENCE

If, as we posit, one of the crucial problems for women of color feminisms lies in the perpetuation of an essentialized reading of the Chicana in terms of a hypostatic absence/presence, then one of the urgent tasks beginning to be undertaken by committed Chicana writers is precisely that of reclaiming all the multiple Chicana subjectivities in all their multiple voices, including the homely voices of the women like Arlene. "Shit, mija, I dunno," she says as she smacks her gum in front of the Miss Clairol display with its tantalizing choices of a beauty packaged under names like "Ash Blonde" or—ironically—"Sun Bronze." "What do you think?" Her aggressive, bell-bottomed, platinum-tipped presence leaves the reader slightly off balance. What do we think? Gloria Anzaldúa neatly captures one typical response to women like Arlene:

> Nothing is more difficult than identifying emotionally with a cultural alterity. . . . Nothing scares the Chicana more than a quasi Chicana; nothing disturbs a Mexican more than an acculturated Chicana; nothing agitates a Chicana more than a Latina who lumps her with the *norteamericanas*. It is easier to retreat to the safety of difference behind racial, cultural, and class borders. ("En Rapport," 145)

Arlene is the very figure of the acculturated Chicana, an unashamed social and spiritual mestiza. Her unlovely hybrid character and appearance provoke that academic retreat behind the barricades/borders described by Anzaldúa into the safety of an authentic ethnicity defined by its difference from the U.S. dominant norm. And yet Arlene provokes and amuses us by turns; her blowsy full-blown humanity makes us laugh with a start of recognition; her sorrows and dreams touch us deeply. The more we consider her, the more academic debates and claims of greater or lesser ethnic authenticity fall disquietingly flat.

We need to add to our perception of Arlene's departure from the academic ideal of ethnic and cultural purity another recognition as well:

that of our ingrained horror of homely female bodies. Arlene is the perfect receptacle for that horror; she can all too easily be read as nothing but a cartoon figure, an unflatteringly overweight, heavily made-up, killingly peroxided parody of a hip white woman. As such, she inevitably presents a pathetic image. Stuffed into a form of white woman drag, unable to bend over to reach for her next bottle of dreams, she seems little more than an exaggerated and awkward Chicana mimicry of white femininity.

Still further, Arlene can only imagine herself as a woman in relation to a heterosexual system of thought that, in her own mestiza culture as well as in the white dominant culture she mimics, exploits women's bodies through their dreams. Viramontes says it explicitly when she has Arlene meditate on two contrasting stories of her sexual initiation:

> Arlene is a romantic. When Champ begins her period, she will tell her things that only women can know. She will tell about the first time she made love with a boy, her awkwardness and shyness forcing them to go under the house, where the cool, refined soil made a soft mattress. . . . She was eleven and his name was Harry.
>
> She will not tell Champ that her first fuck was a guy named Puppet who ejaculated prematurely, at the sight of her apricot vagina, so plump and fuzzy. "Pendejo," she said, "you got it all over me." (104)

Arlene retains a romantic perspective despite a lifetime of experiences that to this point more closely approximate the unbeautiful story of sex with Puppet rather than love with Harry. It is a story written on her body with the death wish in her hair's dark roots, the mask of foundation that covers her face, the insectoid false eyelashes she wears to enhance her eyes, the rolls of fat that stretch the seams of Pancha's blue dancing dress. Yet, each time she colors her hair she washes away the unpleasantness of her past and can set herself dreaming again. Because Arlene is a romantic, she can continually rewrite her life; once a week she can "dance spinning herself into Miss Clairol, and stopping only when it is time to return to the sewing factory, time to wait out the next date, time to change hair color. Time to remember or to forget" (105). If Arlene the woman is neither attractive nor particularly empowering for her readers, nevertheless she makes us think: about the conventions of the beauty system, about the stifling constructions of femininity, about the racist assumptions that underpin much well-meaning Chicana feminist theorizing about Chicanas.

"Miss Clairol," however, also describes another Arlene—the mother. In much of Mexican folk tradition motherhood is inextricably linked to abnegation, so that loving one's mother is linked to the degree of the mother's purity and to her ostentatiously silent self-sacrifice for her children. Shockingly, for Arlene love is equated with sex and her children are the recipients of her generally benign neglect. Not only is she anything but a traditional model of maternal abnegation, the heart and soul of her familia, she is a sexually active woman, and with more than one man. From the point of view of traditional constructions of motherhood, as an acculturated Chicana mother, she is even more unlovely than as a dream-ridden young sweat factory laborer. (We might add in parentheses that unlike Viramontes, much Chicana poetry and theorizing skips Arlene's generation, idealizing and memorializing the abuelita at the working mother's clear expense.) After all, Arlene's idea of a mother-daughter excursion involves choosing a new Miss Clairol haircolor at the local K-mart, and in her imagination a touching mother-daughter conversation in which she passes on the wisdom of her years to a newly pubescent child consists entirely of telling her daughter graphically about the joys of sex.

Fierce, needy Champ inherits her mother's toughness as well as her romanticism. The title story of the collection opens with an image of the ten-year-old girl in her home, looking longingly out the window for a glimpse of her brother or her mother. When Gregorio/Spider invites her out to the movies, at Champ's expense, she leaps at the opportunity to accompany her brother. "We don't leave no note or nuthin," Champ informs us. "We don't even go to church or feel bad when we pass it and peoples waiting all inside and out. Arlene didn't come home anyways sos we ain't gonna leave no note cause we don't care bout no bodies or nuthin" (2). Champ juxtaposes two of the most powerful traditional forces in Mexican culture—motherhood and the Church—and purposefully remembers-forgets them both in a sweeping gesture of rebellion. Strikingly, Champ, whose resentment of maternal abandonment is clear, evokes the neighborhood church specifically in a moment when that public institution reaffirms and consolidates the force of intimate, individual ties. Simply put: when a Roman Catholic church has "peoples waiting all inside and out," it's probably either for a wedding or a funeral. In fact, Champ's self-definition as a care-for-nobody is premised precisely upon her ability to recall such homely, comforting traditions, customs she observes or dimly recalls from the example of popular cultural markers—"Hey you Willy," she yells at a school companion dressed up in his going-to-church clothes, "La Llorona's behind you!" (3)—and then to negate them, thus positioning herself as an outsider to these two great institutions that tend, even in her rejection of them, to run in tandem. At the same time as she rejects the promise of Motherhood and the Church, she forges the boundaries of a new social contract in the magical "we" of Champ-and-Spider, the tough outsiders. She cannot imagine herself inside a church; her mother and aunt found it irrelevant to their lives and never steeped the children in its teachings. By the same token, she cannot love her mother since the only definitions for such love depend from the alternatives of the abnegated Madre Santa, who lives through her children, and La Llorona, who is condemned to haunt the world frightening living beings precisely for her failure in this regard.

"Tears on My Pillow" melds Viramontes' version of the tale of La Llorona with the weepy lyrics of the rock song that give the story its title. It offers, first of all, a story of inexplicable loss: of loss through death—La Llorona's kids, Grandpa Ham, Lil Mary G.—or through unpredictable and unexplained disappearances:

> Just they never say hello and they never say goodbye. Mama María never said goodbye, she just left and that's that and nobody to tell me why tío Benny don't live with tía Olivia any more or when is Gregorio gonna come home or if Arlene is fixed up to go dancing at the Palladium tonight. No one to say nuthin'. . . .
> See what I mean? They just never say hello and never say goodbye. They just disappear, leaving you all alone all ascared with your burns and La Llorona hungry for you. (115)

All sorts of people in Champ's world disappear—or are disappeared, but the story focuses particularly on the women, on their fleshy excesses and on their mutilation. In the central incident of the story, Lil Mary G., a classmate's mother, is raped and murdered; Champ catches only a glimpse of bloodstained sheets as the ambulance arrives. This memory triggers another, as her classmate's abandonment by the mother takes on mythic resonances. In Champ's version of the La Llorona story, the hapless ghost-mother wanders around with no feet, seeking victims to pull out of their rooms if they are so careless as to sleep with their feet toward a window.

Most prominently, however, the story is dominated by women's breasts, which in this story are massively and grotesquely present. Champ crawls into bed with her mother when they hear La Llorona screaming and seeks comfort by pressing her head to her mother's generous breasts (111). Arlene takes Champ shopping again in this story, this time for a new bra: "cause the thing that makes the straps go up and down broke and so her chichis hang down like a cow's. . . ." Lil Mary G. and Arlene joke about "this kinda crippled bra for beginner chichis," and Lil Mary G. "grabbed Veronica's chichis and Veronica gets all bare-assed, unknots her hands and flapped Lil Mary G.'s chichis back" (112). The most obvious physical marker of femininity, thus, resonates as one of Viramontes' potent homely images; attractive women in this world have large, firm chichis, while girls have small, crippled ones. Moreover, the presence or absence of chichis defines a womanly existence even as they deform the female into something not totally human. After Lil Mary G.'s murder, her daughter Veronica "just wants to be left alone til everybody forgets she's around. . . . Then she can disappear like Lil Mary G. without no one paying no attention. You don't need bras or nuthin' when you just air" (113). Champ's fear of disappearing is just the other side of the coin of Veronica's desire to disappear; both derive from the same hunger for security and the same nightmares.

## UNSPEAKING MACHO CHICANO REPRESENTATIONS

While the woman's body describes a homely excess, the men in these stories are referenced only sketchily (Grandpa Ham, tío Benny, Willy the schoolkid) or, in the case of the most important male character, Gregorio/Spider, defined by insufficiency. "To me," Champ tells us in the opening of "Paris Rats," Gregorio looks "like a balloon not blowed up all the way, like his bones need more air." More extended descriptions of him focus on his scarred face "what makes him look always real mad, jest real mean, like he ain't ascared of no knife no gun no nobody" (1), and on the tattoo of a spiderwoman covering his back. The spiderwoman is, if anything, still more ominous than the scar: "the woman's purple hair extend[s] like tentacles into a web" and when he "takes off his white tank top, and the young girl sees the spiderwoman transform from insect to woman, light to dark, woman to insect, dark to light, taunting her with his every move" ("Spider's Face," 33). Spider, then, has two faces that he shows the world; the mean, scarred face of the frightening gang member and the cruel, purple-lipped face of the fiendish spiderwoman. And while Champ fears the tattoo and knows what the scar portends, she loves the man her brother becomes when he covers the spiderwoman with his shirt and comes into the house for the night. Then he is Gregorio, a frightened boy, and not Spider, the gang member.

The visual aggressivity of the scar and the tattoo tend to obscure Gregorio, the thin, homely boy, and turn the Spider into an instantly readable figure of criminality. Spider emphasizes this homeboy image with the impeccable t-shirts he bleaches and irons himself to a pristine sharp whiteness, and with his trademark "pendleton . . . ironed real smooth, looking bitchen. Gregorio likes it buttoned up to the neck and even up to his hands, even when the hot so hot you could fry your toes on the tar street" ("Paris Rats," 1). The clothes articulate a powerful masculine identity, creating a meaning structure out of his disguised body, turning himself into the spectacle of that very figure people expect to see when they see the scar.

In an important article, Angie Chabram-Dernersesian reviews the history of the Chicano movement and signals the typically masculinist bias that has historically imbued it until very recently. She describes what has frequently been understood to be the essential Chicano subject as "a combined genealogy of Spanish conquistadores and Aztec Warriors without a trace of a Chicana/Mexicana authenticating root," and cites Armando Rendón's *The Chicano Manifesto* as one influential document among others which, "while contesting racism, economic exploitation, and political domination, . . . reinforces dominant ideology by identifying 'machismo' as the symbolic principle of the Chicano revolt and adopting machismo as the guideline for Chicano family life" (82–83). This myth undergirds even the interactions of those acculturated Chicanas, Arlene and Champ, with the boy they tend to see as the man of the family, their protector. And yet, such a reading of the young man, even if it is the reading Spider himself promotes, reflects an essentializing of his character that ignores not only important aspects of his ethnic background and his fatherless family situation, but also his own private misgivings.

If the homeboy is threatening, he is also seductive; still worse, from his point of view, he is subtly seducible. In a telling scene, Champ watches the homeboys hang on a Saturday night and listens to their talk: "Quiet sets in until someone brings a radio and the oldies caress the boy-men like slow dancing lovers, whisper, 'you're mineeee—and we belong together'; watches Spider Oooooo baby . . ." ("Spider's Face," 33). The music seduces the boys, and does so in a manner that specifically casts them into a passive, feminized role when their guards are down and the music caresses them. It would be easy to read elements of what Eve Sedgwick calls "homosocial panic" into the subsequent behavior of the boys. The intensity of the male bonding in Spider's gang, the initiation rituals used to cement such ties, and the violence that perpetuates them recall lifestyles both machista and openly gay. Yet these two unreconcilable extremes are brought home in Viramontes' text in the slow-dance seduction of boy-men riding the undercurrents of flash and desperation. Spider's body is a text, already written and rewritten in the facial scars and spiderwoman tattoo, in the pain and violence that reaffirms his masculinity and his worth in the HM gang. The streets belong to him, at least in that part of the barrio upon which he has staked territorial claim, and that space remains intimately his, even if the boundaries are defined and policed by others. Yet this defiant body/text is reread at least twice in the spectacle of the quiet Saturday evening with the homeboys. It is reread in the peace of the evening and of Champ's gaze who sees past the cruel spider to her beloved brother; it is reread again in the caress of the music that defies the latent violence and replaces it with frank appreciation.

Once again, it is this homely scene in the heart of the barrio that marks Viramontes' vision. She matches the struggle to define virility in a situation of oppression—a grim tale and one often told in memoirs, novels, and films about gang wars in U.S. cities—with a seductive sidestep into the embrace of the oppressor's music. Once again, as with Arlene, as with Champ, Viramontes describes a mestizaje that goes much further than an identity constructed against U.S. dominant and traditional Mexican customs. Spider is not the stylized figure of an ambiguously expressed phallic potency; he is not an Aztec warrior, nor a

Chicano militant, nor a pachuco rebel. Like his mother and sister, he is a romantic, susceptible to sentimental songs and the stirring sexuality of the dance.

Poignantly, like Champ, who reads herself against the models of Church and Motherhood, Spider too reads himself against others. In his case, he locates his presence in the dislocations and discomfort of passersby, in their silence when he lights up an illegal Camel cigarette on the bus, in their refusal to look at him for fear of drawing attention from that scarred face. He reads himself as that empty space opened in front of him for his passage: "He was dragged into the dark ages years ago, catacombs of the nightmare, since. Of course, he must have been afraid. Because he's not really a spider, although at times he wishes he were. . . . But that's enough for the street warrior. It confirms his existence, like the placas on the walls. He is tired of being invisible" ("Spider's Face," 34). His placa is, of course, Spider, and "the way he writes Spider, the S looking like a thunderbolt, differentiates him from Spider of Flats" (33). He writes "Spider" on the walls of his barrio, and a cruel woman-spider grins fiercely from his back. "Spider" defines at once a gang member's visibility and his invisibility; it allows him to take charge of his home, to own his streets through the warrior's symbolic presence. But what visibility is that for a skinny, frightened boy-man named Gregorio? And it is Gregorio that both Champ and Viramontes insist upon in these stories, the spider-presence fading in and out like the tattoo on his back: dark to light, spider to boy, light to dark, child to warrior. Spider writes his placa on the walls, taking measure of his world and bringing it within his control; Viramontes' homely storytelling takes cognizance of that writing and, while noting its power, bends her talents to unwriting Spider, the warrior, writing Gregorio, the boy. Trinh T. Minh-ha writes, in words that seem equally applicable to Spider as to the postcolonial woman she describes: "In trying to tell something, a woman is told. . . . And often [she] cannot *say* it. You try and keep on trying to unsay it, for if you don't, they will not fail to fill in the blanks on your behalf, and you will be said" (79–80). The homely reality is this: whatever Spider chooses to write, he betrays himself.

Nevertheless, the woman's mutilation and the man's mutilation respond to different abstract systems, and different modes of objectification, and while both the excessively lush mother and the tightly pared-down son use the presentation of their bodies, and the masking of their shapes and features to create meanings, such meanings shift with circumstance. Especially interesting in this regard is a scene in "Dance Me Forever" that parallels the seduction by music in "Spider's Face." In this story, it is Champ and Gregorio's tía Olivia who allows herself to be seduced away from her bitterness and sense of failure by the stories and the dreams Gregorio outlines, until the two of them dance each other into a temporary wholeness:

> "When Benny and me married, we had a big wedding. . . . Anyways, Gregorio, come the dollar dance, Arlene gives you a dollar to dance with me. You looked so sharp, mijo. I get your dollar and we dance. Kinda dance. And then someone else comes with another dollar to dance with me. But you got so jealous, mijo, you wanted to dance with me forever, and Arlene ended up dragging you off the dance floor. . . .
>
> "Sabes que? Afterwards I tell Benny. Dance me like that, like it's forever."
>
> "Some things change, Tía," Gregorio offers, leans forward and removes the butt from her hand. . . . "And some things don't," Gregorio finishes.
>
> And Champ notices that Gregorio's scar is gone. It is hidden under Olivia's cheek and for once his face is whole. (G20)

The homely romantic again offers a bittersweet happy ending, erasing the scars and holding violence at bay, just for a time, in the narrative forever of the dance. Male and female discourses about the body, while separate and distinct, prove that they have healing, as well as mutilating qualities. Gregorio makes his aunt a present of the attractive self he imagines for her; she, likewise, gifts him with the young man he could be, freed from Spider's disfigurement.

SPIKING LANGUAGE

"I think we would all agree that Chicana criticism and theory are still in a state of flux, looking for a theoretical, critical framework that is our own," wrote Tey Diana Rebolledo a few years ago (350), before going on to survey the contributions of such writers and thinkers as Norma Cantú and Norma Alarcón to this emerging Chicana understanding of its theoretical basis. Likewise, Angie Chabram-Dernersesian evokes Margarita Cota-Cárdenas and Viola Correa as well as the work of politically committed poets, artists, and community activists to explore the question of what happens when writing women enter the Chicano script. They all agree: writing women cannot merely be written into an existing script; by existing, and in the acknowledgment of their existence, they rewrite the script itself. The problem, as Rebolledo so succinctly puts it, is to identify a workable framework for theorizing Chicana writing from within the flux. Clearly, a shift to a female narrative point of view and a focus on circumstances and metaphors drawn from a woman's life are two such strategies. The rewriting of feminocentric legends like those of La Malinche and La Llorona is another. So too, as Rebolledo writes, is "dealing with the significance of language use and silence within our literature" (351).

Helena María Viramontes has always deployed the multiple possibilities of silence as an effective narrative technique.[2] In "Paris Rats" this hyperawareness of the values of the spoken and the unspoken is even more highly developed and is tied both to a bodily calligraphy and to the author's awareness of the physicality of writing the story:

> His placa is Spider. Because of those little eyes black as petrified wood. His eyelashes are as thick as spider legs, jet black and long and contradicts a face punctured with challenge; a rude contradiction like the thorns of a rose. The scar begins near his left eye like a teardrop, as if the knife was held there for sometime, as if it had been twisted into the soft flesh of a twelve year old, then the tears open down his cheek under his chin and straight to his jugular. Then it stops with nothing more to say: full sentence. ("Spider's Face," 33)

Gregorio is compared metaphorically to petrified wood, to a spider (a comparison he invites not only in the unwitting cooperation of his eyelashes but also with the redundancy of the grimacing spiderwoman tattooed on his back), to a thorny rose. The scar is a sequence of teardrops puncturing his face; it is a sentence complete with its fleshly punctuation. Grimly, Viramontes evokes the getting of the scar with a phrase that bridges the imaginative realm of the fiction writer and the reality of the barrio. She writes the scar's sentence in the form of a contrafactual "as if"; and, strangely, what follows the "as if" is not a metaphoric and impossible comparison (e.g., "as if he were a Spider in fact"), but a cotidian horror: "*as if* the knife was held there for sometime, *as if* it had been twisted into the soft flesh of a twelve year old," as indeed it almost certainly *was*.

Economically, Viramontes' swift characterization of Gregorio/Spider points toward an informing logic as well as a theory and a method for writing Chicano/a. Language itself solidifies in the barrio streets, marks out space with the placa, becomes cruelly angular, cuts like a knife. The two words that frame Gregorio for his world—*placa* and *scar*—words that make/mark/mask his identity, are also words that should never have escaped the dictionary, and that now, ineradicably, shape the real.

In "Spider's Face," as well as in others of these stories, the awkward syntax points to the violence done against a young boy, that is then adopted as a defiant inscription and used to rewrite a certain form of intensely masculine personal identity: the placa. At the same time, Spider's territorial marker mocks him with its reminder of the gang's paradoxical impotency, its frustrated fear of feminization lurking outside the territorial boundaries in the realms of the other gangs, the Anglo authorities, the spiderwoman behind his back. Furthermore, the triangulation of the gang members and the streets through the vision of the young girl looking down upon them from the window reminds us in still another way of the constructedness of "Spider," as it is not the mean, scarred gang member who eventually comes into the house, but the beloved brother, Gregorio. Still further, the estranging grammatical structure, the awkwardly inappropriate "as if," foregrounds Viramontes' own writing practice. This style reflects an implicit critical methodology to some extent consonant with that described in Los Angeles' streets not only by the youthful gangs, but also by the increasingly celebrated Chicano/a artists integrating groups like ASCO. Marcos Sánchez-Tranquilino and John Tagg describe ASCO's project thusly: "ASCO's was a calligraphic gesture that, at the same time, mocked itself: marking, in the gap between *signature* and *placa* its own impossibility. . . . ASCO marked, resigned, but refused to occupy the spaces, genres, and languages disposed in advance 'for Chicanos'" (563). Viramontes, too, marks the gap between signature and placa, but she does so unmockingly; her "stitched sentences" (I borrow the phrase from "The Jumping Bean," 9) bring together the edges of the gap, marking the tear-shaped scar tissue that for her makes meaning.

Viramontes not only signals the strange shape of an embodied language but also continually foregrounds its gendered quality. Spider has his word, his estranging placa. In another story, the wounding word has no such ambiguously empowering outlet: "The young girl cried. If only she had the capacity to walk barefoot on broken and jagged words like

María, then she wouldn't have to release the words, and she could smash them into a thousand pieces of glass, just like she wanted to smash the window" ("The Jumping Bean," 9). The young girl in this story also imagines herself in the context of an embodied language, and yet her contrafactual imagining of words like glass leads to no physical cut, but only and again to the deep spiritual wounding of a Chicana woman. In the depiction of the wounded boy who finds refuge in what hurt him, the wounded girl who has recourse only to a literalized "unbroken silence," Viramontes outlines a radical questioning of the nature of representation itself. Substance, in these stories, is an abiding illusion, just as illusion offers a foundational reality.

Finally, the English itself in these stories is stitched and cobbled. As Juan Flores and George Yúdice remind us, "even for the most monolingual of Latinos, the 'other' language looms constantly as a potential resource, and the option to vary according to different speech contexts is used far more often than not" (75). While Viramontes uses Spanish sparingly in her stories—with the exception of crucial cultural markers like "amá," "tía," "mija," and "placa" her works are written almost entirely in English—the syntax and word choice echo with the rhythms of the Mexican Spanish that serves as her characters' resource and refuge. Occasionally this muted bilingualism also wounds. It is impossible not to remember, for example, that in Spanish, unlike English, gender marks all nouns. For Viramontes, however, the implications of gendered language are far from neutral. The given names of the two central characters in this linked series of stories are "Ofelia" and "Gregorio": both of which are names that carry the typical Spanish gender marker of "-*a*" for the feminine and "-*o*" for the masculine. This gender-marker is hidden, but not forgotten, under the nicknames "Champ" and "Spider." Furthermore, the reader can be counted upon to remember (and the tattoo reminds us) that in Spanish *Spider* ("araña") is also a word that not only carries the feminine gender marker, but metaphorically recalls a deadly female force (evoking something like a "black widow" in Hollywood B-movies). Thus, the English placa with the thunderbolt *S* encodes masculine force in the written word, even as the graphic visual metaphor of the spiderwoman reminds us of the feminine power of the "araña." The reader, of course, sees both the placa and the araña.

The resulting complicity on this count between Viramontes and her (Chicana) readership suggests something very like a counterpoint and corrective to what Flores and Yúdice see as Richard Rodriguez's most prominent flaw:

> Rodriguez draws a tighter and tighter net around that which he (and the dominant culture) has defined as private until it is strangled out of existence and he emerges as his own abstracted interlocutor. . . . Who is this interlocutor but the symbolic Other (the law of the Anglo father or teacher) with whom he has identified after his linguistic and cultural "castration." (66)

In the castrating culture, Anglo teachers downgrade or punish Mexican American children who use the wrong words, the home words, and Spanish speakers stumble over English words and are reduced to "Spiks." In Viramontes' world, as her characters are well aware, language is thorny; it has spikes, and it stabs the incautious or the weak. At the same time, Viramontes' characters, the acculturated Chicanas and Chicanos of the stories, offer a muted dialogue with the dominant culture in speech, in musical tastes, and in the graphisms of their bodies and bodily adornments. Viramontes' readers, like Champ at the window, are both inside this dialogue and participant-observers upon it. And the readers' qualification, like Champ's most significantly defined quality, is adhesiveness, making a web that goes round and round, picking up stray parentheses ("Miss Clairol," 102). At any rate, they/we celebrate the homely richness in this spiky/spicky language, in the intentionally awkward syntax and doubly evocative word choice that calls attention to its unspoken bilingualism, to its words broken and stitched together across the gap of two different cultural systems.

But let us go a step further, as Viramontes does. For she not only places these homely tools in our hands, but implicitly asks us what we intend to do with them. Viramontes puts us all, puts herself as well, in the position of observers upon the 1960s barrio scene, and the fact of our reading, writing, and thinking about it identifies us ineluctably as outsiders to it. Outsiders then: the point-of-view character is Champ, a child noted for her difference, for her testing of boundaries of self and world, for her ability to build a web linking resisting objects and persons into a language that speaks (for) her. Outsider now: a generation or more has intervened between Champ's barrio and that of today. Outsider in another sense, too: at this point it becomes harder and harder to maintain the abstract concept of "readers" or even of the "Chicana reader." Viramontes' intimate experience of the East L.A. barrio is not a knowledge she can expect all her readers to share.

In the United States's academy, white liberal guilt has taken a curious turn, and a safely distanced marginality is "in." Fredric Jameson is as good a reference as any for an articulation of this mode. He writes: "The only authentic cultural production today has seemed to be that which can draw on the collective experience of marginal pockets of the social life of the world system" (148). Jameson, of course, has been criticized for his academic tourism in these marginal pockets, and for his tendency to fit the souvenirs of these trips into his own previously constructed theoretical niches. And while it is relatively easy to critique Jameson, especially the straw man depicted here, Viramontes reminds me that we are all-too-frequently in Jameson's position. Much feminist thought in recent years has been bent toward helping us understand that the social and cultural structures of theorizing are neither evident nor universal. Such insights do not always help us, though, here in universities where we can appropriate works like those of Viramontes for a feminist analysis without any arduous rethinking of the means by which we produce an explanation of it that allows us to insert it into a given course syllabus. To misquote Hortense Spillers: We might ask not only where Viramontes belongs in an American/U.S. order of things, but by what finalities of various historico-cultural situations are we frozen forever in precisely defined portions of culture content? (16)

Feminist thinkers concerned with the cultural production of Chicanas are becoming more and more uneasy with this scenario, and are beginning to agitate for a more rigorous and attentive rethinking of epistemological, existential, and methodological questions alongside challenges that are as political as they are intellectual. But these are unhomely words, and Viramontes is a homely writer. Her contribution to this emerging theory will have something to do with a woman's seeking, and speaking, with her attentiveness and adhesiveness, and sometimes with the frustration of having to make a meaning out of a broken dream, a hole in a shirt, a tattoo, a missing dress, or even nothing at all (and "nuthin" is another of those insistently repeated and multiply valenced words in these stories). Let us give Champ the last word:

> Champ is in the closet. There are piles of clothes on the floor, hangers thrown askew and tangled, shoes all piled up or thrown on the top shelf.

Champ is looking for her mother's special dress. Pancha says every girl has one at the end of her closet.

"Goddamn it Champ."

Amidst the dirty laundry, the black hole of the closet, she finds nothing. ("Miss Clairol," 102–3)

# 7. Solidarity

*Demetria Martínez*

My first obligation in understanding solidarity is to learn her
mothertongue.
— *Gayatri Spivak,* Outside in the Teaching Machine

All of the writers whose works are highlighted in this book offer us the
opportunity to meditate on a theory and a poetics for rethinking the
construction of ethnic discourse and national identity at the conflicted
intersection of various simultaneously held and often mutually contradictory roles. In *Mother Tongue,* her prize-winning novel about the tortuous relationship between a Chicana Sanctuary worker and a Salvadoran
refugee man, Demetria Martínez puts us in the position of observers
upon the recent events in El Salvador and on the U.S. Sanctuary movement, testing our memories of near-contemporary history as she asks
us to look at the specific qualities of this relationship between a Central
American man and his Chicana lover. Martínez is a poet, and language
itself solidifies in this novel, becomes cruelly angular, tears the soul.
"Words had a barbed wire feel to them," says the narrator (23), or "the
unspoken words were turning into hooks, they were caught in my
throat" (55). These barbed words frame/make/mark/mask identity and
ineradicably shape the real. Both the Salvadoran man and the Mexican

American woman suffer from traumas that are both political and linguistic, both find themselves torn by circumstances between two identities: a U.S. name and U.S. life, and a Mexican or Central American
heritage. The shocking and in some ways inevitable outcome of this
pain is that in their mutual love they hurt each other as a reaction to
the estrangement each feels. Yet, while Martínez writes sympathetically
of the anguish felt by the displaced refugee man, her point of view is
that of the Mexican American woman, and her style reflects an implicit
critical methodology in which she not only signals the strange shape
of this cruelly embodied language, but also continually foregrounds its
gendered quality, its relation to the "mothertongue." Martínez's poetic
concern with the gendered quality of language and her deep sympathy
for the sheer humanity of committed personal intimacy between very
different individuals is matched as well with an implicit reminder of the
often vexed and underanalyzed relation between personal decisions and
political commitments.

The brief one-paragraph epigraph/prologue to the novel puts the
narrative in the context of the ten-year civil war in El Salvador and the
U.S. government's support for a repressive regime that targeted its own
civilians in a bid to retain control of the country. Martínez writes: "the
characters in this novel are fictional, but the context is not," and this
simple statement can be paired with another, at the end of the novel,
where the author's brief biographical note tells us, "[I]n 1987 Martínez
was indicted on charges related to smuggling Central American refugees
into the United States. A jury later acquitted her on First Amendment
grounds" (123). With these two framing comments, Martínez brings the
world of the novel into contact with her own life and asks us to look
back to the historical conjuncture that gave rise to U.S./El Salvador
policy, to her indictment, the acquittal, and this novel.

The Sanctuary movement in the United States officially began in
March 1982 when Reverend John Fife's Southside Presbyterian Church
in Tucson, Arizona, declared itself a sanctuary for Central American
refugees fleeing political persecution in their own countries—mostly
Guatemala and El Salvador—and who were denied political asylum by
the United States.[1] The government position on the movement was that
the Sanctuary workers were no different from any other "coyotes" who
helped illegal aliens cross into the United States, and thus they were
subject to arrest and legal charging on those grounds. In 1985 sixteen

Sanctuary workers in Phoenix were indicted on smuggling charges, and the 1985–86 trial of eleven of them and conviction of eight gained the program wide sympathy among an international and interfaith group of churches in Europe as well as the United States, Mexico, and Canada. By 1986–87, at the height of Sanctuary's informal network of operations— a loose set of community contacts often likened to the Underground Railroad that functioned in the mid-nineteenth century as a network of safe houses for escaping slaves—60,000 to 70,000 people were involved in the North American Sanctuary movement. More than four hundred religious congregations and twenty-two cities formally proclaimed themselves Sanctuaries, openly declaring their intention not to cooperate with the Immigration and Naturalization Service (INS).[2]

Because Sanctuary originated in, and remained dominated by, church-sponsored support groups, the movement inevitably brings into question the parameters of church-state relations in the United States. As Hilary Cunningham notes in her book on the movement, "Sanctuary . . . encompassed not only acts of compassion toward Central American refugees but also a much deeper questioning of the relation of faith to nationalism, Christianity to Americanism, and individual conscience to the law" (xvii). By its very nature as a (conceptually) imagined besieged site, Sanctuary requires, as she says later, "a process of 'articulation,' one that created a distinct kind of cultural 'space'" (137). This "cultural space" of Sanctuary overlaps with discrete geographical spaces (churches, refugee centers, city limits), with particular historical precedents (medieval sanctuary practices in Europe; the underground railroad in the pre–Civil War United States; safe houses for Jews in World War II), with legal and intellectual spaces (conscientious objection, civil disobedience, division of church and state). This conflation of intellectual, historical, spiritual, and geographical spaces with political action is one of the richest and most significant contributions of the movement, and one that serves as an intellectual balance to the recent conservative church domination of popular press debates about the relationship of religion and politics. This articulation of actual and symbolic space with a particular political-religious-social movement provides the underpinning for the binational, multicultural explorations of ethnic and national identity undertaken by Martínez in *MotherTongue,* where the embattled microcosm of Sanctuary serves as an understood, but understated, transcultural referent.

Yet, as Cunningham notes, and Demetria Martínez movingly reminds us in her novel, the Sanctuary movement was neither univocal nor homogeneous. Many Latino supporters felt both empowered by their ability to assist Central American refugees and disempowered by a largely white leadership. Furthermore, for many Sanctuary workers, especially women, the structure of the organization unattractively mirrored the male hegemony in U.S. Christian churches, and the media, in focusing on the roles of Reverend Fife and Jim Corbett, underscored this gender bias in newspaper reports. Adding to the discomfort of many of the women who worked with refugees, much of the Sanctuary coverage implicitly divided the workers into the U.S. stereotypes of the outlaw-hero of popular Westerns and the moms who worked behind the scenes to prepare the meals and wash the clothes. Once again, as in the movies, the men got all the good roles.

This structural imbalance gave rise to poisonously hurtful combinations of paternalism and male gender bias. The paternalism of Sanctuary was already recognized from within the movement, as the following anecdote and commentary clearly demonstrates: "'A refugee woman was coming to speak to us and we heard she'd been raped,' a Sanctuary workshop participant told us, 'but when she made her presentation, she didn't talk about it, so we didn't know whether or not it was true.'" The writer quite correctly poses the important question, "Would this North American woman, if she were raped, be able to stand in front of a crowd of strangers and relate particulars of her pain and humiliation?" (Malcolm, 22). Marion Malcolm's story hints at more than the gender bias of much of Sanctuary; it also reminds us that the movement, even at its best moments, tended toward an unconscious paternalism. The refugees became objects of North American political-religious commitments rather than empowered subjects, to the point that the North American woman cited in this anecdote was unable to put herself in the place of the Salvadoran refugee. Unkindly, she expected a good show in payment for her charitable assistance. The Central Americans' cultural otherness and their traumatic *testimonios* become reinscribed as exotica, as performances geared for a well-intentioned but unconsciously biased audience. On the other side, and understandably, refugees complained that they never became part of the decision-making circles of Sanctuary, that Americans seemed to feel more comfortable treating them as children than as responsible, politically aware adults, and that Anglos in particular were so firmly convinced of their own superiority that they could not conceive of treating refugees as equals (Cunningham, 141–42, 154–55).[3] Once again, the refugees are perceived not so much as the agents of their own history, but as its victims, who function primarily as the objects of knowledge for an alien people.

All of these conflicts point precisely to the kind of process of functional overdetermination that Homi Bhabha defines as the typical mode by which discourses of sexuality and race become imbricated within a resistant or unconsciously perpetuated colonial structure ("The Other Question," 79). To the degree that Sanctuary fixed on the image of the refugee as the childlike-object-to-be-helped, it created a fantasy in dissonance with its own primary objectives, but one that remains deeply emotionally satisfying to the inbred guilt and unrecognized prejudices of many liberals. This stereotyping must be masked or concealed from consciousness, but the conflictual positions it engenders continually disrupt self-other representations and affect relationships with the objectified and infantilized other. It is precisely at the level of the individual negotiation of these difficult and conflictive dramas that Demetria Martínez poses her novel.

*Mother Tongue* is constructed around a series of textual fragments put together by an English-speaking Chicana named Mary, who in 1982 provides support for a Salvadoran refugee she calls José Luis. Twenty years later she composes a memoir of that time to order her own memories and to offer an auto/biographical inheritance to her son. Mary uses whatever pieces of the past she has available in putting together this bifocal, bicultural reconstruction of her recent past. She recreates her memories of that time, and confesses to the blanks in her memory; she transcribes letters, postcards, tape recordings, scraps of her journal and of his; she copies Amnesty International documents, poems, newspaper clippings; she describes photographs, and sorts through a shoebox of varied treasures. By the end of the novel, Mary comes to terms with her "ordinary" name, that she has at various times considered a blessing, a curse, and a sign of her assimilated identity; she learns that José Luis hid himself in the United States under the mask of his real—although presumedly invented—name; and her son from that long-ago liaison finds his real name in his father's actual last name: Alegría. As always, Martínez's use of languages carries with it a poet's overdetermined sensibility. The patronymic "Alegría," which at the end of the novel replaces the airline pseudonym of "A. Romero," substitutes a feminine-gendered noun meaning "happiness" for the masculine-sounding name, "Romero," that pays tribute to the martyred Salvadoran archbishop while it evokes the most significant quality of the Salvadoran's stay in the United States: pilgrimage. At the same time, in returning to his own name, José Luis also remembers his own poetic heritage, one that brings him into spiritual and political contact with his well-known countrywoman, poet and activist Claribel Alegría, whose work is cited in this novel. The mothertongue, then, is not simple or single, but coheres around a prickly border of half-forgotten, half-remembered cultural markers leading from the English Mary to the Spanish Alegría and permitting their reconciliation across multiple religious, political, and ethnic borders.

Thus, this story constructed from fragments of memory and the equally important gaps between those memories reveals itself as a family romance with an only slightly untraditional happy ending. The story of the political affiliation with Sanctuary and of the consequences of that commitment becomes as well a story of filiation: of a heritage passed on from mother to son. In this way, through political/religious affiliation and personal filiation, the woman who initially felt in many ways an exile in her own land, cut off from the language that should have been her mothertongue, finds a belated wholeness in her own fragmentary life tale, a completeness that comes full circle as her son takes up the challenge of beginning to learn Spanish, the language of his father, the language partially lost to his mother. In so doing, he acquires the desired cultural and physical markers absent in his parents. Thus, in the first paragraph of the novel, Mary says of the Salvadoran refugee, her future lover, "His was a face I'd seen in a dream. A face with no borders. . . . I don't know why I had expected Olmec. . . . No, he had no warrior's face" (3). In her first impression upon seeing the Salvadoran refugee there is a curious superimposition of expectations and the frustration of these expectations. José Luis initially represents for Mary a particular cultural site associated for her with her own incompletely understood, romanticized Mexican past (Olmec warrior). Despite (or perhaps because of) her own embattled ethnic identity, Mary conceives of her charge as belonging to this clearly delimited ethnic group entirely unrelated to El Salvador and, at the same time, as a man whose face and experience transcends borders. Her conclusion, based on the contradictory evidence of José Luis's face, is that the warrior she hoped to find in him, and which she needs to fulfill her own dreams, is unnervingly absent. Nevertheless, she knows, and the reader knows, that José Luis is in fact a warrior and a survivor of war. This contradictory structure of visual cues and psychological need responds to Mary's own motivation for hosting a refugee man. She explicitly conceives of her task as the archetypal one of the temple prostitute, of "tak[ing] a war out of a man" (3) in offering him her body. Insofar as it responds to the articulation of a deeply felt need on her part, this conjunction of whore/war haunts the entire novel despite the inaccuracy, and it serves as one of the clues to define the distinctive quality of the mothertongue. The mismatch of face and function is not resolved until the son makes whole the breach between dream and reality with his own generational conflict, his own warrior's face: "Right there, one terrible afternoon, my baby grew up and be- came himself: Olmec with a warrior's helmet, raging against me and the powers that had laid waste his Earth" (87).

And yet, the son's happy ending, both Olmec and Alegría, his em- bodiment of a narrative whole out created from his mother's fragments, comes only artificially, projected into a narrative future that had not yet arrived (2002), after the mother has given herself a twenty-year span for meditation that sets the time of narration at eight years later than the novel's date of publication (1994). This temporal dislocation reminds us that the novel is historicizing near-contemporary events, which, as the epigraph notes, really occurred, while it also points toward a his- tory that has not yet happened. At the same time, the main narrative of *Mother Tongue* passes through a sequence of aporias, of narrative frag- ments that cannot quite locate themselves or articulate themselves as a linear, sequential auto/biography. It is as if all historical timekeeping in itself becomes relative when the subject of that history is terror, identity switching, and the erasing of boundaries in terms of a legal establish- ment, but not ethnically or psychologically.

Fundamentally, then, the novel enacts the dislocating effects of spac- ing and of displacement, as three people and two temporal markers occupy the same narrative space in this family tale. This dislocation or overdetermination concerns differential political and gender readings of people and events as well. Martínez's point-of-view character is careful not to impose her judgments on others in any pseudo-omniscient way. Instead, she tries to construct a discontinuous family history in which agents and objects continually shift locations. Simply put, we see how

Mary sees herself and how she sees José Luis and how she thinks he sees her; we see how José Luis sees himself and her and how he thinks she sees him. We see how the son sees them both and how others see them. Each identity is both admittedly partial and more than usually multi-faceted, inextricably bound to the contingencies of the moment and the linguistic and cultural models that provide an individual's context for expression. In this contrapuntal play of voicing, Martínez suggests the absolute crucialness of situating such structures of imagination and desire with reference not only to what is said or observed, but also with respect to when and where and who. Here, for example, is Mary's reading of how she imagines that José Luis sees her after reading of the nuns' murder in El Salvador:

> He saw in me an image of a gringa whose pale skin and tax dollars are putting his compatriots to death. My credentials, the fact that I am Mexican American, don't count now; in fact, they make things worse. In his anger he looks at me and sees not a woman but a beast, a Sphinx. Earlier in the morning, he had made love to a Chicana. But after telling him the news of the nuns' deaths, I am transfigured. For a terrible, disfigured moment, I am a yanqui, a murderess, a whore. (75)

In counterpoint, in his journal, José Luis describes his anger this way:

> I acted as if it were her fault that the sisters were killed. I suspect the real reason for my anger is that I have no idea what to say to make her understand that my world is falling apart around me. I am too proud to say, María, there are reasons why I get cold whenever I hear helicopters or sirens. . . . The problem is that we are not seeing or hearing the same things. . . . It is not her fault that her culture has made her who she is. (77–78)

For both Mary and José Luis, what they see, and how they see it, is embedded in their national and ethnic identities, the impact of their individual experiences of oppression, and in their culturally determined expectations about the other. Both the man and the woman agree that he met her distress with anger. She sees the anger as denaturalizing her, stripping her of her Chicana or Mexican American identity to leave behind that stereotypical image of the U.S. woman for stereotypical Latin American men: the gringa whore. With this move, a complex historical process is reduced to the feminine projection of a masculinist bias: the nuns stand in opposition to the whore, and José Luis's country is being destroyed implicitly because in the United States women are seducing or being seduced. Mary's reading reflects, then, her own insecurity about her acculturated double identity as Latina and as gringa, as well as her sense of political insufficiency to Latin American reality. In addition, it also deconstructs her self-representative dream-image of herself as a romanticized temple prostitute. José Luis understands his anger to be a reaction out of his own male pride to his own fear, a fear that he suspects she does not recognize because her culture (singular) has conditioned her differently.

This strategy of continuous embedding interrogates the issue of identity precisely at the nexus of social, political, and gender constructions. "Looking back now," Mary asks herself, "I wonder what troubled me more, the fear that the Border Patrol might see José Luis or that the tourists in his midst could not see him" (35). Like those gringo tourists, Mary is unprepared to see the whole José Luis. While she admittedly sees something other than the small, dark man who passes fleetingly through the visual scope of the gringo tourist, when Mary looks at him she too sees something other than his own ethnic and national and personal identity. She sees instead the not-Olmec, the not-warrior, the sensitive poet. It is only when he reveals the story of his torture to her that she comes to understand that the strange markings on his body are scars, and even then she cannot see them:

> Beneath my hands was a constellation of markings that in any other life-time might have been the momentary flushing of skin in the fire of passion, marks left by a woman's fingernails. And as I so often did in those days, I refused to believe my own eyes. I refused to believe that what I was seeing was a pattern of scars, the legend to the map of his life. (81)

Here Mary's refusal to see her lover's scars causes her to misread them as passion's inscription on the man's body, a reading almost frighteningly consistent with her self-castigation in misreading José Luis's anger as an effect of sexual intimacy displaced over a consent to commit murder. In an analogous manner, her loving interrogation of José Luis also mimics the brutal interrogation of the Salvadoran torturers. In her reading of him, his personal history has less to do with the events that mapped his life, but rather with the dislocation of the spectacle—of love, of torture—that signifies by way of distance and displacement. His body does not signify in itself or to himself. It is a sign only insofar as it exists in dialogue with the spectacle of its ambiguous testimony. Delicately, Martínez marks out the ethics of this testimonial reenactment that signifies only to signify differently, because the spectator/audience comes to the event with an alien cultural bias.

The map of José Luis's life in the United States has already been violated in at least two ways by the time he tells Mary, slowly, with shame in his voice and tears in his eyes, about how he came to be scarred. In the first violation, he is asked, as Salvadoran refugees supported by Sanctuary were routinely advised, to pretend to a nationality that is not his: "remind him that if anyone asks, he should say he's from Juárez. If he should be deported, we want immigration to have no question that he is from Mexico" (5). He is also asked to give meaning to the life of a young woman who admits, "before his arrival the chaos of my life had no axis about which to spin. Now I had a center" (4). Mary is charmed by the romance of Sanctuary's mission and seduced by the irony in the name of the refugee's home country, El Salvador/the savior, and she immediately imagines herself in the powerful role of his personal savior: *la salvadora del salvadoreño* as it were. In the first case, pragmatics dictate the shape of his mask; if he were to be discovered and deported, Mexico would be safer than El Salvador, and return to the U.S. would be more feasible. In the second case, Mary's need for order and meaning in her life propel her into a relationship with this man from a very different, and deceptively similar, culture. It is no wonder that in his own reflections on their subsequent relationship, José Luis comes to see that Mary has created him in one way, not through objective truth, but through desire. In turn, his notebook and Mary's rereading of it twenty years later betray her need to herself while retaining the secret of his identity (54).

Even before Mary meets him, José Luis defines the structure of her need; it is she who inaugurates their physical relationship, turning him into the object of her sexual fantasy. She admits that she is "utterly unoriginal" (17) in her passion for this man, and tells us that her selfishness about wanting him sexually eventually broke down his physical reticence, but only at the point where her desire turned to a kind of love: "from the very beginning I wanted him. . . . José Luis would have none of it. . . . In the end, I had no choice but to love him. Desire was not good enough" (13). And yet, what Mary loves first of all and most of all is her idea of him as a needy, wounded warrior. She loves her projection of herself as the compassionate, healing prostitute; she is thrilled by the sharp plea-sure found in the violation of her own Catholic ethical standard against unmarried sex. She finds a certain comfortable safety, or romantic poi-gnancy, in repeating her mother's story of desire and loss in a different, more open and empowered way: "When I was three, a woman lured my father from home. This story is not about them, but it would be dishon-est to disregard the role their ghosts played in my life, maybe still are playing; I had to make something beautiful out of abandonment" (57).

In this revision of her mother's abandonment, Mary alternatively views herself as the alluring woman and the woman left behind with a small child, as the agent and as the object in her own romantic retelling of the old story. It is precisely at this moment, in which Mary projects her future abandonment of/by José Luis, that she mentions briefly and in passing that she now has a new love: "real love is quiet as snow, with-out chaos, hard to write about. Perhaps that is why I haven't mentioned the man I have been seeing for a year" (58). Finally, in Mary's dreams, it is not José Luis who abandons her, but she who must finally take the choice to let him go free. Calling him by "his true name, *desaparecido*" (54), Mary erases the audiotape on which she had recorded his *testimonio* of war and torture, symbolically erasing as well the worn-out remnant of a voice and a history that had almost obliterated any trace of the real man, the man whose face was not that of a warrior, the man she had once loved, or thought she loved, without ever knowing him. Still fur-ther: this missing/erased tape serves as an important strategic void in her text, marking one of those memory blanks that Mary signals but refuses to discuss. In erasing the concrete physical representation of her lover's voice, Mary reminds her son and us that the "real man" (her lover, the father of her child) can be revealed only through *her* reinterpretation of his writings and her interpretation of his actions; at all times it is the voice of the mother, of the mothertongue, that shapes the image of the father.

It is entirely consistent with this outpouring of the play of naming into the "true" name, *desaparecido,* that the text itself is likewise full of disappearances and invented details that, like the name of the border city, Juárez, signify a conveniently masked identity, or an insufficient one. The narrator warns us at the outset: "I am good at filling in the blanks, at seeing meaning where there may have been none at all. In this way I get very close to the truth. Or closer still to illusion" (8). Later she says, "What I can't remember, I will invent, offer up my tales for those who were not granted time enough to recall, to mend" (91). Sometimes the effort at recall and invention breaks down under the pressure of words too painful, too violently overdetermined: "I might never recall everything. But see the blank spaces between sentences?" (103).

For it happens that, unexpectedly, Mary too is a *desaparecida*, a survivor of another and intimate gender war that taught her too early the meanings of those resonant "barbed wire words" that structure her later understanding of her relationships with men, and particularly with José Luis. She, too, has hidden her identity from herself, allowing the illusion of the compassionate prostitute to define that nineteen-year-old girl, to help her find an ordering principle in an alien face, to invent a narrative on the surface of the unrecognized skin of a torture victim. It so happens that his scars are also, in a different register, hers. As a seven-year-old child, Mary was violated, in her case by a smiling neighbor in whose care her mother left her, and she has repressed that memory of sexual abuse until an eruption of violence between her and her lover shocks her into recall of that earlier, unrepresentable pain:

> A finger in a place you hardly know exists is a knife. A knife in a place for which you have no word is the most lethal of weapons. It carves words on your inner walls to fill the void. Words like *chaos, slut, don't tell, your fault*. . . The girl is alone in the house, alone with the man. . . . She learns to fear being alone long before she learns to say *abandonment*.
> (103)

In this shocked moment of recall, "abandonment" looms like the secret cipher of her life, overdetermining at the same time as it unpacks all the other signifiers of her sense of self. "Abandonment" is the name of that forbidden memory and of the structure of unrecognized reinscription or iteration that shapes her subsequent actions, even to the displacement of the seven-year-old "slut" into the nineteen-year-old "temple prostitute." In this respect, naming the secret violation provokes the whole of the narration at the same time as it points to the narrative aporia at its most critical moment; it is the story of the mother, archetypally played out across time, in the absence (abandonment) of the father. And yet, because the iteration is also an interrogation and a recuperation of lost memory, it frames and instates a different history, a compassionate mothertongue that responds powerfully to fatherlaw.

Crucially, this narrative agency occurs as a created entity—a child, if you will—produced between the incommensurable positions of the Salvadoran man and the Chicana woman, between their gender-marked *testimonios* (electric shocks to the genitals, finger in the vagina), between their objectified status and their achievement of agency, between their twinned experiences of memory and forgetting, their ultimate possession of space and self through names both true and invented. Derrida writes:

> "Memory" is first the name of something that I shall not define for the moment, singling out only this feature: it is the name of what for us (an "us" which I define only in this way) preserves an essential and necessary relationship with the possibility of the name, and of what in the name assures preservation. (*Memoires,* 49)

Memory, then, is not only that which in itself names a particular quality of mind, but also a reminder of all that naming evokes. Thus, to name a friend is to call up, for example, the entire inchoate sequence of memories that identify the particularity and essential truth of the person named. It is because naming is so powerful and problematic in all its potential contextualizations that it becomes the most potent figure in *Mother Tongue* for the necessary, impossible, and impossibly overdetermined remembering of the story, of all of the stories and histories of political and sexual conflict. Consider the following:

> I said, we have to pick a name for you, one you would answer in your sleep. . . .
>       He said, Roberto, Juan, any name will do. I said, why not Neftalí or Octavio? I wondered, why not pan for gold. . . . He said, in my country names turn up on lists. . . . Pick an ordinary name. (8–9)

> He said, any name you pick will do. I said, it's not my place to decide. . . .
>       He picked the name, José Luis. (10–11)

In this sequence a spurious and undefined "we" sets off the discussion, and the repetition, "He said," "I said," establishes the parallel lines of this pseudo-dialogic anecdote. Neither of the two participants in the conversation seems to hear the other; Mary wants the choice of the name to be a collaborative effort ("we") or by preference his choice ("it's not my place to decide"). José Luis ostensibly defers to the woman he has just met, counting on her good sense to choose him an "ordinary" name, not knowing that for her "ordinariness" is a sign of repression and pain, whereas in his own experience it is the unusual name that endangers. Mary, in accord with her own romantic nature and with unconscious prescience, wants to choose the name of a poet (Octavio [Paz], Neftalí [Ricardo Reyes: Pablo Neruda]) for her refugee. José Luis wants a name that is like no name at all: anonymous and undifferentiable. Though they speak at cross purposes, each speaks more truly than they know, and each finds salvation of sorts in the other. In the final analysis, José Luis's journals open onto poetry; Mary is rescued from her ordinariness and from her unremembered trauma:

> I needed a mystery, someone outside of ordinary time who could rescue me from an ordinary life, from my name, Mary, a blessing name that became my curse. At age nineteen, I was looking for a man to tear apart the dry rind of that name so I could see what fruit fermented inside.
>
> This is what happened back then to women who didn't marry or have babies. They begged to differ. They questioned their own names. (11)

> Twenty years later I still go by the name, María. When I said to José Luis, it's me, María, I remembered. And the ghost of the man with the minus sign smile fled. . . . He could not bear the sound of my true name. (104)

Here the ordinary name "Mary" gives way to the "true name," María, the name given to her by José Luis and one that she associates with her identity as an empowered Chicana rather than the child-victim of the perverse neighbor and the object of his deeply wounding secrets. "María" does indeed crack open the secret in "Mary" and releases the poisonous words fermenting inside. Her true name also opens onto his:

> He asks, have you ever kissed a man whose name you did not know?
> I say, I knew the name but not the man. (38)

Indirectly, through this process of articulating the problem of naming and knowing, José Luis and Mary address the change in their own relationship as they become lovers. Unbeknownst to her, the ordinary and anonymous name that the Salvadoran refugee chose is his own name, unacknowledged. His question to her, then, poses a circumstantial problem. To kiss a man whose name she does not know presumes minimal acquaintance, or, alternatively, the kind of necessary masking of someone in José Luis's own situation. In fact, in kissing the man she calls "José Luis," Mary kisses a man whose name she does not know she knows. Her response to his question once again echoes the deep connections between knowledge of a person and knowledge of that person's true name; Mary in the past has kissed a man whose name was familiar to her, but whose true self was hidden. What she hints at but does not say is that in loving José Luis she knows the man, so the name will in some sense reflect the truth of that love. It is this memory of love, conflictually tied up with the memory of true and invented names, of physically and psychically scarred bodies, that becomes the untranslatable experience Mary/María struggles to bring to her son:

> There are some memories I would rather fight to the death. Fight, rather than say to my son, mijito, once upon a time I gave you the name José Luis in order to make it real, to make a made-up name real. (92)

> But look, Ma, look at his name. It's José Luis Alegría. José Luis. It's not a made-up name after all! . . . Ma, you never gave me a real middle name. I've got one now. Alegría. Happiness. (115)

Despite her earlier assurances to José Luis, for Mary names are crucial. To make love to a man with a made-up name violates her sense of what is good and proper. By giving the invented name to her son, she makes the name real, attaching a true name to the appropriate body. When the correctness of her choice is confirmed with her discovery of José Luis's real name, her son is also freed to take the final step and complete his own name, providing the novel with its "happy" ending.

This happy ending, the restoration of the proper name, provides the healing balm spread over the still-aching wounds of a relationship that had ended twenty years past. Yet, as Mary reminds us in reminding her son, there is a new love in her present, a true love that has not found words to define it. The relation with José Luis, then, for all its tortured authenticity, can be remembered and written because it remains essentially hidden under the tortured mark of an invented name and an invented, poetically tinged history. This story can be voiced and given form by the mothertongue because in some sense it is already written, in the form of a romantic novel with a strong, brave hero. In his notebook José Luis writes: "I wish there were a way I could tell her. Say to María,

you're inventing José Luis. And your invention may be very different
from who I really am. She sees my scars and thinks I was brave. . . . She
doesn't understand that you don't always have to be brave to survive"
(51). He is scarred in ways she does not understand and which he doesn't
want her to know; he is on the verge of breaking apart under the pressures of this new life, including the pressure to be heroic for her. Twenty
years later, Mary/María is still inventing José Luis, although as a more
complex character in a more interesting novel. He says further: "she
won't give me the gift of flaws" (53). Again, there is a strategic void both
marked and avoided in Mary's citation of José Luis's painful confession;
does she or does she not give him "the gift of flaws" in her compassionate rewriting of their history of misprision? The culturally and sexually
tinged translation of experience, from man to woman, from tortured
political prisoner to sexual abuse victim, from El Salvador's civil war to
the United States's ethnic conflicts, can only intuited in the cautious
articulation of those insufficient and inefficient barbed-wire words that
describe his communication with/about her and hers with/about him.

Even at the moment of their greatest mutual gift of self to the other,
they do so across a border: "We opened each other up like sacred books,
Spanish on the one side, English on the other, truths simultaneously
translated" (41). Despite the conventionally romantic literary metaphor
of opening each other like books, the very need for marking the translation effect suggests the cultural and linguistic divide between them and
reminds the reader of the untranslatable element in their very different
concepts of the truth. Thus, at this point in their relationship, the book
each individual imagines s/he is opening is no more and no less than
the masked grapheme of his/her own need, projected on the other in
the invented image of mutual understanding. Mary's story is admittedly
a partial account of two people whose identities are only partially and
gradually revealed; there is, ironically, no moment less simultaneously
translated than their first sexual encounter. Likewise, the story passed
from mother to son carries the sign of an aporia of meaning at the point
in which a love that does not recognize itself as selfish need intervenes in
the narration. Then too, and very briefly, Martínez's character reminds
us also that her current love, a real love, and one that defines a different
"truth," is "blessedly nondescript" (58). Strikingly, this truer love likewise carries the mark of the untranslatable (undescribable, undescribed,
unscribed), although for different reasons.

Signposts of untranslatability are everywhere in this novel. On an obvious level, Mary's Spanish is, as she admits, less fluent than she would like—José Luis eventually gives her classes, following upon her friend Soledad's practical, if somewhat facetious, advice: "Mijita, if you must lose your head over that boy, at least apply yourself and use the experience to shore up your Spanish" (25). More crucial is the young woman's inability to translate his struggle against his native pessimism into her naive North American optimism about cultural bridges. "It is difficult to recall the day-to-day exchanges by which we transcended the borders of culture, language, and history," she tells her son, but the example she gives of one such exchange indicates that she understands very little after all. José Luis is passionately committed to his political ideals; Mary recalls "late evenings on the couch, swirling spoons of molasses in black coffee, and talking about la revolución in Nicaragua. Don't ask me what he said. I couldn't have cared less about politics" (31). What Mary understands is the passion; what compels José Luis is the politics, and yet, there they were, far apart in their togetherness, drinking coffee on a couch. It is, in this context, amazingly hurtful as well as gauche when Mary comments, "At last I said, We're married, no?, to la revolución" (36), in her apoliticality making a trivial cliché out of her partner's deep commitment, out of the deaths he has seen and the torture he still lives. José Luis's enigmatic response to her comment displaces the pain: "Yes, why not, he said as a smile swept across his face." José Luis thus resists her appropriation of the Central American revolution by turning away the question and refusing her too-facile identification with him. Nevertheless, each individual has a different translation of this enigma. In her interpretation of that smile, Mary says, "I knew at that moment that José Luis was seeing and wanting all that would come between us" (36). Her reading of the smile is both prescient (the revolution will eventually come between them) and inaccurate (it embodies a heroic reading of his character that he has already rejected, as well as an interpretation derived from her own overdetermined understanding of "abandonment"). Significantly, Mary's commitment to *la revolución* remains in a utopian realm, where she can imagine herself as a powerful woman, a guerrillera fighting alongside her man. José Luis has seen and been crushed by the reality of civil war where the guerrillera could easily die in bloody agony at her lover's side. In his journal he notes, "María doesn't want advice. She wants a whole new self. It's too great a burden for me. It's all I can do to keep my own mind in one piece" (53).

The crux of this untranslatability comes when Mary realizes that in her efforts to identify with her lover (apolitically), to embody her self-image as a sacred prostitute who heals the war injuries of her man, she must also confront the abyss beyond which José Luis lived another life, with another woman, one who loved him and the revolution, one whom Mary fears has been disappeared and killed, and whose trace she discovers in a poem that burns itself into her memory:

> When at last my man
> gets out
> to become a new man
> in North America,
> when he finds a woman
> to take the war out of him,
> she will make love to a man
> and a monster,
> she will rise
> from her bed,
> grenades
> ticking in her. (82)

This "lamentation" signed by "Ana" predicts Mary's inevitable existence and her purpose in José Luis's life. As Mary herself comments in the first paragraph of this work, her function is "to take the war out of him"; what she did not realize at the time was that her romantic dream of rescue also involves taking the war into herself and choking on its linguistic representation. We soon learn that Ana represented José Luis's dream of the ordinary before war came to interrupt his life, to destroy her, and to change him irrevocably: "We were going to get married. All we wanted was an ordinary life" (99). Mary's blithe "We're married, no?, to la revolución" reminds José Luis of the marriage that did not take place because of the revolution. Her yearning for an exotic warrior who needs her to take the war out of him contrasts with Ana's love for an ordinary man and her hopes of an ordinary life with him. Mary faces Ana across the unbridgeable abyss of that destruction of the ordinary, and with her mention of that name, "Ana," she releases the grenade ticking in José

Luis into an explosion of violence directed against her. And yet, it is that violent act that frees up Mary's hidden memories of her own personal war, when a smiling neighbor raped her with his finger.

Hilary Cunningham writes, "[M]any Sanctuary communities did not know how to handle some of the deep psychological problems refugee family members were manifesting as a result of torture, witnessing massacres, having family members 'disappeared,' or leaving children behind. Nor did they know how to respond to pervasive domestic violence within Central American families" (66). Demetria Martínez looks unflinchingly at these issues and explores them in her novel with sensitivity and compassion. "This war syndrome thing is very complicated," Soledad notes in a letter to Mary, but she advises her friend, "Better to have scars from living than from hiding" (105–6). Mary's flip identification with "la revolución" hides her own personal war even from herself, and if her experience is untranslatably different from José Luis's, and their *testimonios* (in churches, in this notebook for her son) are likewise different and incommensurable, nevertheless his pain and hers are, she says, "part of the same pattern. Of people loving power, or some such thing, more than life" (107). Mary/María's knowledge, twenty years after José Luis has left, follows the reasoning of that pattern, and she learns to love José Luis better, for himself rather than for the lifeline he can throw her. She accepts the untranslatable, the still painful, as specifically situated and necessarily situational. Her hesitant mothertongue transcribes this experience for her son with all its skips and gaps, all its truth and all its masks. By including José Luis's notebooks as well as hers, by uncovering his needy invention of her as well as hers of him, she juggles the untranslatable silences in the two languages.

Most important, while this story is composed of lasso letters (29) and barbed-wire words that tear at her throat (55), the loving mother realizes that her writing is the medicine she needs to complete her own journey from past to present. Some wounds must be torn open by language so that learning can take place, so that healing can occur. "Every story has its medicine," she advises her son; "you must figure out what you most need from this one so you can take it and let go of the rest" (100), repeating the wise words of her own teacher and mother-figure, Soledad: "every remedio, she said, has elements of both, of the sickness and its cure" (69). And while the story is ostensibly for her son, the mother realizes that in recreating it for him, she is also curing herself of accumulated poisons. "I must tell myself the rest of the story, chew on it like oshá root, sweat it out" (91), she says, echoing her lover's prescription. "José Luis said he needed to get old poisons out of him, and so he has been chewing on oshá root" (106).

It is, finally, this homely image of the oshá root, a curandero's remedio to sweat out the sickness, that comes to stand as the correlative of those bitter memories that must be chewed over so as to arrive at a more healthy understanding of the self in all its complexity. In this sense, the novel fulfills the function of mourning, as described by Jacques Derrida: "a meditation in which bereaved memory is deeply engraved." The French philosopher continues: "Funerary speech and writing do not follow upon death; they work upon life in what we call autobiography. And this takes place between fiction and truth" (*Memoires*, 22). One of the functions of this novel is to come to a gender-conscious understanding of the work of mourning and of memory in the construction of the past; another is to recognize that all such work is at least partly fictional, composed of vagaries involving situational response and personal recall, the tropological substitution of self-interest for the bitter root of consensual truth.

The frame of this novel—founding the mothertongue by reminding the reader of the victims of El Salvador's civil war and of Martínez's commitment to help—also asks us to think about how gender and politics are imbricated together in specific cultural sites. She raises the crucial question of how issues of ethnic identity, political necessity, gender bias, cultural appropriation, and differentially constructed understandings of truth are all at stake in this implicitly feminist undertaking. There are two countries, two genders, two generations, and several multiply conflicted cultures and languages represented in this novel, all hinting that single-issue politics have important limits as an analytic category and that traditional narrative practices are too univocal for the more nuanced representations Martínez undertakes. At the same time as she engages in a specific version of feminist theorizing marked as Mexican American, she also identifies and confronts persistent problems in a narrowly conceived feminist political practice so as to make it both more accurate and more useful. Mary's mistake is to try to make the Salvadoran man her object, to attempt to possess him and his culture as a way of waging a spiritual war against her own oppression as a Mexican American and as a woman. José Luis's error is to accept the idealistic young woman for what she gives him, while still fighting out the mental traumas of the Salvadoran military abuse and the U.S. government policy across her body. Such frustrated attempts at projecting the self into the other represent the untranslated threshold both man and woman must cross. As Spivak acutely notes in writing of the political positionality assumed by First World feminists with respect to their counterparts in other parts of the world, "My first obligation in understanding solidarity is to learn her mothertongue" (191). This is a lesson that Martínez knows very well.

# 8. Utopia

*Regina Swain and María Novaro*

These are the spaces that tend to make one believe that the rest of
Californian life is not a fiction.
—*Michel de Certeau, "Californie"*

In August 1997 the *presidente municipal* (mayor) of Tijuana, José Guadalupe Osuna Milán, received the following communication from the
head of the city's judicial department as the final stage in a series of municipal discussions and negotiations that had been going on for months,
much to the consternation and bemusement of local press:

> Atendiendo la instrucción girada en su momento y habiéndose con-
> cluido el trámite, anexo al presente me permito acompañar original del
> Título de Registración de Marca número 555863, expediente 300027 por
> el Instituto Mexicano de la Propiedad Industrial, bajo la clase 35, nomi-
> nativa, vocablo "TIJUANA" que protege publicidad y negocios, difusión
> de material publicitario, folletos, prospectos, impresos, muestras, pelícu-
> las, novelas, videograbaciones y documentales, a favor del Ayuntamiento
> de Tijuana.[1]

The mayor's office clarified that under no circumstances would that office charge royalties for the use of this newly registered term, and that

189

the purpose of this legislation was purely to protect "el vocablo Tijuana para evitar su mal uso" [the word "Tijuana" so as to avoid its ill use]. The elected officials' concern with the good name of Tijuana, of course, inevitably reminds us of the city's less-than-pristine reputation; indeed, such legislation can only be imagined in the context of the considerable adverse publicity that has made the name "Tijuana" a byword for the worst stereotypes of excess associated with Mexico's northern border: Americanized inhabitants, tacky commerce, bad food, sleazy sex joints. This stereotype, somewhat differently conceptualized from two domi-nant cultures (United States and central Mexico), combines with the local anxious rage against being caught helplessly between two giant propaganda machines. The resulting volatile mixture constitutes what Jorge Bustamante in another context calls the "síndrome de Tijuana" ("Et-nicidad en la frontera México")—which, after August 1997, would theo-retically have to be called the Tijuana Syndrome®—the hapless feeling of living on the wrong side of the defining edge of national culture while at the same time persisting as an obsessive object of discourse.

The area seems almost fatally predisposed for such obsession, given the lucky or unlucky circumstance of its hyperdetermined geographical loca-tion, its always-already liminality to traditionally sanctioned discussions of national power and gender right, long before the small settlement on the U.S./Mexico border became a boomtown and international sin city at the beginning of the twentieth century. In 1535 Hernán Cortés wrote the name "California" on a map, identifying a strip of land on the west-ern edge of New Spain and paying homage to one of the more intriguing mythic sites invented for the immensely popular chivalric romance cycle dedicated to the adventures of Amadís de Gaula and his progeny, in this case, Garci Rodríguez de Montalvo's *Las sergas de Esplandián:*

> á la diestra mano de las Indias hubo una Isla, llamada California, muy llegada á la parte del Paraíso Terrenal, la cual fué poblada de mujeres negras, sin que algun varón entre ellas hubiese. (539)

> [on the right-hand side of the Indies there was an island called Cali-fornia, which was very close to the region of the Earthly Paradise. This island was inhabited by black women, and there were no males among them at all.] (457)

Montalvo's California, thus, before its specific geographic siting—to the left of the West Indies, but indeed, in a global perspective on the right-hand of the fabled East Indies—was already marked out as a fabulous and incomprehensible site, fiercely guarded, woman-ruled, liminally paradisical, racially differentiable.

Louis XIV of France's court geographer, Sanson d'Abbeville, warns in the introduction to his description of California that returned travelers' and knightly conquerors' reports are not always to be accepted at face value:

> These opposite descriptions about these areas show us how dangerous it is to trust those who return from far away. We should not be deceived by people who make such claims, regardless of how well dressed these people may be, or regardless of how well they speak, or of how good looking they are. We should not trust them even if they give much assurance of the truth. (55)

In the concluding paragraph of this little work, the geographer gives one example of such inaccurate reporting. It seems that folks believed for many years that California was a peninsula; however, Sanson d'Abbeville has privileged information from a Dutch ship that had captured a Spanish ship that had complete charts showing that California was an island after all (65): interestingly enough, as Montalvo had already presciently foreseen in "Las sergas de Esplandián." (It is worth noting that the French also read Spanish chivalric novels, which were the bestsellers of the time, and almost immediately translated into the major European languages.) The place name "California," then, evokes a temporal, spatial, gender-marked anomaly outside normative domestications of the American wilderness as (male) conquerable spaces. It is a markedly, uneasily feminine space, unusually subject to the superimposition of, or veering between, distopic and utopic visions, reactionary and avant-garde political and social perspectives, nostalgia for an invented past and anticipation of an imagined future.

As political interest in and attention to the border region grows, Debbie Nathan asks, "[D]oes such a turnabout then mean that life on the *frontera* is actually the avant-garde of our larger cosmopolitan *mañana*?" Nathan's comment, is, of course, a tongue-in-cheek question about the modalities increasingly associated with modern late-capitalist production and, as such, puts a finger on an issue that is only beginning to be addressed seriously. In addition, one of the things we particularly like about her form of expression is that it offers a paradigmatic instance of a highly self-conscious border discourse at play, one in which a French-derived high art literary term ("avant garde") jostles with colloquial phrasings from both sides of the linguistic and political border, implicitly bringing into question the stereotypical cultural presuppositions about cosmopolitan (implicitly U.S.) and *mañana* (Mexican) cultures.

Much of the discourse of/from the *frontera* in general, and about Tijuana in particular, has this shadowtext quality, that is, from a space ambiguously in/outside dominant discourse(s), it echoes those issues that both societies uneasily abject or repress. On the one hand, dominant discourse about the *frontera* tends to look like the dark side, the hidden attachment to a discourse otherwise cast in bright light. Sometimes this play of light and shadow is overtly described. "Mexican cynicism is an aspect of the Mexican habit of always seeking the shade," says Richard Rodriguez in his discussion of Tijuana, "In Athens Once" (in *Days of Obligation*). "Americans distrust Mexican shading. The genius of American culture and its integrity come from fidelity to the light" (88). On the other hand, the shadowtext gives contour, if only in a dangerous, phallic, and fetishized manner. Ortega y Gasset's much cited definition of the polis in his 1930 *Revolt of the Masses* is apposite: "the most accurate definition of the *urbs* and the *polis* is very like the comic definition of a cannon. You take a hole, wrap some steel wire tightly around it" (151). In the border text, analogously, you would take a whole and wrap a steel fence along it. The military metaphor for this dark space is particularly apt, not only in terms of the United States's language of the "wars" on drugs and against undocumented aliens, but also in its evocation of a space that is both contained and at the same time associated, from the moment of its invented origin, with an othered bellicose nature. This latent violence is echoed even in the U.S. tourist imaginations, where Tijuana frequently figures as a sort of cinematic Wild West outpost, and in centrist Mexican conceptions, where it persists as a convenient trope for the provincial city full of violent men (Tijuana was where PRI presidential candidate Luis Donaldo Colosio was famously assassinated) and lawless women (its infamous place in the centrist imagination as a rattled prostitute of a town).

Tijuana border writing—and here we intentionally confuse writing *on* with writing *from*—is, furthermore, a peculiar kind of shadowtext, one projected simultaneously into an anticipated future: "avant garde," Nathan says; "cosmopolitan *mañana*" that is also and at the same time a refused past. The Tijuana Syndrome reflects those stereotypes about itself that each society has refused, while readmitting the stereotypes about the refused other; it also reflects the border as a well-known site of refusal—the literal and figurative dump for each society's urban, industrial, toxic, and sexual wastes. In one such formulation Tijuana is described an "inedible city" where "street vendors offer unclean enchantments" (Rodriguez, 92), capturing in this manner the image of a sexualized abundance of things and people (women) to chew and suck, which nevertheless must be refused. And yet, because the refused (repressed) always returns in some future moment, because the refuse is inextricably linked to the most personal and private details of modern life, dominant cultures' refusal is doomed to shadow itself, past and future. Trinh says: "If, despite their location, noun and verb inhabit the two very different and well-located worlds of designated and designator, the space between them remains a surreptitious site of movement and passage whose open, communal character makes exclusive belonging and long-term residence undesirable, if not impossible" (6). Who can live on a waste dump? Or in a cannon's mouth? Is it not the lure of "unclean enchantment" that draws a significant percentage of Tijuana's tourist industry to the city?

Metaphors rapidly get even more mixed but, curiously, continue to follow similar lines of argument, presenting variations on the theme of an abjected shadow other as projected future self. Writing from the U.S. side, Richard Rodriguez posits that "Tijuana is where Mexico comes to an end." Immediately following upon this statement he summarizes what he considers the Mexican centrist view of the northern border city: "People in Mexico City will tell you, if they have anything at all to say about Tijuana, that Tijuana is a city without history, a city without architecture, an American city" (83). He concludes that "taken as one, Tijuana and San Diego form the most fascinating new city in the world, a city of world-class irony" (106). Rodriguez's trajectory here is fascinating; Tijuana is at one and the same time "the end" (of Mexico) and the beginning of something else. Furthermore, Rodriguez does not dissent from the view of Tijuana he puts in the anonymous mouths of Mexico City's inhabitants, but he shadows and elaborates on it in relation to his own peculiar take as English-favoring, U.S-identified son of a Mexican father. From that point of view, in some respects like Rodriguez and his father, Tijuana is the shadow that defines Mexican national character by antinomy—unlike Mexico City with its long historical trajectory, its pyramids and skyscrapers, its absolute hegemony as the site of national culture, Tijuana has no history, no architecture, no claim on the national imagination. Rodriguez takes this catalogue of negatives and turns it into a positive attribute. Tijuana–San Diego (analogously with the gay American son of the macho Mexican man) is the model for a transcultured, transexualized identity: the city as rhetorical trope, the heartlands of po-mo irony.

Writing from Mexico City, Néstor García Canclini posits two different models of Tijuana, both of which enter into dialogue with Rodriguez, as again one dominant culture shadows itself and its complementary dominant culture counterpart in the bordertext. For García Canclini, Tijuana, along with New York City, represents "uno de los mayores laboratorios de la posmodernidad" (293) [one of the biggest laboratories of postmodernity (233)]. It is also, in an alternative metaphor, "la casa de toda la gente" [everyone's house]. Here too, as in Rodriguez's text, Tijuana is both exceptional and paradigmatic, both not-Mexico and globally transcendent. Tijuana is everyone's house precisely because in this formulation it is not a symbolic house at all, but rather a huge laboratory for aesthetic contemplation from outside, where scientists can do field work in postmodern reality effects. We suspect that John Welchman would categorize García Canclini's version of a border theory alongside the position he aligns with the Baudrillardian spectacle in which "'home' is thus evaporated" and the "'borderama' is vaunted . . . as the governing trope of the postmodern" ("The Philosophical Brothel," 175). Please note Welchman's appropriately San Diegan scare quotes as ironic commentaries on this archetypal First World po-mo position—like Nathan, and unlike either Rodriguez or García Canclini, he lives in the wasteheap of western civ, in the can(n)on's mouth, with all its attendant shadow rites and responsibilities.

Baudrillard, along with Lyotard and other luminaries of French high theory whose travels in America figure prominently in their analyses of the (post)modern condition, in fact do make important appearances in García Canclini's discussion of the Tijuana borderlands as a privileged site of postmodern production. His conceptualization of the region centers on the term *deterritorialization* (borrowed from Gilles Deleuze and Félix Guattari, though unattributed), is elaborated through reference to Michel de Certeau, finds support in Guillermo Gómez-Peña, turns to seminal quotes from Baudrillard and Lyotard, and concludes with reference to "mayo del 68 en París (también en Berlín, Roma, México, Berkeley)" (314–15) [May of '68 in Paris (also in Berlin, Rome, Mexico City, Berkeley)] (249–50). In the conjunction of, for example, Néstor García Canclini (Argentine scholar living in Mexico City) and Michel de Certeau (French scholar relocated in San Diego) we can readily see the complicities and alliances among various dominant cultural discursive practices and politics which determine the valences ascribed to particular cultural modes.

A quote from Michel de Certeau, "life consists of constantly crossing borders" (11), serves as García Canclini's opening into the assertion that Tijuana, along with New York City, is one of the two great laboratories of postmodernity. The essay from which García Canclini took the de Certeau quote, "Californie, un théâtre de passants," is an ambiguously located travel narrative in which text shadows text to a unusual degree. Written for a French audience upon de Certeau's return to France and French after two and a half years in San Diego, the article describes the author's Californian writing block and the release from that inability to write once back in the homeland, and does so through positioning itself with reference to yet another text, a poem in which California becomes an imaginary space (he might just as accurately have evoked Montalvo's splendid description of California in *Esplandián*):

> I have been in California for two and a half years. Up to this point I have abstained from writing about it. Back there, the sentences get lost in the Pacific's waves. On returning to France I have the impression that the lunar country from which I come cannot be introduced nor spoken about in the closed text of my Parisian villages. . . . Perhaps California must be described as a dream, in the style of Edgar Morin, in his California Journal, the poem of an imaginary country. ("Californie," 10)

Interestingly enough, de Certeau can only write about California from France, for a French audience that is incapable of understanding a place so foreign, approaching it metaphorically through a poem in which California becomes an imaginary country. If it is important to discover the direction of the guiding metaphor for the construction of border theory, then de Certeau's orientation is clearly eastward, back in Paris, where writing can occur, rather than in the too-real California that swallows up his commentary. Furthermore, he can only write about California as a certain kind of fictional effect, filtered through the metaphorical appropriations of poetic expression. It is also interesting to note that the dominant image he chooses to organize this discussion, "théâtre de passants," evokes U.S. California's most famously stereotypical association with a certain Hollywoodesque theatricalized play of identity, alongside Mexican California's stereotypical association with illegal migrants, who in their efforts to avoid the border patrol not only attempt surreptitious border crossings but also hope to "pass" as U.S. nationals. Certainly it is this multiply textually shadowed French appropriation of an imaginary country that García Canclini finds so postmodernly productive in his own reading of the border area. In this context, it is not surprising that the Argentine critic located in Mexico City comes to Tijuana through the French thinker and ends up, discursively at least, in Paris (or Berlin or Berkeley) in May 1968.

The purpose of this chapter is not to undertake an anthropological or ethnographic effort in the search for a genuinely locatable authentic fronterizo (artist/thinker), even as an elided shade haunting the dominant shadowings of the border as text,[2] but rather to signal the processes by which border theorization seems to require a transcultural dialogue between dominant cultural discourses in which the border culture is invented, projected as an imaginary space, and reread in the engagement between shadowtexts. To speak about the border in such a context is, as the Ortega y Gasset metaphor suggests, to empty it out, retaining the projected residue of a refused and powerful violence. It also, as de Certeau quite rightly recognized, "brings us back to a ubiquitous problem . . . Where does one speak? What can be said? But also, in the end: Where do we speak? This makes the problem directly political, because it makes an issue of the social—in other words, primarily repressive— function of learned culture" (*Heterologies*, 135). Tijuana can be both a battleground for this will to knowledge in the most traditional formulations and a place from which to speak otherwise (e.g., in a postmodern ironic mode); in either case, as de Certeau intuits, the competing models of discourse both operate from the premise that they speak from or against the time and place of a dominant culture.

But it is time to become more specific about the contours of this shadowtext, this obsessive object of discourse. Learned culture offers us several metaphoric points of departure for an indagation into the imaginary California, among which we highlight converging comments by

Richard Rodriguez (Mexican American), Néstor García Canclini (central Mexican), and Michel de Certeau (French). After this theoretical peregrination, we look to two creative artists from the border—María Novaro and Regina Swain—to complement the travelers' outlooks with those of native informants on the Tijuana scene.

## JOURNEY TO A LOST ISLAND

Over and over, the lost island imagery inherited from the earliest inventions/ representations of California returns, often in a contradictory fashion as a localizable spatial node with fluid temporal qualities. Tijuana is simultaneously represented as Mexico's disavowed past and its distopic future. Thus, for example, Rodriguez comments that "Tijuana and San Diego are not in the same historical time zone. . . . Papa crosses over into the twenty-first century; Mama raises the kids at the edge of the nineteenth century" (84, 93). Here, Tijuana—the space of women—is temporally and geographically marked off from the progressive future associated with the United States and with male endeavor. In another, more positively valenced version of this recurrent metaphor, de Certeau defines California as Europe's other: "For Californians . . . the American East is already Europe. The true internal division of the Western World is not the Atlantic Ocean but the Rockies and their deserts" ("Californie," 13). In this version, the mountains and deserts substitute for the ocean, creating cultural and temporal divisions that serve as convenient loci for imaginative projection.

## VISIT TO A WILD WEST MOVIE SET (MADE FOR GRINGOS)

"How does one depict the history of so unmonumental a city?" asks Richard Rodriguez early in the chapter of *Days of Obligation* focusing on Tijuana (86). Implicitly, we are asked to approve the postulate that the terms *city-history-monument* are cognate and inextricably connected. And yet it is clear that the absence of monumental architecture in this most visited of cities is a liability primarily for those visitors for whom tourism necessarily includes prescribed culture doses, so as to satisfy the nagging guilt that travel is supposed to broaden one's knowledge. The reinforcement of this connection between travel and learning history and the assuagement of tourist guilt readily leaps to the fore in the five-cities-in-seven-days tours of Europe, for example, or in group trips to central Mexico. In each case, "seeing the city" primarily involves instantly forgettable canned guides to large public structures. Yet, contradictorily, Tijuana is a heavily tourist-oriented city—though clearly not for the ideologically and ethically correct, monumental-historical tours. What to do?

Since there are no monuments to catch the eye, entrepreneurs construct a false nostalgic idea of the "old Mexico" for tourists, as this Tijuanan quoted by García Canclini indicates:

> Ante la falta de otro tipo de cosas, como en el sur, que hay pirámides, aquí no hay nada de eso . . . como que algo hay que inventarle a los gringos. . . . [T]ambién remite a este mito que traen los norteamericanos, que tiene que ver con cruzar la frontera hacia el pasado, hacia lo salvaje, hacia la onda de poder montar. (300)

> [Faced with the lack of other types of things, as there are in the south where there are pyramids, there is none of that here . . . as if something had to be invented for the gringos. . . . it also refers to the myth that North Americans bring with them, that has something to do with crossing the border into the past, into the wilderness, into the idea of being able to ride horseback.] (236)

As this businessman recognizes, tourists come to Tijuana not to see another, othered (monumental) history, but rather to travel into their own imaginary past, where—implicitly—men were white, women were cantina whores, and Mexico was the place evil bandidos hid out from the Wild West cowboys. This past, in turn, is projected into the nostalgic superiority of past-as-future where, for instance, on the famous Revolución strip, gringo men and gringa women can take turns getting photographed with zebra-painted donkeys so they can go home and tell all their friends about the truly tacky things contemporary Mexicans try to sell to savvy northamericans.

In Tijuana's notorious "zona norte," the Adelita Club (now with its own website!) stands in for the internet-aware sex clients as the handiest representation of this kind of created-authentic Mexican-ness, of a living culture read as if it were a movie set invented to respond to U.S. consumer dreams of the picturesque. One internet "researcher" into the region calls Adelita "pure South of the Border," and another client elaborates: "When the taxi dropped us off . . . we knew we weren't in Kansas anymore. This was the Mexico of the movies . . . steamy streets, food vendors everywhere, ladies more than everywhere." Still another writer describes it as "like walking into a brothel in some old Western." Interestingly enough, Adelita's clientele is mixed Mexican and United States, and if for the U.S. client the bar evokes the imaginary Wild West, for the Mexican client it creates a parallel but different image of a Revolutionary past ("Adelita" is, of course, one of the most instantly recognizable ballads of the Mexican Revolution, and one that specifically highlights the exploits of a famous soldadera).

The Mexican Revolution is, of course, one of the unrecognized and unstated backdrops to a fair amount of Wild West footage, just as the Revolutionary general Pancho Villa is the unnamed villain whenever Mexican bandidos appear to perturb the peace. In the shadowing of text upon text, the Wild West cowboy is an anglicized version of the Mexican immigrant vaquero (why else would blond men in movies have a diet based on beans and run around "lassooing" cows, horses, bad guys, and women?), back-projected onto a Tijuana that looks to U.S. tourists like a rundown version of a Hollywood film set.

BACK TO THE FUTURE IN MINNEAPOLIS (FOR MEXICANS)

Writing from Mexico City, culture critic Carlos Monsiváis reminds us that in traditional centrist discourse not only is the national identity firmly located in central Mexico, but so too is the imaginary projection of that identity. Thus, the capital city is associated both with the authentic repository of Mexico's past and with the progressive conception of Mexican future. The provinces become the repositories of unassimilated, chaotic partial identities along with a rejected, and implicitly inauthentic, past. Nevertheless, while Mexico City by its geographical location is somewhat insulated, the northern border states

> refrenda[n] a diario las limitaciones del localismo y de lo nacional. En los estados fronterizos las semejanzas son intensas: el shock cultural en algo compensado por la relativa abundancia de empleos; la ausencia certificada de tradiciones regionales y el hecho de que 'lo norteño típico' deriva directamente de la industria cultural; el uso oportunista y comercial del nacionalismo. (Monsiváis, "De la cultura mexicana," 202)

> [debate on a daily basis the limitations of localism and of the national. In the border states the similarities are intense: culture shock to some degree compensated by the relative abundance of employment, the certified

absence of regional traditions, and the fact that the "typical northerner" derives directly from cultural industry, the opportunistic and commercial use of nationalism.]

Still, in this mobile and continually transforming border redefinition of the national future lies precisely those elements of national restructuring that central Mexico needs to refuse in order to maintain primacy of its own vision of the national identity: "The manager of one assembly plant by the airport predicts that all of Mexico will soon look like Tijuana. . . . Tijuana is an industrial park on the outskirts of Minneapolis" (Rodriguez, 94). Uncannily, it is some version of Minneapolis that crystallizes Mexico City's technocratic imaginings about the centrist-based progressive future, but in that dominant discourse both industrial Tijuana and the U.S. Midwest need to be carefully expelled.

TOURING MIGRANT ZONES

Tijuana is a magnet for workers from other, poorer states, some of whom come to live permanently in Tijuana, others who come with the hope of crossing over into the United States. It is, thus, a migrant zone in two senses, as people migrate to and migrate through the city. These migrant zones are sharply divided by gender. Thus, for example, 70 percent of maquiladora workers are internal migrants from other parts of Mexico; 80–90 percent are women; and worker-hiring efforts are concentrated on single women between the ages of 16 and 24. Maquiladora hiring strategies "target a category of workers whose age and gender ensure a consistent lack of workplace experience. This strategy facilitates their replacement without creating serious labor problems" (Iglesias Prieto, *Beautiful Flowers of the Maquiladora,* 36). Young women are encouraged to migrate to Tijuana and, once there, to migrate in and out of the labor market, in and out of the various assembly plants. A certain "look" is promoted by employers, as witnessed by the Queen of the Maquiladora beauty contests (74–76), consistent with the unstated goals of machining young women as available objects for male consumption.

On the other hand, 94.4 percent of the immigrants to the United States are men, concentrated particularly in the age group from 25 to 34 years old. Here, too, the correct "look" is essential, if for other reasons:

> Border patrol agents are only supposed to stop you on the street if they can put into words why they think you act or look illegal. . . . But their decisions about who's got the Look of acceptable citizenship can be

pretty arbitrary. . . . The dilemma creates self-doubt and image anxiety in mojados and citizens alike. . . . It's even more bizarre to conceptualize dressing legally. (Nathan, 25)

Young men, too, are machined—but for the U.S. labor market.

Michel de Certeau, writing from the other side of the other border (across the line, across the Rockies and the deserts, in France), highlights the metaphor of migration as the dominant strand in his elaboration of Californian identity. In his case, however, and despite his recent stay in San Diego, the metaphor of migration and movement clearly focuses on the migration from east to west rather than south to north. He emphasizes the role of cars, mobility in jobs, and second-hand books in defining the Californian "passant," points to credit cards and driver's licenses as replacements for the familiar French "carte d'identité," and highlights jogging (rather than, say, stoop work in fields) as his favored image of physical side of migration:

> One never ceases passing from one history to another, from one language to another, and from one region to another. The entire society is passing. In this respect, jogging is only the physical metaphor of a daily activity. . . . But immigration is a more internal experience, one that characterizes Californian socializing. ("Californie," 11, 14)

SIDETRIP THROUGH "DISNEY CALCUTTA"

Once again, it is Richard Rodriguez who crystallizes this modality, in transferring one of the most readily available images of commercialized utopia from one side of the border to the other: "It is more fun, perhaps, to approach Revolución with adolescent preconceptions of lurid possibility. Marrakesh. Bangkok. . . . A quick shot of the foreign. Unmetered taxis. Ultramontane tongue. Disney Calcutta" (82). There is, of course, an unintended irony or bilingual pun in the conjunction of fun-revolution-possibility, as well as the intentional or unconscious shadowing of another well-known traveler from the United States who went into Mexico searching for the lurid potential of an earlier utopian project. We refer here to the unsolved mystery of the nineteenth-century soldier, journalist, and short story writer Ambrose Bierce, who, after announcing his intention to tour South America, crossed the border, joined Pancho Villa, disappeared into the chaos of the Mexican Revolution, and never returned. In one of his last letters Bierce writes:

I go away tomorrow for a long time, so this is only to say good-bye. I think there is nothing else worth saying; therefore you will naturally expect a long letter. What an intolerable world this would be if we said nothing but what is worth saying! And did nothing foolish—like going into Mexico and South America.

Good-bye—if you hear of my being stood up against a Mexican stone wall and shot to rags please know I think that a pretty good way to depart this life. It beats old age, disease, or falling down the cellar stairs. To be a Gringo in Mexico—ah, that is euthanasia! (196–97)

Like Bierce, Rodriguez theatricalizes a trip into Mexico as a journey from staid normality (and middle-class morality) into a revolutionary realm of an interestingly degraded utopic potential. Bierce calls it "euthanasia"; for Rodriguez it is "Disney Calcutta." Like the Wild West film set, Rodriguez's Disney Calcutta evokes an artificial and contained space, though the film set involves a trip to one's own imaginary past while Disneyland evokes a commercialized dream of the future. In each case, U.S. popular-culture dreams are exoticized and projected onto another and foreign space, one that reaches out to enable them through skewed and commercialized shadowings of its own: Disney, but reimagined in Calcutta.

Michel de Certeau also evokes Disney as a metaphor for understanding his Californian theater. Putting together two large public spaces, he says of Disneyland and supermarkets, in the words we quoted as the epigraph to this chapter: "These are the spaces that tend to make one believe that the rest of Californian life is not a fiction" ("Californie," 17). A curious twist to this phrasing suggests once again that California itself and life in California are, in fact, irremediably fictitious, and that only encounters with hyper-real public commercial utopias ameliorate this pervasive imaginary quality. While he recognizes and underlines the utopic quality of the Disneyland experience—and remember, he includes California supermarkets as a kind of Disneyland—the primary function of this real pseudo-utopia in de Certeau's analysis is not to secularize a semi-religious attachment to the idea of California as Earthly Paradise, but rather to signal commodification as its central and most significant mode of operation.

Both García Canclini and Monsiváis ask about methodologies for associating popular culture with national identity formation. Both writers also signal the danger and opportunity involved in the material and commercial qualities of deploying certain theatricalized roles as salable iconic representations: what Celeste Olalquiaga in her essay on "Vulture Culture" calls "the displacement of referentiality by simulation" and the "valorization of surface, immediate gratification, and highly iconographic codes over the tradition of depth, contemplation, and symbolic abstraction" (92, 94). Both García Canclini and Monsiváis register and discuss the dominant Mexican culture's concern that a contaminated, Disneyfied version of popular culture will obstruct access to real national culture, and stifle progress. Among the oppositions these authors set up between Mexico and the First World, they signal the still-current debates around the poles of colonizer versus colonized and cosmopolitanism versus nationalism. In a parallel manner, Monsiváis elaborates on the binary oppositions still undergirding official national understandings of the conflict between central Mexico and the provinces. In this view, the conflict capital versus province carries with it the baggage of civilization versus barbarism, culture versus desolation, national consolidation versus aborted history. New complicating factors make these dichotomies harder and harder to maintain; both authors point to demographic explosion, industrial development extending into formerly isolated zones, the influence of mass media, creeping Americanization "tan temida desde la ingenuidad y tan sacralizada desde el consumo" [so feared by the ingenuous and so sacralized from the point of view of consumption] (Monsiváis, 201), and, in more general terms, the "deslocalización de los productos simbólicos por la electrónica y la telemática, el uso de satélites y computadoras en la difusión cultural" (García Canclini, 289) [the delocalization of symbolic products by electronics and telematics, and the use of satellites and computers in cultural diffusion] (229).

Briefly, then, Tijuana becomes the space where popular-culture icons of Mexicanness can be reified, refried, and sold, so long as these iconic representations also concatenate with U.S. cultural stereotypes of Mexican identity in their Disneyfied variations. Mexican centrist culture fears border contamination; Tijuana becomes the realm of fearful possibility and of rejected affinities. Tourists, on the other hand, want to go across the border to see the "real" Mexico, as long as the real Mexico looks and sounds like a down-market Speedy González.

Yet, by holding in abeyance these two texts and their shadow others, by representing for both cultures the place of opportunity and the site of refusal, Tijuana also slips outside the norming processes of popular-culture absorption. As Michel de Certeau notes, "'Popular culture' presupposes an unavowed operation. Before being studied, it had to be censored. Only after its danger had been eliminated did it become an object of interest" (*Heterologies*, 119). He concludes: "This takes us to the root of the problem: popular culture can only be grasped in the process of vanishing. . . . These blank spots outline a geography of the forgotten. They trace the negative silhouette of the problematics displayed on black and white in scholarly books" (131). California, no matter how imaginarily constructed, no matter how Disneyfied in the popular and official imaginations, never quite disappears entirely; its geography is and has from the beginning been blurred but always sited on the maps.

CITY OF WOMEN

Tijuana almost too neatly conflates symbolic geographic and moral exclusions from the healthy body of the state. Most potently, Tijuana becomes a powerful shadowtext defining the whole of Mexico as a passive whore to be fucked over: "Mexico lay down and the gringo paid in the morning" (Rodriguez, 88). Rodriguez's phrase succinctly captures U.S. male fantasy as grounded in racist misogyny and reinforced in a gendered structural inequality between nations, while at the same time it echoes a Mexican inferiority complex about its relation to the United States as most strikingly captured in Mexican misogyny about traitorous females who sleep with conquerors—even if payback time eventually rolls around.

There is a strong note of (postmodern?) ironic *ubi sunt* in Richard Rodriguez's introduction to Tijuana as he describes his arrival in that city. Though he imagines the city as "a metropolis crouched behind a hootchy-kootch curtain" (81), his trip through the *zona norte* fails to live up to its advance billing:

> Mexican men loiter outside the doors of open bars. From within come stale blasts of American rock. Is this all that is left of the fleshpots of T.J.? We are a generation removed from that other city, . . . a succubus that could take [American men] as far as they wanted to go. At the turn of the century . . . there were whores and there was gambling and there was drink. (87)

Strikingly enough, Rodriguez's plaintive voicing of his disillusionment involves both Mexican men and American rock, which have presumably and unforgivably replaced American men and Mexican whores. García Canclini marks a similar change and dates the reformation of the old image to a recent shift in public perception:

> Desde principios de siglo hasta hace unos quince años, Tijuana había sido conocida por un casino . . . , cabarets, dancing halls, liquor stores a donde los norteamericanos llegaban para eludir las prohibiciones sexuales. (294)

> [From the beginning of the century until fifteen years ago, Tijuana was known for a casino . . . , cabarets, dance halls, and liquor stores where North Americans came to elude their country's prohibitions on sex.] (234)

In each case, the illicit relations between U.S. men and Tijuanan women are relegated to the past. Furthermore, regardless of the effects of industrialization and modernization that have changed the face of the city, both Rodriguez and García Canclini find it necessary to remind their readers of the recent past, if only to tell us that this past is no longer representative of contemporary reality. In effect, then, both writers have found an answer to Rodriguez's question (cited earlier) on how to write the history of so unmonumental a city; they set up a contrast between the distanced and romanticized calumny that overlays upon the city through the images of the past as a depraved female and the contrasting image of macho modern industry. The rattled or vampiric whore becomes the rejected image that must be obsessively called to memory along with the abjuration that it is no longer either accurate or adequate.

Interestingly enough, in this manner, the "unhistorical" Tijuana offers a prominent example of the operations of centrist historical discourse that have been so ably dissected by Benedict Anderson, although Anderson's work develops without the necessary additional nuance of attention to history's gender politics: "Having to 'have already forgotten' tragedies of which one needs unceasingly to be 'reminded' turns out to be a characteristic device in the later construction of national genealogies" (201). Unsurprisingly, in the context of Anderson's observation, Rodriguez's other metaphors for Tijuana also bring up remembered/

forgotten peoples that found national genealogical projects: Tijuana is "silent as a Trojan horse, inevitable as a flotilla of boat people" (106).

Ann Laura Stoler would add to this analysis a reminder of the significance of gender politics in the construction of these historical models, and John Welchman's admirable overview of the "philosophical brothel" in western thought helps bring some of these imaginary overlays together:

> Remembering Derrida's etymological association of the border, the plank, and brothel, Picasso's image *[Demoiselles D'Avignon]* can be read as an arrest and incarnation of the non-processional border, the purest moment of modernist border fetishism. This brothel/border is a place of violence and consumption which objectifies and consumes both women and others. It is this *bordello* that is the scene of the masculinist metaphorics of war and combat, of the appropriative transplantation of so-called primitive faces onto the already fractured bodies of the so-seen deviant women. It is here that the western fantasies of philosophy, the non-western other, and sexual violence converge on the territory of the border. (Welchman, 180)

Tijuana speaks most allegorically, and most clearly, to its old image as an abjected feminine presence, and it is the continuing resonance of this image that must and cannot be forgotten which has motivated José Guadalupe Osuna Milán and the other members of the Tijuana municipal council to take the extraordinary step of attempting to register "Tijuana" as a trademark name. Like the Wild West image, the vampiric whore meets barely articulated needs that derive from outside the municipal limits by which U.S. pornographic fantasies can be safely projected across the border onto an exoticized other. Tijuana has "a more graceful sense of universal corruption," says Rodriguez (90); and while graft is a painful reality for Mexican nationals struggling day after day to live and raise their families, "graceful universal corruption" has an exotic and erotic attraction for the gringo tourist. In the good old/bad old days evoked by both Rodriguez and García Canclini there were plenty of whores/succubi to trap and victimize innocent U.S. men into the sinful fleshpots of an entire city given over to decadence; now, in contrast and by a pathetic devolution, Mexican men are corrupted by American rock—a point also made by García Canclini in his lucid reading of the ambiguities infesting the street sign, "Rock en tu idioma los jueves"

(298–99) [Rock in your language on Thursdays] (237). There is a loss of poetic resonance and erotic force in the shift from fleshpots to American rock, from elegant whores to loitering Mexican men.

Objectively speaking, of course, the closing of the Agua Caliente casino during the Lázaro Cárdenas administration only symbolically brought an end to all that glamorous corruption. In Tijuana today there are estimated to be 15,000 women working in prostitution, on the street in some sectors, as well as in 210 nightclub/brothels (Castillo, Rangel Gómez, and Delgado, 403). In the bars and streets of Tijuana at least two dominant (United States, Mexico) and two marginalized (underclass) versions of male and female stereotypes meet in the grating of various sets of cultural mores against each other. When we try to understand the concrete situation of real women in that particular city, we are thrown back upon ambiguously framed narratives about lives that implicitly or explicitly rub up against all these social, theoretical, cultural, historical frames in a sometimes complicitous, often contestatory manner. To talk about Tijuana involves a complex history in which all of these magic signs, discourses, practices, and struggles are filtered through a particular border-site with its own metaphorical overlay of feminization and abjection, its own legal history, its own racially inflected past and present, its own biculturally determined exchanges. Traditional fictional representations of Tijuana echo these themes obsessively as well, and in the final section of this chapter we look at Tijuana through two representative fictional texts from different genres and perspectives: María Novaro's film; and Regina Swain's collection of short stories.

María Novaro's film, *El jardín del Edén* (1994, The garden of Eden)— tellingly, in terms of a practice of border-crossing work, a joint Mexico-Quebec coproduction—opened to mixed reviews in Mexico, but in the United States has been very favorably received by U.S. Chicano/a scholars, where it has been interpreted as important contribution to the "nuevo cine mexicano" as well as a significant shift of perspective on "immigration movies" and on the hackneyed representation of Tijuana–San Diego. For David Maciel and Rosa García-Acevedo, however, *El jardín del Edén* "because of [its] structure and individuality, does not fall into the classification of genre films, but rather under the concept of *auteur*." (184). In this respect, Novaro speaks to the tradition, but with an individual voice. At the same time, as Claire Fox notes, "the Mexican and Canadian [Quebecois] anti-imperialist politics that inform this feature make its portrayal of the border richly complex" (9). Despite this complexity (and we agree with Fox on this point) in this film Tijuana once again becomes flattened out as the standard bearer for "a borderless continent" to follow the argument of Claire Fox (9), or as the utopic zone familiar to us from so many studies done by Chicano/a and postmodern theorists. As Fox reminds us in her lucid analysis, "this is a predominantly celebratory view of border culture that was popularized on the eve of free trade by artists such as Guillermo Gómez-Peña (who, not surprisingly, has a cameo in the movie) and progressive academics such as Néstor García Canclini" (10–11).

Despite these somewhat obvious flaws, *El jardín del Edén* takes seriously its ethical mission of regrounding a cinematic tradition of stereotyped images of the border in general, and of Tijuana and its women in particular, and subverts them through setting in motion a rich and diverse set of characters whose destinies crisscross in this border city. In earlier films, Tijuana's women (and border women in general) were subjected to the male directors' and/or scriptwriters' wishes, where women's roles were almost exclusively limited to eye candy. Consequently, movies about the border would always be defined by melodramatic plots set in the same limited locales, and we would always see filmic portrayals of prostitutes, thieves, pimps, exotic dancers, drug dealers, smugglers, or their almost-as-sensational opposites: *mater admirabilis,* redeemed prostitutes, or rehabilitated dealers and smugglers. In her film, Novaro presents a handful of women from different ethnicities, nationalities, class, and personal interests sharing the same geopolitical space and their everyday life. By doing this, Novaro not only deconstructs the paradigm border = brothel but also "attempts an unconventional and creative approach to the immigration question" (Maciel and García-Acevedo, 184). Moreover, as Fox notes, the film offers anything but a comfortable viewing experience for an audience attuned to melodrama; instead, Novaro's "is a kaleidoscopic world of mutually unintelligible linguistic registers and sexy, surreal juxtapositions" (10).

Reviewers from the Mexican side celebrated it as an excellent film where Tijuana, finally, is not portrayed as in the tired clichés of the whorehouse or the "wild west."[3] Isabel Arredondo sees the film as a celebration of feminine images that had been introduced in other Novaro films. Likewise, the image of Tijuana in *El jardín del Edén* resists that earlier landscape presented in innumerable Hollywood or national Mexican films where, as we noted earlier, Tijuana was the city of chaos and damnation or, in Tim Girven's words, "Hollywood's heterotopia."[4] One of Novaro's most signal achievements is that Tijuana in her film is no longer Hollywood-identified at all, but, rather, a nuanced and complicated rereading of the prelapsarian garden of Eden.

Other Mexican readings focus on the aesthetic side of the film but criticize the stereotypes and the lack of representation of the "real" people from the border and their everyday life.[5] These readings suggest that one of the most important contributions of the film is to offer a dynamic view of the U.S.-Mexico border and its themes. Because the film presents a balance regarding what many consider stereotypes alongside depictions of "real life," these differing and often contradictory readings are easily understandable. The film shows a glimpse into the lives of a Chicana and her daughter (Liz and Lupita); two Anglo siblings (Jane and Frank); a family from Mexico City (recently widowed Serena, and her children Julián, Luis, and Paloma); an immigrant from Zacatecas (Felipe); a group of Huave Indians (Margarita and her fellow coworkers); and the "token" local (Juana). In that same context the movie projects the way in which Mexican border cities have been settled from the beginning: through national and international migrant flows.

The most visible and most-highly debated topic in the film is that of immigration, since the majority of the characters coincide in Tijuana with this intent. But for María Herrera-Sobek, although the movie is "one of the most artistic films belonging to the undocumented Mexican immigrant film genre . . . , the genre has not achieved its full potential" ("Corrido as Hypertext," 243). And perhaps the film is not fully realized in this sense because the undocumented Mexican immigrant is not the main character, nor does his story lead the plot. At the same time, and despite the focus on this question, for Mexican audiences from the borderlands Novaro's point of view on migration and emigration continues to be derived from central Mexico's dominant cultural perspective without a more nuanced or profound understanding of the phenomenon. From the perspective of the Mexican border dweller, Novaro's vision slips all too easily into a Gómez-Peña-like construction in which the prospective undocumented worker, Felipe, turns into a playful, funny, Don Juan figure. These characteristics help displace the real problematic of the migrant worker, and at the same time they effectively erase the images of his mother and brother and their struggles on their farm in Zacatecas, replacing them with a more intense focus on the Tijuana scenes with Julián and Jane. In this sense, Novaro's project of creating a film based on and organized around the theoretical concepts of postmodernity falls short with the border audience, precisely because these concepts, as we noted in the introduction, dissolve their own ethnographies. Thus it is, paradoxically, the attempt to represent the dynamism and change typical of postmodern urban life that causes the border viewers to feel defrauded, for while they applaud the complication of the image of Tijuana beyond hoary stereotypes about the brothel, the Wild West, and the life-threatening border crossing, the film does not yet accurately represent "the social realities of immigrants crossing the border and their work experiences, [nor] the individual human complexity of 'being' a Mexican immigrant" (Maciel and García-Acevedo, 184).

In *El jardín del Edén* Montalvo's imaginary California is subverted; while Novaro's Tijuana is indeed a city populated by women "sin que algún varón entre ellas hubiese," they are not at all the kind of women Montalvo had imagined. Serena has just lost her husband; Liz is divorced; Jane oscillates between an affair with Felipe and one with Margarita; and Juana is a single woman. The fabulous and incomprehensible sixteenth-century construction transforms itself into a space in which women of different races and ethnic backgrounds, different aspirations and professions, cross paths and rub along with each other. No longer are we dealing with feminine images marked with Montalvo's exoticism or the stigma attaching to nineteenth- and twentieth-century imaginary figurations, but rather these are women of our time, with their own problematic existences.

Novaro's film does slip into stereotype at times, however. For example, *El jardín del Edén*'s portrayal of the gringa precisely fits the well-known structure of the dumb, friendly blonde woman who is totally enthralled by the exotic otherness of the border. This is the case with Jane, a "typical gringa" who arrives in Tijuana looking for "her voice." Jane encounters aestheticized versions of typical Mexicans, especially indigenous women, like the Huave woman Margarita from the restaurant El pescado mojado and the bird seller in the penultimate scene in the movie. Jane also encarnates the concept of "Alliance for Progress," as she stands ready and willing to help the "Third World natives" in their struggle for economic stability, even at the risk of falling into prison. For example, she helps Margarita leave the restaurant and takes her to Rosarito so she can "earn dollars" from the Americans that live in that town. And she takes Felipe and Julián illegally across the border in the trunk of a car which she purchased on the spot precisely for this purpose.

Through her portrayal of Liz, Novaro reelaborates a familiar and much-used image in Mexican film with respect to Chicanos/as: that of the lack of fit with Mexico. Novaro rearticulates Mexican interpretations of filmic Chicanas such as María del Consuelo from *Espaldas Mojadas* (1953); Alice from *Los desarraigados* (1958 and 1975) or Lupe from *Acá las tortas* (1951), among many other similar films. These movies typically show the Chicana as a woman from the lower middle class, who has rejected anything Mexican (traditions, language, culture, people). In these older depictions, characters like Lupe and Alice buy into the rhetoric of assimilation with the U.S. dominant culture, and María del Consuelo lives in a permanent identity conflict because she is marked as a "pocha." María del Consuelo ultimately resolves this conflict in the approved Mexican manner; she decides to assume a Mexican identity, move to Mexico, and marry a Mexican man. In addition, all these women exist at all times in relation to, and dependent upon, a man: father, husband, boyfriend, lover. In contrast, Novaro is very careful to avoid falling into another cliché about the Chicana's fatal attraction to affairs with Mexican men. Liz retains her sexual autonomy; despite her obvious sensuality, she decides not to pursue a closer relation with Felipe.

Liz is a Chicana artist who appears in the movie for the first time while she is setting up an exhibition in the Tijuana Cultural Center (Centro Cultural Tijuana or CECUT). Later, we learn that she works on "lo tocante al arte chicano y sus videos alternativos" [things related to Chicano art and alternative video]. A Chicana intellectual, her characterization suggests she has a university career and (probably) a subsidy to conduct research in Mexico. In the juxtaposition of these characters, we can see Novaro's complication of the old "us/them" dichotomy found in earlier depictions of Chicanas and gringas in Mexico; she explores the lack of a connection with Mexico through the lens of a personal and intimate search rather than a quest imposed by others. Here there is a psychological reflection about ancestry; Liz is searching for a connection "con [sus] abuelitos" [with her grandparents]. In addition to her desired reconnection with indigenous Mexico, Liz also wants to reconnect with the language, and the film marks her frustration with her inability to speak Spanish correctly. In this respect, she retraces a common narrative in Mexican-Chicana discussions which frequently point to the use of "corrupted" Spanish or Spanglish as one of the principal vectors by which (central) Mexicans heap scorn upon Chicanos.[6]

Novaro's film marks this conflict as one of the repeated subtexts in the background of the movie, and the film as a whole is subtly constructed so as to allow the audience to freely position ourselves as "us" or "them," to elect one language over the other or give our tacit support to the use of Spanglish. Thus, for example, at one point the viewer hears the voice of Gómez-Peña coming from a television, with his characteristic exaggeration of his Spanish accent on speaking English: "I speak Spanish therefore you hate me; I speak English therefore they hate me; I speak Spanish . . ." and the sound fades as Jane and Liz greet each other. At the same time, the subtitles in Spanish that appear on the screen while Gómez-Peña is speaking are interrupted after his Spanglish commentary and switch to the translation of the greetings between the two characters. María Herrera-Sobek has also commented on this point in the film, and observes: "when she [Liz] acknowledges her inability to be fluent in Spanish and speaks in a mixture of Spanish and English the song 'Hey baby qué pasó' is played. The song, rendered in a mixture of Spanish and English, reiterates the Spanglish theme introduced by Liz" ("Corrido," 242). One further point: there is a striking displacement of this typical narrative deriving from a centrist gesture of looking down on returning or visiting Chicanos/as, to a confrontation about language that is inaccurately located on the border. In Novaro's film it is always Juana, the token Tijuanense, who corrects Liz's Spanish, when more correctly the prejudice about Chicano Spanish reflects a central Mexican, rather than a border, concern.

Serena is another of the atypical (in the traditional U.S. and Mexican film history) women who appear in the filmic space of Tijuana. She arrives from Mexico City looking for economic stability for herself and her children, as she has just lost her husband. With this character we can trace two important ruptures with the hegemonic Mexican cultural discourse. On the one hand, Novaro presents what is now a well-known social phenomenon documenting the migratory pattern that since 1985 has brought large numbers of internal migrants to the border area. These internal migrants have been attracted especially to Juárez and Tijuana, drawn by the combination of the push-pull factors relating to the destruction of their homes in the 1985 Mexico City earthquake and the growing opportunities provided by the maquiladora industry in the border area. In this respect, Tijuana no longer represents the urban abject, the blight on Mexico's otherwise pristine reputation, but rather an attractive and prosperous city, especially for the poorer segments of the population, who were never able to recover from the economic crisis of 1982. On the other hand, Serena represents a different type of woman from Montalvo's Amazons or the mature widow of previous border films. In exact contrast to the typical representation of border women in films like *Aventurera* (1949), where Rosaura, after becoming widowed, finds herself running a brothel in Juárez, Serena has a professional career and lives from it successfully. She opens a photographic studio and is able to support herself and her children from the proceeds. Here Novaro complicates the traditional picture of the mother-widow by suggesting the possibility of a full life, including a relationship with another man. This aspect is not well developed in the film—perhaps because Gabriela Roel's acting is undistinguished—but there are hints of a possible relationship with Frank, Liz's brother, although, like the relation between Jane and Felipe mentioned earlier, the hint never comes to fruition in the film.

One of the most important and pervasive image structures in the film can be accessed through Novaro's allusions to popular culture. Throughout the movie we are introduced to numerous typical images: the Virgin of Guadalupe seen through a taxi window or tattooed on the arm of a low-rider, the low-rider parade itself, the popular "quebraditas" in a dance party, the "corridos" that serve as background music to present characters or themes. One of the most salient of these images is the venerated figure of Juan Soldado, the "santito" associated with Tijuana, who receives a credit line at the end of the movie "por habernos permitido terminar la película" [for having allowed us to finish this film]. There are two potential readings for this insistence on specific popular-culture icons. One would emphasize these elements in the context of the dominant culture discourse asserting straightforwardly the familiar cliché that in Tijuana (and on the northern border in general) there is no Culture; the other would concern itself precisely with the reverse reading, by recognizing and authorizing these popular-culture expressions. Both readings hold a double edge, one by reaffirming the national stereotype of the "cultural desert" and the other by leading us to believe that, as always, any kind of cultural manifestation in Mexico exists only to the degree that it has already been evaluated and accepted by the center.

Here the figure of Juan Soldado holds particular interest. By acknowledging this border figure as an integral part of the narrative, Novaro implicitly displaces the more obvious alternative patron: the Virgin of Guadalupe. It is an interesting move on her part. The Virgin of Guadalupe has a power and a presence in general Mexican culture that a marginal figure in the cultural-religious canon like the 100 percent Tijuanenese Juan Soldado can never hope to achieve; likewise, the Virgin has an important cultural signification among both Chicana and Mexican intellectuals. This use of the Tijuana icon, and relative downplaying of the Virgin, could signal María Novaro's emphasis on certain canonical formulations that are, or should be, displaced or rearticulated so as to take into consideration formerly marginalized discourses that are beginning to gain a presence and a voice in the national consciousness.

The play between popular- and high-culture images occurs throughout the film in the counterpoint, for example, of the exhibition in CECUT, Gómez-Peña's videos, Iturbide's photographs, intertextual references to the paintings of Frida Kahlo, the "intelectual sonido de las ballenas" [intellectual sound of the whales], the references to Milton, the use of dictionaries, the presence of indigenous languages without translation, and the constant dialogue between artistic and commercial photography on the one hand and between photography and film on the other. These are cultural elements that simply coexist in the film, as a play of images in space, without any explicit ideological stance or critical intent.

Novaro's Tijuana, at the same time, rearticulates the Tijuana of Richard Rodriguez, of Sanson d'Abbeville, Paul Theroux, and José Vasconcelos. The famous topic of nightlife on Revolución transforms itself in this film. Acting against the persistent background consciousness of the nightclubs and the evening activities on Revolución Avenue so typical of other discussions of the city, Novaro takes us to different sites in the city and focuses on activities during the day. The night scenes, in fact, are minimized. The camera takes us on a tour of the downtown streets, stops in on the peripheral suburbs, continues through the Zona del Río, stops in at the Plaza de Toros and CECUT, and, almost as an afterthought and only for about a minute, Revolución Avenue by day and by night. It is also important that in her nighttime scene, Novaro focuses exclusively on the callers outside the nightclubs and their invitations to passersby to come into the cabaret or discotheque where they work. At no point in this short nighttime scene does Novaro focus on any women whatsoever, except for the face of Serena, who is nervously seeking her son Julián throughout the city.

One place that stands out in the film is the borderline between Mexico and the United States, including the dike in the suburb of Playas de Tijuana abutting on the international boundary line, and the section of the border near the lighthouse where previously there had been no fence, no metal divider, and where at Border State Park families from both sides of the border were once able to meet and picnic. In this space, Novaro narrates the story of "nameless immigrants waiting for the opportunity to cross to the American side at night" (Maciel and García-Acevedo, 184), as well as part of Felipe's tale. This territorial space underscores the "drama" of the migrant worker, as Maciel and García-Acevedo call it in their analysis of the first scene in the film, in which U.S. Border Patrol agents return attempted migrants back to the Mexican side of the border. We would like to focus briefly on this scene of exchange, and on the way in which Novaro projects the figure of the migrant and of the border agents.

Mexican audiences tend to squirm uncomfortably at Novaro's mostly sympathetic depiction of the U.S. Border Patrol. For example, in the first scene, several agents intercept a group of Mexicans who are attempting to cross over into the United States and return them to the Mexican side of the border. While they are crossing, the Mexicans throw stones and mock the U.S. agents, while the patrolmen respond in heavily accented, broken gringo Spanish: "adiós amigos, see you tomorrow, vaya con Díos." In another scene, the camera focuses on two U.S. patrolmen who are sitting on the U.S. side of the border watching a group of children as they play baseball on the Mexican side. When Serena's son Luis hits a home run, the border patrolmen jump up and down and scream just as loudly as the Mexican fans on the other side. These depictions, while from the Mexican side tend to undercut the sinister stereotype of the border patrol, show a human face while also leaching away their power and their mystery. The scene also gives evidence for the image of the "good Samaritan" that the U.S. dominant culture wants to project, especially as articulated by people like Silvestre Reyes, the former head of the border patrol in El Paso and the key figure in Operation Blockade and Operation Hold the Line. At the same time, of course, Novaro's sympathetic portrayal erases the very real violations of human rights, the rough treatment and the deaths of undocumented migrant workers at the hands of border patrol agents throughout the years.

The migrants' image of the border patrol appears in the film in a conversation that occurs precisely at the borderline, among a group of people who are deciding whether or not to chance crossing the border. In this conversation, one of the most important elements is the Mexican cultural perception of Chicano otherness, a discourse that permeates all social strata in different ways:

"No, si son más cabrones los que se ven como nosotros."

"Todos son iguales de cabrones."

"No se crea, si hay unos que hasta le dicen a uno cuándo correr."

"Los más cabrones son los texanos y ahora han traído mucho texano."

["The ones who look like us are the biggest assholes."

"They're all just as bad."

"Don't believe it. Some of them will even tell you when it's OK to run."

"The worst assholes are the Texans, and they've been bringing in a lot of Texans lately."]

In this exchange of impressions we can see, in addition to a clear anti-Chicano sentiment, two distinct variations: "todos son unos cabrones" and "los texanos son los más cabrones" versus "unos nos dicen cuándo correr." Here the general perception of the migrant workers matches that of Mexican culture in general: the members of "la migra" as arbitrary and abusive. Linked to this point is a general sense that some of the agents are more corrupt than others, or more sympathetic to the Mexicans' plight. This feeling is captured in the voice of the character who comments, "No se crea, si hay unos que le dicen a uno cuándo correr." In context, however, it becomes clear that his observation directly subverts the image of the Silvestre Reyes–type "good Samaritan." The agents who are letting some people through not only are not complying with their duties with respect to Operation Hold the Line, they are also part of a network of corruption and trafficking in undocumented workers that is seldom if ever discussed on the U.S. side of the border because of a widespread U.S. preference to see their officials as incorruptible.

In this migrant-migra relation the audience is also exposed to a far more ludic interpretation of the hazards of border crossing than in previous films. In *El jardín del Edén* there is a marked vigilance on the part of the migrants with respect to the U.S. agents. Some migrants serve as sentries, subverting the border agents on the other side by patiently watching for their moments of inattention so as to cross the line and lose themselves in the United States. At the same time, when the prospective migrants call attention to themselves by openly making fun of the patrolmen, yelling at them and throwing stones, we can see an inversion of the stereotypical pattern of the passive, fearful migrant up against the powerful border patrol. In this sense we can begin to imagine a rearticulation of the migrant worker confronting the aggressive discourse of the U.S. politics with respect to Mexico and intervening, at least minimally, in the asymmetrical relations between the two countries that are clearly pointed up in the physical presence of the wall and the constant patrol presence. This response to—and lack of respect for—U.S. authority is reflected in the fact that both the migrants and the patrolmen occupy the same space and are placed in the same position: each makes fun of the other, each is aware of the positional nature of their exchanges, and each knows that it is a kind of game that takes place to some extent outside of dominant culture expectations and requirements. Furthermore, as María Herrera-Sobek adds, "each participant knows that it really doesn't matter who wins because the game will continue to be played indefinitely" (*Northward Bound*, 211).

Each of the cultural theories, autographical notes, and films focusing on Tijuana that we have examined above includes an awareness of two dominant cultural discourses—that of the United States and that of central Mexico—as well as of the most common stereotypes that each of these dominant cultures has created about the other. As we put these discourses and stereotypes into relation with each other, they come to shadow each other with varying degrees of intensity, in their discussion of the discursive equivalent of the no man's land: the fetishized and abjected border other. However, María Novaro in *El jardín del Edén* applies "an important aspect of cultural studies, which is that it does not dismiss cultural clichés and stereotypes in a search for authenticity and more original and powerful cultural production" (Robinson, xv). In other words, in this film, Novaro takes up these stereotypes and gives them an original twist. Perhaps one of the most interesting departures in this respect is Novaro's reelaboration of the metaphorical image of Tijuana as, in García Canclini's words, "la casa de toda la gente." Novaro rearticulates this image not only through the use of the geographical space of the city as the background to her film, but also by focusing it through one of her characters, Juana, the only character in the film who does not arrive in Tijuana. She was already there. Juana is the token Tijuanense of the movie, the only character in the film who does not have an existential conflict, is not desperately looking for ways to earn dollars, is not in search of her identity, her voice, or her father. Juana already has all these things and, curiously, it is in her house(s) that many of the film's characters cross paths. We very much doubt that Novaro chose this name for her character by chance, when the movie as a whole reconstructs an image of Tijuana so close to de Certeau's and so distant from Montalvo's. She is the "tía Juana"[7] and her house is "la de toda la gente."

From our point of view the most significant achievement of the film is its dismantling of overly familiar and trite clichés about the border. It avoids the temptation to present a linear history of Tijuana, focus on any specific site in the city, develop any single character in depth. *El jardín de Eden* pulls together multiple histories, in different locations throughout the city, to project the city's dynamic quality, the constant sense of movement and change that best fits this busiest of the world's borders. Additionally, this film contributes in important ways to the relocation of traditional filmic and dominant culture stereotypes about the border. *El jardin de Edén* projects a more complex and nuanced vision of the border space that operates both in awareness of and as a countervening voice to the familiar image of the border as an unredeemable hell from which one has no recourse but to escape, so typical of films like *Aventurera, Espaldas Mojadas,* or *La frontera del terror.*

Regina Swain's collection of short stories, *La señorita Superman y otras danzas* [Miss Superman and other dances] complements Novaro's film in that in addition to its explicitly female-gendered take on these issues, her point of view is also unmistakably that of a border Mexican. In contrast with Novaro's concept of the region, which is somewhat more nuanced, but still centrist in orientation and dependent on metropolitan theoretical elaborations, Swain's practice requires a different metaphor, perhaps (with apologies to Quetzil Castañeda for retooling his term) an aesthetics of the doughnut hole. As Castañeda notes, "This uncanny pastry is a presence defined as an absence and an absence materialized as a presence" (26). The comparison of this narrative project with a paradoxically named fatty, yeasty confection is borne out in the history of traditional discursive encrustings that project onto Tijuana a no-culture imaginary presence: from the U.S. side, an illusory reality as the Third World's three-dimensional concretization of a Hollywood dream of the real Mexico, and from the Mexican side, a sinister place without culture that nevertheless serves as the site of cultural contamination from the United States that must be contained. In other words, Tijuana is scandalous from two cultural points of view because it is an absence (a no-culture culture) and an overdetermined presence (a too two-cultured culture, in which the dominance of one culture over the other is precisely calibrated from the opposite space: Mexico for the United States; the United States for Mexicans).

What Swain does in these brief stories is to trace critical nodes in these contradictory and complementary discourses, recovering their concealed or forgotten genealogies, and setting them side by side in a site where everything and everyone is dangerously, disruptively out of place. Like the pastry, a fatty presence and nominal absence, her stories are both overly allusive and vaguely ungrounded. A doughnut hole aesthetics also has some of the qualities Judith Butler ascribed to the performance of realness in drag balls: "the contest (which we might read as a 'contesting of realness') involves the phantasmatic attempt to approximate realness (or, alternatively, merely to 'do' realness), but it also exposes the norms that regulate realness as themselves phantasmically instituted and sustained" (130). It is precisely this phantasmic quality that regulates the gap between "Miss" and "Superman" in the collection's title, with its evocation of other staged rituals of performative femininity such as beauty contests and with its grating gender transgression (this is explicitly not about Supergirl, the comic book's cop-out confection of a cousin for the Man of Steel). It is also this phantasmic quality that supports the text's contestatory relation to the doubled set of institutional norms that undergird its textual practice.

The city is never named in Swain's story, though it is mythically located in California, which is identified as an island both in the Amazon Calafia's letter to el conquistador Balboa (57–58),[8] and in an implicitly more contemporary re-siting: "La Frontera sigue siendo la misma, Zona Libre desde que era sólo una pequeña isla llamada California" [The Border is still the same Free Trade Zone ever since it was only a small island named California] (23). The unnamed city, like Tijuana, is subject to floods in the downtown area (18), has a suburb called "Playas" (29), and is described as "una ciudad enorme y caprichosa, cuyos pobladores vivían al filo de dos mundos distintos pero similares" with "casas construidas a lo largo de un gran cerco de alambre de púas" [an enormous and capricious city, whose inhabitants lived on the knife edge of two distinct but similar worlds (with) houses constructed all along a barbed-wire fence] (18). It is fundamentally a "ciudad nocturna" [nocturnal city] (18) inhabited by "criaturas nocturnas" [nocturnal creatures] (52). Contemporary inhabitants of this unnamed city include a troop of García Márquezian gypsies, the "hombres-lobo" (wolfmen), and "niñas Clairol" (Clairol blondes) who hang out in the bars, and the Amazon queen Calafia herself, along with a special guest appearance by "la negra Angustias," who has exited the pages of Rojas Gónzalez's eponymous novel to do a strip-tease in the Aloha bar.

In these unauthorized juxtapositions, Swain's short stories economically provide a parodic displacement of both "authentic" (i.e., noncommodified precapitalist) Mexican culture and its postmodern ironic shadow-text supplement. Here, too, Swain offers allusive sketches for alternative histories of unachieved potential and of loss. In a punning allusion to Lázaro Cárdenas's closure of the famous casino, Señorita Superman gets up one morning only to discover "NO HAY AGUA CALIENTE" (51). In another story, referencing the colonial period, the Amazon Calafia writes a letter to Balboa:

> En este Imperio de Norte, las tardes aún se despeinan sobre el reflejo del agua. Nada las perturba. . . . Aquí las palmas mecen fronteras que siguen siendo alcanzables; aquí, el reflejo de los sueños sigue siendo igual, no importan salidas o llegadas. Aquí, caballero errante, el conquistador sigue siendo conquistado por los ojos grandes de las de mi raza. Mujeres hechas de deseo y metal, de piel y llama. (57–58)

> [In this Northern Empire, the afternoons are still disheveled in the water's reflection. Nothing bothers them. . . . Here the palm trees rock borders that remain reachable; here the reflection of dreams remains the same, regardless of entrances and exits. Here, wandering knight, the conqueror is still conquered by the large eyes of the women of my race. Women made of desire and metal, of skin and flame.]

In each case, a feminine voice remembers/forgets a preexisting dominant cultural discourse. In the first case, a controversial (and, from some perspectives, hypocritical) moralizing action by one of Mexico's greatest presidents becomes domesticated in a punning overlay with a young woman's frustration at not being able to take a hot shower in the morning. In the second case, Calafia writes back to both the chivalric novels that in some sense provided a discursive context for narratives of the colonial encounter, and to the Spanish colonial chronicles themselves. Calafia's letter describes the imagined utopia of the Californian island, where conquerors' dreams are reflected back into a common pool, and at the same time hints at the duplicity of such encounters between a fictitious wandering knight and a dream lover. These women represent the entirely reachable dream, insofar as it serves both the conqueror and the conqueror's woman to imagine such a traditionally lyric space; yet, these seductive, large-eyed women have a cybernetic dissonance that interrupts the island idyll. They are women of desire, skin, flame—and metal.

At the same time that these brief texts serve as counternarratives to an established discourse, they are contestatory in a specifically female-centered way. Swain uses her brief tales as a medium to hyperclarify that traditional dominant texts like the ones to which she alludes are irremediably male-centered constructions. Thus, she ironically presents the border woman as consumer and as consumer product, in her home and even more particularly in the bar setting, where eroticism is most strictly understood through commodity culture. Here, for example, that great lyric theme of Love is reimagined through the metaphor of a can of Nestle condensed milk: "El amor, Amor, es una lata Nestlé de leche condensada, por eso te empalaga y luego, después de la tercera cucharada, la pobre lata de amor termina siempre en la basura" [love, my Love, is a can of Nestle condensed milk, that's why it sweetens you up and then, after the third spoonful, the poor can of love always ends up in the garbage] (37). In a later story, one of the characters muses that "la Nestlé reparte la cultura . . . y se lanza a vivir un amor látex a fuerza de sexo enlatado" [Nestle divides up culture and one throws oneself into living a latex love through the demands of canned sex] (54). In Swain's world, Campbell's soup and Nestle love are identically instantaneous, equally disposable commodities.

Read together, Calafia's letter and Señorita Superman's meditations speak powerfully to each other and help the reader comprehend an edgy, feminine, bordered discursive context for Swain's work. Calafia's

Amazon women live in a (male) prefabricated paradise where traditional lyric dreams jar with visions of metal women. In this world, the abandoned Nestle can provides another context for imagining the undertext to Calafia's seductive cybernetic scene; it points to the canned sex, the throwaway love that defines commercialized sexual relations between local women and visiting conquerors. It is no wonder that Señorita Superman comments that "le han salido arrugas en el alma" [wrinkles have appeared in her soul] (52). In contrast with Richard Rodriguez's lament for the lost putas of yesteryear, Swain's narrator complains to the archetypal "madrerreina" (motherqueen):

> Pero, ¿y las sopas instantáneas, madre, y las carreras de perro por conseguir trabajo? . . . ¿Dónde guardo las prostitutas de la Zona, mamá, dónde pongo las angustias? . . . ¿Y la amenaza del SIDA, madre, y los condones de colores, y el borracho de la esquina, dónde, dónde colocarlos? . . . ¿Dónde guardo la presión del trabajo, y las muertes de migrantes, la mujer de la maquila? ¡Ya no caben con las Barbis!
>
> Y es que vivimos en una generación de sopas instantáneas y amores instantáneos que no duran más de cuatro copas. (53–54)

> [But, instant soup, mother, and the dog-eat-dog races to get a job? . . . Where do I put away the prostitutes from the North Zone, mom, where do I put the anguish? . . . And the threat of AIDS, mother, and the colored condoms, and the drunk on the corner, where, where can I place them? . . . Where do I save the pressure from work and the deaths of the migrants, and the woman from the assembly plant? They don't fit on the shelf with the Barbie dolls!
>
> And the thing is that we live in a generation of instant soup and instant love that doesn't last longer than four drinks.]

Swain captures well the cost of living in a site of contested meanings, specifically those deriving from both dominant discourses that include a perception of the border as place of no culture. Nevertheless, Nestle milk, instant soups, Barbie dolls, and other material analogues of U.S. cultural influence are understood even in this assumed no-culture context as scandalous contaminations that do not fit and cannot be appropriately placed in the proper Mexican house. At the same time, while these products allegorize a perceived scandal, they are already entirely naturalized in Swain's world; Nestle is a metaphor for love, and Barbies already have their assigned place in the girl's room; the problem remaining for the narrator of the story is how to incorporate other, homegrown scandals. In effect, then, Swain points to the intricacies of regional politics that traditionally tend to decry a superficial scandal while ignoring a profound one.

In his discussion of the workings of cultural imperialism in the Mexican Yucatán, Quetzil Castañeda uses Coca-cola as a convenient shorthand reference for this unequal form of transculturation: "Because Coke has become a synecdoche for a specific culture, this situation is often nostalgically or angrily lamented by some culture-bearers of the metropolitan core as cultural loss or cultural rape. . . . The analogy is not that Coke is Culture, but that Culture is like Coke." Castañeda extends this conclusion, and asks his readers to imagine "the invention of Culture whether locally or globally as if it were Coca-cola," what he calls "the Coke theory of culture," that is as "a heterogeneous entity constituted in and through the contested crisscrossings of borrowings across boundaries forged by such transcultural traffic" (37). Castañeda's point, we take it, is that Coke (taken as a symbolic marker) has a conventional cultural association in U.S. dominant culture and in U.S. contestatory cultural commentaries, while in other sites it has been infused with other significations. In Swain's stories, too, imported consumer products are infused with new meaning. Like Nestle condensed milk, Coca-cola plays a small but important role in these fictions, where it too becomes a synecdotal marker for a scandalously naturalized cultural product.

In Swain's collection of short stories, the tale of the Amazon Queen of California, Calafia, is told twice; once in the pseudo-colonial letter already cited above, and the second time in the final story of the volume, a pseudo-folktale entitled "De cómo se creó el río Amazonas (o ¡Ay, Calafia, no te rajes!)" ("On how the Amazon River was created, or, Don't back down Calafia!"). In the second version of the story, the island utopia gives way to the modern border city and the protagonist has a much harder life. This Calafia was named after the bus on which she was born, and her mother's fellow passengers "la llamaron reina porque jamás llegaría a princesa" [called her "queen" because she would never become a princess (beauty queen)]. Growing up, Calafia buys her treats in the Chinese grocery, "El Palacio" (the palace), "donde, a pesar de encontrarse alejado de los maravillosos reinos del Norte, se podía encontrar diet coke, cherry coke y coca-cola clásica" [where, despite being located far from the marvelous kingdoms of the North, she could find diet coke, cherry coke, and Coca-cola classic] (61). If in the earlier story, the conqueror Balboa serves as an organizing focus for narration, in this more contemporary Calafia's story, a cultural context is built out of missed connections and reassigned significations. Calafia's name comes from a public transport bus; she is nicknamed queen as a consolation for her lack of beauty; her palace is the corner grocery; riches means being able to choose among the various Coke products. Here Swain economically alludes to the conventional meanings of such cultural signifiers as (concretely) Coca-Cola and (abstractly) the myth of the Little Princess, and at the same time exposes the constructedness of these conventional meanings, while reinfusing them with alternative discursive contexts.

The first Calafia, Esplandián's and Balboa's Calafia, is an Amazon queen; this latter-day Calafia becomes a fortuneteller. Each of the women loves and is abandoned by a foreign man; in each case there is a misrecognition of a brief conqueror's visit for true love, an exchange of drunken imaginings for solid human bodies, a transposition of genealogies and cultural mappings along with a conjunction of the foreign man and the Californian woman. "Sepa usted, Conquistador Balboa," says the first Calafia at the end of her letter, "que aquella negra en blanco a quien llamó Evohé, no ha sido otra que la amazona Calafia" [Know this, conqueror Balboa, that the black woman in white you called Evohe is none other than the amazon Calafia] (58). The second Calafia reinvests the attribute of "amazona" with another context: "Aprendió a querer a Homobono por zonas," says the narrator, and when he leaves her: "Lloró tanto que sus lágrimas hicieron un riachuelo . . . que se llamó AMA-ZONAS en honor al mapa fabuloso de la anatomía de Homobono" [She learned to love Homobono by zones. . . . She cried so much that her tears made a stream . . . called AMA-ZON (LOVE-ZONES) in honor of the fabled map of Homobono's anatomy] (64). Cortés honored Montalvo by giving the name California to a distant western province of New Spain; Swain picks up on this old misappelation and gives it her own twist. Montalvo's liminally paradisical island is the home of legendary warrior women who live without male counterparts. In Swain's version of this legend, the women, discarded metallic cans of Nestle love, must make do without men, and their suffering is comically, hyperbolically transmuted into a flood of tears that turns the Río Tijuana into the Amazon.

Finally, one of the qualities of the doughnut hole and its perfect nutritional partner, Coca-Cola, is to fill us up with empty calories. Swain's doughnut-hole-and-Coke aesthetics continually evokes its stagy no-culture culture backdrop, often through reference to another controversial U.S. export: Hollywood movies. One character is described as "muy James Bond" [very James Bond] (24); a certain bar is "simplemente una película de Capra" [simply a Capra film] (30); another character explains her inability to sustain a relationship as: "yo prefiero el TV-Guide a la televisión y los cortos en cine a las películas" [I prefer TV Guide to television and the trailers in the movie theater to the films] (37). Swain's narrative technique is full of similarly parodic cinematographic references. For example, at one point her narrator explains: "de pronto, como en las películas de Warner Brothers, podemos apreciar una escena retrospectiva" [suddenly, like in Warner Brothers films, we can enjoy a flashback] (52). If one of the modalities for inventing Tijuana in modern U.S. and Mexican dominant culture discourses is a bad imitation of second-rate Hollywood movies, Swain's response would be to explore the implications of such overlays through a textual shadowing that overdetermines them. In shadowing the shadowtext, Swain's female-centered narratives do not pretend to step outside dominant culture—an impossible enterprise—but to shake up conventional attributions of signification and hint at the unrecognized premises upon which such discourses have been grounded.

While U.S. and Mexican dominant cultural discourses are differentially weighted in Swain and Novaro, in each case Tijuana and its remembered/forgotten shadows objectify the conflict, propel the narrative into existence, and clarify ideological, cultural, and ethical stakes. Even in the fictional context, Tijuana serves as a textual backdrop for reality-as-simulation: a real-life Wild West, a real Disneyland. Like Ortega y Gasset's city-as-cannon metaphor, Tijuana offers a content-less explosive violence that needs to be contained and bracketed off, for the simulated fiction-reality is sometimes just too real, too Third World, too aesthetically contaminated, too unpleasantly disruptive. At the same time, it is this simulated, contaminated, Third World disruptiveness that is Tijuana's major selling point, and the main assurance of its authenticity, for the gringo tourist who crosses the border to purchase a piece of the "real Mexico" instead of taking the family to Walt's Disneyland further north. Sleaze sells in a way that one more northern Californian mall or supermarket would not.

Thus, for example, Gronk's comment that "Borders don't apply now. East L.A. is everywhere" (quoted in Fregoso, 273) resonates in the same cultural register as Richard Rodriguez's "Mexico will soon look like Tijuana. . . . Tijuana is an industrial park on the outskirts of Minneapolis" (94). In each case, the real border is blurred into an abstraction and projected as the shadow of a preferred dominant culture construct. This narrative tic, so common in border discussions ranging from philosophical to pop cultural, is precisely the quality that alert writers like Swain have been able to identify and play with in their texts.

# Conclusion: Shorts

Hace falta una letra.
—*Pátzcuaro fisherman to Balibar*

In short, what do we do with short takes? We began this book with reference to Etienne Balibar's anecdote of the missing letter in the Tarasca language that was somehow (metaphorically? literally?) responsible for the Mexican fisherman's inability to cross the international boundary line into the United States. This phantom letter serves as the sign of a specific linguistic and political interdiction; it also holds open the space that prevents mutual comprehension, unimpeded flow across borders, narrative cohesiveness. In this book, too, we have struggled with the missing letter—or its theoretical analogue—that plagues border theory and keeps practice from pulling together into a coherent body of work. Each of the texts we have examined in this book to some degree forces the consciousness of that absence onto the reader, so that we are forcibly brought back, again and again, to the site of that missing agglutinating factor as held open in fragmentary texts, as well as to the cultural presuppositions that create a collusion between reader and text in the acknowledgment of this missing link and the analysis of its sociocultural import.

*"A dialogue as with a mirror . . ." (Khatibi)*

All these texts play at the borders of disconnection and cohesiveness, whether in the form of a fragmented novel (Martinez), intentionally interrupted autoethnographic or mockudrama accounts (Cantú, Sandra Ortiz Taylor and Sheila Ortiz Taylor, Novaro), interconnected yet independent short stories (Gaspar de Alba, Conde, Viramontes, Sanmiguel), or snippets of narrative that beg for and refuse completion (Swain). A persistent practice that relies on an abutting of fragments is surely significant, though at the same time their traversal by the nonrecuperability of the missing letter hints that what is at stake is more frequently or more likely to be associated with pure interdiction than a refusal to fill in the blanks of a particular cultural script. French psychoanalyst André Green has argued, "One can be a citizen or an expatriate, but it is difficult to imagine *being* a border" (cited in Balibar, 217). It is, however, precisely this almost unimaginable borderbeing that both Chicanas and Mexicanas are asked to inhabit, for the furtherance of centrist thinking about peripheral postmodern states and identities. It is also a figure that they ask themselves to inhabit, as a way of rearticulating alternative forms of be-ing outside dominant culture's ideological imperatives. In a recent article, Norma Alarcón describes the process by which such missing-letter-spaces in Chicana subjectivity, held open and previously perceived as "empty," emerge in provisional decentered solidarities:

> The contemporary subject-in-process is not just what Hegel would have us call the *Aufhebung* . . . as tenuously, Chicanas' consciousness, which is too readily viewed as representing "postmodern fragmenting identities," entails not only Hegel's *Aufhebung* with respect to Chicanas' immediate personal subjectivity as raced and sexed bodies, but also an understanding of all past negations as communitarian subjects in a doubled relation to cultural recollection, and remembrance, and to our contemporary presence and non/presence in the sociopolitical and cultural milieu. ("Chicana Feminism," 67)

There is a particular poignancy to this simultaneous evocation of fragmentation and community, of positioned and positional identities in flux. Alarcón, thus, sets communitarian solidarity against a Western unified consciousness focused on totality, holding tightly to the contingent and provisional structures of what Spivak called "identity-in-difference" (Spivak, "Subaltern Studies," passim). Alarcón's analysis of the role of Chicana subjectivity in contemporary theory also echoes in important ways with Nelly Richard's discussion of how centrist readings of Latin American culture have come to play a crucial role in theoretically "decentered" analyses. Richard talks about the "fractured syntax of postmodernity," which she considers a "perverse inflection of the Center, which aims at appropriating the periphery's alterity and its anti-hegemonic protagonism" ("Cultural Peripheries," 220). In Latin America, she suggests, the terms are different. While Latin American thinkers may play with reappropriating the metropolitan theoretician's appropriation of local realities and identities, the question remains as to "why the identity/difference conflict continues to be arbitrated by the discursivity of the First World. Even when their current hypothesis is that of de-centering, those who formulate it continue to be surrounded by the reputation, academic or institutional, that allows them to situate themselves at the center of the debate at its densest point of articulation." The only escape, she suggests, comes through "a *situational* politics of critical resignification" from outside these First World institutional nodes (222).

The agency ascribed to these border forms and identities in smart, theoretically informed analyses, such as those of Richard and Alarcón, speaks to and seems a model for postmodern fragmentation, but without inscribing textually or subscribing philosophically to the totalizing impulse that continually enforces the will-to-theory in metropolitan discourse. At the same time, both thinkers are well aware that despite service celebration of border modes in metropolitan theory there is surprisingly little real engagement with border texts, and in such analyses as exist the missing letter of the other country's border texts is insistently, and seemingly intentionally, avoided. Even where theory advocates an open and frank discussion of transborder questions, or celebrates the fertility of cross-border exchange, it is all but impossible to prevent dominant culture expectations from overtaking decentralizing thought.

Here Balibar is helpful, at least in parsing out some of the layers in metropolitan border thinking. Balibar examines this concern with relation to what he, in good French psychoanalytic fashion, calls the "real," the "symbolic," and the "imaginary" of the border, which he defines respectively as: "(1) the current vacillation of borders, (2) the interiority and ideality of borders, and (3) the conflict or overlapping of cultures"

(217). We take the first category, the "real" vacillation of borders, to reflect Balibar's meditations on the world as we experience it; the second, or symbolic, category refers most signally to assigned traits of identity, including assumptions about racial and sexual identities as well as posited solidarities around linguistically defined ethnicity. It is here, too, in the slippage between ideality and interiority that the force of the missing letter most achingly holds open the space of its absence.

The third, or imaginary, category is given a specific European context in Balibar's account. However, it seems reasonable to extend his analysis of cultural overlapping to refer to other destabilizations of contested semiotic domains or refusals to settle into a single dominant meaning such as those we have noted in works studied in this book that both figure and describe a real and a symbolic of cultural and linguistic collision. David Hayman helps us to understand how the concomitant stylistic preference for fragmentary forms contributes to a fictional practice that also encodes a theoretical stance:

> Radical parataxis generally puts absence in high relief, advertising what the more conventional narrative plasters over. . . . It follows that in many cases paratactic effects constitute frontal attacks on the reader's expectations and desires, imposing disorder on the verbal field we depend upon to orient our reactions. (150)

While Hayman does not speak directly to this question, Pheng Cheah, among others, has pointed to what he calls the intellectual project of hybridity theorists who "attempt to articulate a political theory of culture as a process or production in language" by which "the subject of culture becomes the site of permanent contestation" (293). This generalization seems even more applicable in sites like the U.S.-Mexico borderlands where both a relocation and a fracturing of language and cultures obtains. Here Cheah hints at the political efficacy of fragmentary narratives, a point sustained on more stylistic grounds in Hayman's observation.

Nevertheless, the point to be made in this context is not so much to reiterate an already tired cliché about postmodern fragmentation, but to point to the interesting alignment of metaphor in accounts of the border imaginary. In Cheah, as in Balibar and in Hayman, borderlands theorists and/or paratactic writers are most powerfully focused through metaphors like "contestation," "conflict," "frontal attack": bellic language that seems to anchor analysis in the strong-arm tactics of the dominant. At the same time, Richard, Alarcón, and Spivak, without eliminating such warlike language from their vocabularies, are more centrally interested in talking about "refunctioning," "solidarity," "in-difference": the "tactics of the weak" (to use Ludmer's phrase) or "tricks of meaning" (Richard's) more often deployed by the subaltern. At issue then, is not just "the" imaginary, but *whose* imaginary and *what* conjunction of overwhelming violence and coalition building aspires to create its own order with respect to perceived reality and creative self-fashioning.

*"A face with no borders . . ." (Martínez)*

This question of self-fashioning is, of course, precisely the theme that has exercised prominent Chicana feminist thinkers like Angie Chabram-Dernersesian in recent years: "it is within this slippery territory that I labor along with many others, refashioning fractured identities and community linkages, retracing critical histories, and reconfiguring social and political geographies" ("Chicana? Rican?" 265). The terms and metaphors here are similar to the ones we have already noticed in Alarcón and Richard. Like her fellow culture critics, Chabram-Dernersesian points to the imbrication of disconnected narratives as a symptomatic expression of marginalized identities, and she points to a form of border gnosis that is created out of the act of suturing together communities, identities, and fragmentary narratives over and against the other, seemingly more sinister, sutures created out of transnational economic concerns and globalizing political practices.[1]

To this discussion Chabram-Dernersesian adds a overt questioning of the terms of analysis for her own insistence on her hybrid Puerto Rican–Chicana identity, which poses a particular problem of cognitive dissonance among theorists who are unable to accept or imagine an individual who claims a dual ethnicity. In fact, the Chicana-Rican (or, we might add, any border subject conscious of the equal and unbalanced pull of the two sides of the border) is particularly well placed to interrogate positional claims precisely because her identity is double, or fragmented. Mimicking typical concerns of other scholars, she notes: "hybrids aren't authentic, they have no claim to an ethnic identity (here a fixed insular ethnicity)" (266). Underlying this concern, of course, is a sense that identity, especially ethnic identity, grounds claims to authenticity and cannot represent a complex or problematic affiliation.

Ethnic identity must be limited, contained, "insular." It should represent a single unproblematically authentic Otherness, against which the dominant culture can project its own neuroses. Despite contemporary scholars and thinkers' rejection of this baldly stated model whereby the subject of oppositional history becomes fetished as the perfectly essentialized Third World Woman, the structure is surprisingly resistant.

The writers in this book, like the critics evoked in the last few pages, resist such subsumption into a pseudo-authentic otherness, whether engineered by Latino thinkers, mainstream border theorists, or dominant culture projects from either North or South. A marginalized, subordinated, othered subject position does not provide sufficient grounds for a structure of knowledge in conventional, universalizing terms. For a border thinker/writer to fall into the cultural location of otherness is to remain, like the Pátzcuaro fisherman, unmarked and outside the exchanges of grounding and grounded knowledge. Border gnoseology, when framed through the recognition of the missing letter, is always and necessarily tinged by "distortion" or "the fantastic."

*"El coagulo de palabras en mi garganta al fin se empezó a deslizar . . ."*
*(Gaspar de Alba)*

And yet, of course, these border women speak and write not only for themselves and to each other, but in an awareness of the fact that there is no escaping the interplay of dominant cultures from Mexico and from the United States that shape the warp and woof of their daily lives and writing practices. To write from the border is to write in awareness of the missing letter in their own language that prevents them from crossing over, but also, and more important, in the awareness of a missing letter (or a whole missing language) in the dominant culture's vocabulary that makes readerly coalitions stumbling, and cautious, and subject to error. Furthermore, it is to suggest a politics of location by which partiality and fragmentation rather than universality or coherence delimit the conditions of possibility for claims to knowledge, whether dominant culture-based or border-inflected. The border is not single, nor can it be reduced to the gnoseology of a single sign; this fact encodes both its rich potentiality and the permanent frustration it causes its practitioners and theorists.

These women write from a background of movement (migration) and thwarted motion (border posts), and the reader's role in these texts is to also follow these flows of halting and sometimes frustrated movement. Aesthetic choices are intimately tied up in social and political realities; political realities inflect an individual's understanding of self and community. The encounter with these texts can result in misreading, but the reader cannot remain passive. She must participate and take responsibility for her readings. Bruce Robbins would agree. He argues forcefully for analytic methods that put far more pressure on theoretical models of liberal academia:

> I am trying to suggest three things. First, that the act of finding "agency" in text after text corresponds to a logic that is as much a part of our professional or metropolitan situatedness as the act of neglecting or denying it would be. Second, that a critic's transmission of this (or any other) cultural value should not disguise itself as a defense of the particular, the local, and the specific, because it involves generalizations that are no less dramatically synthetic . . . than the Orientalist stereotypes they are now marshalled against. And third, that if we do not need "easy generalizations," we do need difficult ones. (252)

We have argued throughout this book that the most cogent articulation of these difficult border theorizations is found in border writers' practice, in the record of their positioning within a fraught and fragmented literary and geographical space, in the tales of their literary and literal passage through the zone and across its borders. Donna Haraway says that "understanding the world is about living inside stories. . . . It's almost like my examples *are* the theories" (107–8). The story-theories of the writers explored in this book open out onto a hermeneutics that resists simplification and resists closure.

Reader, this book is made of bones . . .
—*Sheila Ortiz Taylor*

# Notes

I. READING THE BORDER, NORTH AND SOUTH

1. Claire F. Fox's *The Fence and the River: Culture and Politics at the U.S.-Mexico Border* (Minneapolis: University of Minnesota Press, 1999) highlights a number of canonical texts that have made use of the image of the border: Henry Giroux, *Border Crossings: Cultural Workers and the Politics of Education* (New York: Routledge, 1992); Maggie Humm, *Border Traffic: Strategies of Contemporary Women Writers* (New York: St. Martin's, 1991); Ian Chambers, *Border Dialogues: Journeys in Postmodernity* (London: Routledge, 1990); and Trinh T. Minh-ha, *When the Moon Waxes Red: Representation, Gender and Cultural Politics* (New York: Routledge, 1991). Fox's work helpfully points out the differences between the metaphorical border and the real border. Renato Rosaldo's works complement those of Fox: see, particularly, *Culture and Truth: The Remaking of Social Analysis* (Boston: Beacon, 1989). Other theorists of border issues would include Jacques Derrida, "Living On: Border Lines," trans. James Hulbert, in *Deconstruction and Criticism,* ed. Harold Bloom et al. (New York: Seabury, 1979), 75–176; M. Pierrette Malcuzinski, ed., *Sociocríticas. Prácticas textuales/ Cultura de fronteras, teoría literaria: texto y teoría* (Amsterdam: Rodopi, 1991); Gloria Anzaldúa, *Borderlands/La Frontera: The New Mestiza* (San Francisco: aunt lute books, 1987); Héctor Calderón and José David Saldívar, *Criticism in the Borderlands: Studies on Chicano Literature, Culture, and Ideology* (Durham, N.C.: Duke University Press, 1991); José David Saldívar, *The Dialectics of Our America: Genealogy, Cultural Critique, and Literary History* (Durham, N.C.:

Duke University Press, 1991); and the Rolando Romero articles cited in the bibliography of this book.

2. One thinks of the anthologies by women of color which emerged during the 1980s such as Cherríe Moraga and Gloria Anzaldúa, eds., *This Bridge Called My Back: Writings by Radical Women of Color* (New York: Kitchen Table: Women of Color Press, 1983); Alma Gómez, Cherríe Moraga, and Mariana Romo Carmona, eds., *Cuentos: Stories by Latinas* (New York: Kitchen Table: Women of Color Press, 1983); Alicia Partnoy, ed., *You Can't Drown the Fire: Latin American Women Writing in Exile,* (Pittsburgh, Pa.: Cleis Press, 1988); Asunción Horno-Delgado, Eliana Ortega, Nina M. Scott, and Nancy Saporta Steinbach, eds., *Breaking Boundaries: Latina Writing and Critical Readings* (Amherst: University of Massachusetts Press, 1989); as well as Gloria Anzaldúa, ed., *Making Face, Making Soul: Haciendo Caras/Creative and Critical Perspectives by Women of Color* (San Francisco: aunt lute, 1990), among others.

3. For more information on the dissemination of these texts, especially *Border Brujo,* see Marco Vinicio González, "Guillermo Gómez-Peña," *Semanal de la Jornada* 117 (September 8, 1991): 20; and Jason Weiss, "An Interview with Guillermo Gómez-Peña," *Review: Latin American Literature and Arts* 45 (July–December 1991): 8–13.

4. In other informal interviews with writers from Tijuana the response was similar.

5. Bakhtin points out that the cultural act lives, in substance, on the borders, hence its gravity and importance; "while getting further away from the borders, ground and meaning are lost. It becomes arrogant, degenerates and dies." In Mijail Bajtin, *Teoría y estética de la novela,* trans. Helena S. Kriukova and J. Vicente Cazcarra (Madrid: Taurus, 1989), 30. Subsequent citations from the author are taken from this edition.

6. A conference takes place every two years on the northern border. Its participants are mainly writers from southcentral Mexico and those writers whose careers had been made in Mexico City. Well-known Chicano literary critics and authors are also invited to participate.

7. As was mentioned at the beginning of this chapter, the collection intended to give a broader view of the so-called national literature. This collection pretends to include the literary production of every state in the country.

8. One of the strongest criticisms made on the III Border Seminar, "Mujer y Literatura Mexicana y Chicana: Culturas en Contacto," which took place in Tijuana, Mexico, in May 1989, addressed the lack of comparative analysis among Mexican and Chicana women. For further information, see Guadalupe Huerta and Virginia Bautista, "Un coloquio sin algunas respuestas," *Cultura Norte* 2, no. 8 (February–May 1989), 52–53. In an extensive, if not exhaustive, bibliographical search on this topic, one can only find a handful of articles: Elena Poniatowska, "Puentes de ida y vuelta," presented at the aforementioned

seminar and published in *Esquina Baja* 7 (April–June 1989): 9–14; Poniatowska, "Escritura chicana y mexicana," *La Jornada* (June 28, 1993); María Socorro Tabuenca Córdoba, "Apuntes sobre dos escritoras de ambos lados del Río Bravo," *Cultura Norte* 6, nos. 26–27 (October 1993–January 1994): 35–38; and Tabuenca Córdoba, "Sandra Cisneros y Rosario Sanmiguel: encuentros y desencuentros," *Rutas: Forum for the Arts and Humanities* 2 (Spring 1994): 27–31.

9. *El signo y la alambrada* contains a series of essays that had been reassessed in order to be published in book form in 1970.

10. Because these authors are just beginning to form workshops and because their work is published in chapbooks or "plaquetas," which have small readerships, or in local and regional magazines whose circulation is very limited, we have avoided making a list, as it would not be fair to those authors who are just beginning to develop their literature and who have not come to our attention.

11. It is worth mentioning Gabriel Trujillo Muñoz's work, *Un camino de hallazgos: Poetas bajacalifornianos del siglo veinte* (Mexicali: U. Autónoma de Baja California, 1992), sponsored by the Autonomous University of Baja California, which, although not a critical appraisal of texts, does provide a broad perspective on the poetry of Baja California.

12. During the Binational Conference the geographical delimitation of the "border" was discussed. Francisco Amparán was one of the authors who did not want that classification to be made. The author, who is from Torreón, said, "I cannot say that I am from or of the border. Torreón is equidistant between Juárez and Mexico City. Now then, if I'm not from the border *[fronterizo]*, I'm even less of a Chilango. Rather, I am from the North. Why wouldn't it be better to call it the literature of the North?" In interviews with writers from Mexican border states, writers from Monterrey and Chihuahua have been included, and they have affirmed that there is a difference between themselves and border residents, as well as between border and nonborder cities.

13. Because it is a generalized sentiment expressed long before the border literary "boom," it would be difficult to mention the names of those artists and patrons of the arts who first made this observation.

14. He writes: "un ecotono es una transición entre dos o más comunidades diversas. . . . Es una zona de unión o cinturón de tensión que podrá tener acaso una extensión lineal considerable, pero es más angosta, en todo caso, que las comunidades mismas" [an ecotone is a transition between two or more diverse communities. . . . It is a zone of contact or belt of tensions that could perhaps have a considerable lineal extension, but which is, in any case, narrower than the communities themselves] (101).

15. These observations are made as much from the discourse about the formation of the border in terms of migration as from postcolonial theories proposed by Homi Bhabha, Partha Chatterjee, and Timothy Brennan, among others.

## 2. BILINGUAL

1. Gaspar de Alba's work can in some sense be compared to that of fellow Texan Rolando Hinojosa Smith, who is one of the central figures in the Chicano canon. Hinojosa Smith's commitment to recuperating the orality of the Texas-Mexico border is evident in aggressively bilingual works like his classic *Klail City y sus alrededores* (winner of the Casa de las Americas prize) and his comic masterpiece, *Mi querido Rafa*. However, it is important to note that his work has entered the U.S. canon in the English renditions that precisely and unfortunately flatten out the play of and tensions between the two languages spoken by the characters in his novels.

On another front, both sides of question of the place of Spanish language texts in the U.S. literary canon have been forcefully and clearly argued by Chicano critics in, for example, the difference of opinion between Bruce-Novoa and Arteaga on the one hand, and Calderón and Saldívar on the other with reference to the inclusion or exclusion of colonial conqueror-writers like Cabeza de Vaca and Pérez de Villagrá in the Chicano canon. Ironically, Cabeza de Vaca (along with Columbus) is included in *The Heath Anthology*—the exception to the general unwritten rule that U.S. literature is only what occurs in English.

2. "If you do not understand my many tongues, you begin to understand why I speak them. . . . It [introductory monologue in Spanish] is here to be appreciated or missed, and both the appreciation and the missing are significant. The more fully this playfulness is appreciated, the less broken I am to you, the more dimensional I am to you" (46).

## 3. DISPLACEMENT

1. Foucault has studied language as a series of philosophical and juridical discourses that compose a network between desire and power, and has analyzed how these discourses have served to subjugate different human groups. See his *Historia de la sexualidad*, vol. 1, *La voluntad del saber*, trans. Ulises Guñazú, 18th ed. (México: Siglo XXI Editores, 1991), and "Discourse on Language," in *The Archaeology of Knowledge and the Discourse on Language*, trans. Alan M. Sheridan (New York: Pantheon Books, 1972), 215–37. Discursive orders are configured by relations of power within institutions and in society as a whole. This terminology is consistent with that used in Norman Fairclaugh's *Language in Power* (London: Longman, 1990); he bases his study on Habermas and Foucault, among others.

2. In this chapter all references to the "border" refer to the Mexican side of the line. The term also needs to be distinguished from the more general use of the concept of border often deployed in postmodern theory. For a clear discussion of this distinction see Fox, *The Fence and the River*.

3. The rich body of studies, publications, and creative works in the Colegio de la Frontera Norte testify to this fact, as do the Centros de Estudios de la

Frontera/Estudios México-Estados Unidos (Border Studies Centers/Mexican-U.S. Studies Centers), which are flourishing in universities on both sides of the border.

4. Jesús Barquet explains that the entire volume of *Callejón Sucre* concludes in those *non places* (streets, cabarets, cafés, malls, cars, buses, the border itself), in which the characters experience the transgression of different borders in their own private lives.

5. Clearly the frequency of this type of concerns in Sanmiguel's narrative suggests a rich mine for a psychoanalytic reading; however, such readings would take us outside the theoretical concerns of this current project.

6. Amelia Valcárcel explains that women are taught to make enemies of other women precisely in the conflict over men. See *Sexo y filosofía: Sobre "mujer" y "poder"* (Barcelona: Anthropos, 1991), 127.

7. We recall here that the project of French feminism is most significantly associated with writing the body and with the development of a feminine writing that would have to take into account both the text and the reinscription of one's own body.

8. Paraphase of Virginia Woolf's comment: "pensé lo desagradable que era que le dejaran a uno fuera; y pensé que quizá era peor que le encerraran a uno dentro" (35). In the original English, Woolf writes: "I thought how unpleasant it is to be locked out; and I thought how it is worse perhaps to be locked in" (24).

9. We omit the article since Anamaría, the protagonist, is not located in "la otra habitación" [the other room]; it is Cony, another of the characters, who in fact lives in "la otra habitación."

10. We recall the scene in which the protagonist finds himself in a room listening to the voice of Queca in the neighboring room.

11. On numerous occasions Sanmiguel has noted that Juan Carlos Onetti is one of her favorite writers and that his work has a deep impact on her own desire to write.

12. The basis for this comparison of the two works relies heavily on Amy K. Kaminsky's analysis of *En breve cárcel* in chapter 7 of *Reading the Body Politic: Feminist Criticism and Latin American Women Writers* (Minneapolis: University of Minnesota Press, 1993).

13. In a personal interview, Rosario Sanmiguel says she has Molloy's novel on her list of books to read, but has not yet done so.

14. Gayatri Spivak develops this concept more fully in "Subaltern Studies: Deconstructing Historiography" in her *In Other Worlds: Essays in Cultural Politics* (New York: Routledge, 1988), 197–221.

15. The story is called "La otra habitación (segunda mirada)" [The other room (second view)].

16. The first verse of "Pérdida" by Minerva Margarita Villarreal.

5. UNREDEEMED

1. (Hilda) Rosina Conde (b. Zambada, Mexicali, 1954) is the author of the short story/novella collections *Embotellado de origen* [Bottled at the source], 1994; *El agente secreto* [The secret agent], 1990; *En la tarima* [On the platform], 1984; *De infancia y adolescencia* [Of infancy and adolescence], 1982; *Arrieras somos . . .* (trans. as *Women on the Road*), 1994. There is a considerable overlap among stories in the collections. She has published several volumes of poetry: *Poemas de seducción* [Poems of seduction], 1981; *Bolereando el llanto* [Crying to Boleros], 1993; *De Amor gozoso (textículos)* [On pleasurable love: Texticules], 1991. She has also worked in theater: "Cuarto asalto" [Fourth assault], the fourth act of a collaborative play entitled *En esta esquina* [On this corner], and has written a novel, *La Genara*.

2. Barrón Salido is referring to a specific report on the situation in Tijuana. She quotes Martín de la Rosa's extensive list of marginal persons: "Vamos a ocuparnos en este apartado de los peones, los albañiles, meseros, lavacoches, periodiqueros, las 'marías,' los que 'ya volvieron del otro lado' (metedólares), los que 'quieren ir al otro lado,' las empleadas domésticas, las 'que lavan ajeno,' los yonkeros, los 'cholos,' los barrenderos, los artesanos, los vendedores ambulantes, . . . los desocupados" [We are going to concern ourselves in this report with the peons, the construction workers, the waiters, the car washers, the newspaper sellers, the indigenous women workers, those who came back from the other side, those who want to go to the other side, the servants, the washerwomen, the junkies, the gang members, the street sweepers, the handicraft makers, the street salespeople, the unemployed].

3. Apter is referring to Homi Bhabha's coinage of the word *unhomely* as a way of rethinking the term "Unheimlich" (usually translated as the "uncanny"). For Bhabha, the postcolonial critic/writer's experience of the unhomely follows from "the estranging sense of the relocation of the home and the world in an unhallowed place" and he describes it as a common feature in border culture, in exile literature, and in Third World literature in general.

4. The titillating anomoly of the virgin-whore follows directly from ambiguous legal status of prostitution in Mexico. Federal law makes procuring illegal, but does not proscribe prostitution per se. The result, as Barrón Salido notes, is that establishments "hide" their most notorious function: "únicamente no se registra como actividad económica, aún cuando se presenta de manera abierta" [it is just ignored as an economic activity, even when it occurs in an open manner]. One consequence is an inevitable spillover of function and of public perception. Since the prostitutional economy is "hidden," there is tendency to assume that all women who work in such places are necessarily prostitutes (39).

6. HOMELY

1. "Paris Rats in East L.A. and Other Stories" includes the following: "Paris Rats in East L.A." (kindly provided to me in manuscript form by Helena

María Viramontes), "Spider's Face," *Americas 2001* 1, no. 5 (March/April 1988): 33–34; "Miss Clairol," *Americas Review,* special issue on "Chicana Creativity and Criticism: Charting New Frontiers in American Literature," ed. María Herrera-Sobek and Helena María Viramontes, 15, nos. 3–4 (1987): 101–5; "Dance Me Forever," *L.A. Weekly,* June 24–30, 1988, G20; "Tears on My Pillow," in *New Chicana/o Writing,* ed. Charles M. Tatum (Tucson: University of Arizona Press, 1992), 110–15; and three other stories I have not yet seen: "Candystriper" (in draft), "Watts," and "Underground." Also cited in this paper is her "The Jumping Bean" (in *Pieces of the Heart: New Chicano Fiction,* ed. Gary Soto [San Francisco: Chronicle Books, 1993]), 122–32.

2. See Castillo's chapter on Viramontes in *Talking Back: Toward a Latin American Feminist Literary Criticism* (Ithaca, N.Y.: Cornell University Press, 1992), which focuses precisely on this strategy.

7. SOLIDARITY

1. Information in this paragraph is condensed and paraphrased from two sources: Cunningham's book and the MacEoin volume of proceedings of the January 1985 Sanctuary symposium held in Tucscon.

2. Central American refugees, uncertain of their rights to political asylum, were frequently denied access to lawyers or information about their rights to a deportation hearing. They were incarcerated and encouraged, tricked, or forced into signing "voluntary departure" papers. The U.N. High Commissioner for Refugees, upon monitoring the processing of Salvadoran applicants, found that INS practices were "systematically designed to forcibly return Salvadorans irrespective of the merits of the asylum claims" (quoted in Gary MacEoin, "The Constitutional and Legal Aspects of the Refugee Crisis," in *Sanctuary: A Resource Guide for Understanding and Participating in the Central American Refugees' Struggle,* ed. MacEoin [San Francisco: Harper and Row, 1985], 120). Longtime Sanctuary worker Gary MacEoin describes one example of this abuse, as documented in a November 1981 California lawsuit brought on the behalf of a Salvadoran man by the National Center for Immigrants' Rights: "Crosby Wilfredo Orantes Hernández . . . fled El Salvador after he had been beaten by the National Guard, his mother had her face smashed in with a rifle, and two uncles had been carried off and later found dead with their heads mutilated and their sexual organs cut off. He arrived in the United States to become again—in the words of the brief—'a victim of violence and lawlessness.' In Culver City, California, an INS agent grabbed his arm as he left a bus and twisted it behind his back, and a second agent pistol-whipped him while the first held him, causing him to bleed profusely from mouth and nose. For days, agents tried to persuade him to sign a 'voluntary departure' form, even waking him at 3:00 A.M. and giving him coffee, apparently to deprive him of adequate sleep. He was never advised of his right to consult with counsel, of the availability of free legal services, of his right to a deportation hearing, or his right to apply for

political asylum. . . . The court found that 'Salvadorans are frequently arrested, deposited in waiting rooms, interrogated, put onto buses, and flown back to El Salvador all in a matter of hours. . . . [P]ackets of written materials explaining the legal rights of aliens are routinely confiscated'" (121–23).

Stories of abuse like that described by MacEoin were common, especially during the Reagan administration, and their circulation helped reinforce the commitment of the Sanctuary workers, who became even more convinced of the rightness of their support for the refugees in the face of apparently unlawful actions by government officials.

3. The Sanctuary document, "Resources on Beginning and Maintaining Sanctuary," forewarns of problems of this sort when it reminds Sanctuary communities that refugees are people with complicated emotional as well as economic and legal problems. The document quotes Argentine psychiatrist Laura Bonaparte on the difficulties of survival and of exile: "It is a form of torture. . . . We all have instilled in us a warrior spirit; that one must die on the battlefield and not abandon it. . . . Another thing that can be very humiliating for refugees—especially those who have been active in the struggles of their people—is the sense that the groups offering aid are requiring them to adapt. . . . There is an ambivalence between the desire to adapt and begin a new life and not to adapt because one is the product of a whole history of struggle and must return" (203–4). Cunningham also notes that one of the vexed points of contention for refugees came over the question of learning English; for some Central Americans, learning English was seen as a sellout, and refugees who studied the language were harshly criticized (148).

8. UTOPIA

1. *Jornada,* September 22, 1997, 1, 8.
2. To recap some issues to address in such a search:
(1) The displacement of writers from the border—who, subject to small press runs and inadequate distribution, are less well known and tend to be associated with "regional" themes—by centrist writers about the border whose work is widely read and distributed, while also fitting more neatly into dominant culture constructions/inventions of borderness. This displacement of Mexican border writers is borne out in the series of conferences on border literature that take place every two years on the border, with participation (mainly) of writers from central Mexico and well-known Chicano authors and critics.
(2) Border Art Workshop/Taller de Arte Fronterizo (BAW/TAF). Founded in 1984 by Guillermo Gómez-Peña to bring together Mexican and U.S. border artists, Chicanos and non-Chicanos, many of the Mexican nationals dropped out. Explains Chicano artist David Avalos: "some resistance to the BAW/TAF came from Tijuana artists. They said, hey, we don't think that the border is this wonderful place of exchange. We can't dispense with our nationality, so we can't

join the parade. . . . The BAW/TAF has the perspective of the USA, as do so many of the notions of border that we consume" (198).

3. Norma Iglesias Prieto, author of *Entre yerba, polvo y plomo, lo fronterizo visto por el cine mexicano,* 2 vols., and Miguel Angel Berumen, from the Asociación Fílmica de Juárez.

4. We draw this expression from the title of Tim Girven's article, "Hollywood's Heterotopia: U.S. Cinema, the Mexican Border and the Making of Tijuana," *Travesía. The Border Issue. Journal of Latin American Cultural Studies* 3, nos. 1–2 (1994): 93–133.

5. Interview with José Manuel Valenzuela, scholar from El Colegio de la Frontera Norte, and survey with students of the course, "The Border Image in Mexican Film," at the University of Texas at El Paso.

6. There is an enormous bibliography on this topic; here we point briefly only to a few of the most salient texts: Néstor García Canclini's *Culturas híbridas: Estrategias para entrar y salir de la modernidad* (Mexico: Grijalbo, 1989); Pablo Vila's "Sistemas Clasificatorios y narrativas identitarias en Ciudad Juárez y El Paso," in *Voces de frontera. Estudios sobre la dispersión cultural en la frontera México-Estados Unidos,* ed. Víctor Zúñiga (Monterrey: Universidad Autónoma de Nuevo León, 1998), 137–220; and Cecil Robinson's *No Short Journeys: The Interplay of Cultures in the History and Literature of the Borderlands* (Tucson: University of Arizona Press, 1992).

7. Recall that in popular versions of the founding of the city, "Tijuana" comes from a corruption of "Hacienda de la Tía Juana."

8. This is an explicit allusion to Esplandián, and to the Spanish conquistadores' appropriation of those mythic exploits as models for their own conquest of the Americas. As in Swain's text, in Montalvo's earlier novel, the inhabitants of the island California are black-skinned Amazons, ruled by Queen Calafía (539–40; 456–60).

## CONCLUSION

1. In this respect we acknowledge our debt to Walter Mignolo's lucid discussion of border gnoseology which he proposes instead of border epistemology as "a discourse about colonial knowledge . . . conceived at the conflictive intersection of the knowledge produced from the perspective of modern colonialisms (rhetoric, philosophy, science) and knowledge produced from the perspective of colonial modernities in Asia, Africa, and Latin America. Border gnoseology is a critical reflection on knowledge production" (*Local Histories/ Global Designs: Coloniality, Subaltern Knowledges, and Border Thinking* [Princeton, N.J.: Princeton University Press, 2000], 11).

# Bibliography

Alarcón, Norma. "Chicana Feminism: In the Tracks of 'the' Native Woman." In *Between Woman and Nation: Nationalisms, Transnational Feminisms, and the State,* ed. Caren Kaplan, Norma Alarcón, and Minoo Moallem, 63–71. Durham, N.C.: Duke University Press, 1999.

———. "The Theoretical Subject(s) of *This Bridge Called My Back* and Anglo American Feminism." In Gloria Anzaldúa, *Borderlands/La Frontera: The New Mestiza,* 356–69. San Francisco: Aunt Lute, 1987.

Aldaco, Guadalupe Beatriz, ed. *Literatura fronteriza de acá y allá.* Hermosillo: Instituto sonorense de cultura, 1994.

Amorós, Celia. *Hacia una crítica de la razón patriarcal.* 2d ed. Barcelona: Anthropos, 1991.

Amparán, José Francisco. "Obstáculos y problemas de una generaación perdida: los escritores pre-68." In *Literatura fronteriza de acá y allá,* ed. Guadalupe Beatriz Aldaco, 253–68. Hermosillo: Instituto sonorense de cultura, 1994.

Anderson, Benedict. *Imagined Communities: Reflections on the Origin and Spread of Nationalism.* Revised edition. London: Verso, 1991.

Anderson, Danny. "La frontera norte y el discurso de la identidad en la narrativa mexicana del siglo XX." Unpublished manuscript.

Anzaldúa, Gloria. *Borderlands/La Frontera: The New Mestiza.* San Francisco: Aunt Lute, 1987.

———. "En Rapport, In Opposition: Cobrando cuentas a las nuestras." In

*Making Face, Making Soul: Haciendo Caras/Creative and Critical Perspectives by Women of Color,* ed. Anzaldúa, 142–48. San Francisco: Aunt Lute, 1990.

———. "Haciendo caras: Una entrada." In *Making Face, Making Soul: Haciendo Caras/Creative and Critical Perspectives by Women of Color,* ed. Anzaldúa, xv–xxviii. San Francisco: Aunt Lute, 1990.

———, ed. *Making Face, Making Soul: Haciendo Caras/Creative and Critical Perspectives by Women of Color.* San Francisco: Aunt Lute, 1990.

Apter, Emily. "Comparative Exile: Competing Margins in the History of Comparative Literature." In *Comparative Literature in the Age of Multiculturalism,* ed. Charles Bernheimer, 86–96. Baltimore: Johns Hopkins University Press, 1995.

Arredondo, Isabel. "Women's Eden in Tijuana." LASA 1998, photocopy.

Arteaga, Alfred. *Chicano Poetics: Heterotexts and Hybridities.* Cambridge: Cambridge University Press, 1997.

Avalos, David, with John C. Welchman. "Response to the Philosophical Brothel." In *Rethinking Borders,* ed. John C. Welchman, 187–99. Minneapolis: University of Minnesota Press, 1996.

Bajtin, Mijail. *Teoría y estética de la novela.* Translated by Helena S. Kriukova and J. Vicente Cazcarra. Madrid: Taurus, 1989.

Balibar, Etienne. "The Borders of Europe." Translated by J. Swenson. In *Cosmopolitics: Thinking and Feeling Beyond the Nation,* ed. Pheng Cheah and Bruce Robbins, 216–29. Minneapolis: University of Minnesota Press, 1998.

Barquet, Jesús. "La frontera en *Callejón Sucre y otros relatos* de Rosario Sanmiguel," *Revista de literatura Mexicana Contemporánea* 1, no. 5 (April–July 1997): 85–93.

Barrera, Eduardo. "Apropiación y tutelaje del la frontera norte." *puentelibre, revista de literatura* 4 (Spring 1995): 13–17.

Barrón Salido, Patricia. "Las 'María Magdalena': El oficio de la prostitución y su estrategía colectiva de vida." Draft of bachelor's thesis. Colegio de la Frontera Norte, Tijuana, 1995.

Barthes, Roland. *Camera Lucida: Reflections on Photography.* Translated by Richard Howard. New York: Hill and Wang, 1981.

———. *El grado cero de la escritura.* Translated by Nicolás Rosa. México, D.F.: Siglo XXI, 1987.

Bayardo, Patricio. *El signo y la alambrada: Ensayos de literatura y frontera.* Tijuana: Entrelíneas, 1990.

Benjamin, Walter. "On language." In *Reflections: Essays, Aphorisms, Autobiographical Writings,* trans. Edmund Jephcott. New York: Schocken Books, 1986.

Berumen, Humberto Félix. "El cuento entre los bárbaros del norte." In

*Literatura fronteriza de acá y allá,* ed. Guadalupe Beatriz Aldaco, 93–118. Hermosillo: Instituto sonorense de cultura, 1994.

———. "La literatura que vino del norte." In *Borderlands Literature: Towards an Integrated Perspective,* ed. Harry Polkinhorn, José Manuel Di-Bella, and Rogelio Reyes, 15–31. San Diego: Institute for Regional Studies of the Californias, 1990.

Betancourt, Ignacio. "Literatura en la frontera." In *Borderlands Literature: Towards an Integrated Perspective,* ed. Harry Polkinhorn, José Manuel Di-Bella, and Rogelio Reyes, 33–41. San Diego: Institute for Regional Studies of the Californias, 1990.

Bhabha, Homi. *The Location of Culture.* London: Routledge, 1994.

———. "The Other Question: Difference, Discrimination and the Discourse of Colonialism." In *Out There: Marginalization and Contemporary Cultures,* ed. Russell Ferguson et al., 71–87. Cambridge, Mass: MIT Press, 1990.

———. "The World and the Home." *Social Text* 10 (1992): 141–53.

Bierce, Ambrose. *Letters.* Edited by Bertha Clark Pope. 1922. Reprint: New York: Gordian, 1967.

Bradotti, Rosa. *Nomadic Subjects: Embodiment and Sexual Difference in Contemporary Feminist Theory.* New York: Columbia University Press, 1994.

Bruce-Novoa, Juan. "Metas monológicas, estrategias dialógicas: La literatura chicana." In *Literatura fronteriza de acá y allá,* ed. Guadalupe Beatriz Aldaco, 11–17. Hermosillo: Instituto sonorense de cultura, 1994.

———. "The U.S.-Mexican Border in Chicano Testimonial Writing." *Theoretical Studies in Media and Culture* 18, nos. 1–2 (1995–96): 32–53.

Burgin, Victor. *In/different Spaces: Place and Memory in Visual Culture.* Berkeley: University of California Press, 1996.

Bustamante, Jorge. "Etnicidad en la frontera México-Estados Unidos: una línea heche de paradojas." In *Reflexiones sobre la identidad de los pueblos,* ed. Ramón Ruiz and Olivia Teresa Ruiz, 36–64. Tijuana: COLEF, 1996.

———. "Frontera México-Estados Unidas. Reflexiones para un marco teórico." In *Decadencia y auge de identidades,* ed. José Manuel Valenzuela Arce, 91–118. Tijuana: COLEF, 1992.

———. "La aceptación de valores tradicionales es mayor en las ciudades norteñas." *Cultura norte* 2, no. 1 (August–October 1980): 32–36.

———. "Uso del idioma español e identidad nacional. Encuesta en siete ciudades." CEFNOMEX research report, 1982.

Butler, Judith. *Gender Trouble: Feminism and the Subversion of Identity.* New York: Routledge, 1990.

Calderón, Héctor, and José David Saldívar, eds. *Criticism in the Borderlands: Studies on Chicano Literature, Culture, and Ideology.* Durham, N.C.: Duke University Press, 1991.

Cantú, Norma Elia. *Canícula: Snapshots of a Girlhood en la Frontera.* Albuquerque: University of New Mexico Press, 1995.

Carpentier, Alejo. *Los pasos perdidos.* Barcelona: Barral, 1972.

Castañeda, Quetzil E. *In the Museum of Maya Culture: Touring Chichén Itzá.* Minneapolis: University of Minnesota Press, 1996.

Castellanos, Gabriela, Simone Accorsi, and Gloria Velasco, eds. *Discurso, género y mujer.* Colección Estudios de Género. Santiago de Cali: Editorial Facultad de Humanidades, 1994.

Castellanos, Rosario. "Meditación en el umbral." In Castellanos, *Meditación en el umbral,* 73. Mexico, D.F.: Fondo de cultura economica, 1985.

Castellanos Guerrero, Alicia, and Gilberto López y Rivas. "La influencia norteamericana en la frontera norte de México." In *La frontera del norte. Integración y desarrollo,* ed. Roque González Salazar, 68–84. México, D.F.: El Colegio de México, 1981.

Castillo, Debra A. *Talking Back: Toward a Latin American Feminist Literary Criticism.* Ithaca, N.Y.: Cornell University Press, 1992.

Castillo, Debra A., María Gudelia Rangel Gómez, and Bonnie Delgado. "Border Lives: Prostitute Women in Tijuana." *Signs* 24, no. 2 (1998): 387–422.

Castillo, Homero, ed. *Antología de poetas modernistas.* Englewood Cliffs, N.J.: Prentice-Hall, 1972.

Castro-Gómez, Santiago. "Modernidad, latinoamericanismo y globalización." *Cuadernos americanos* 12, no. 1 (1998): 187–213.

Cervantes, Lorna Dee. *Emplumada.* Pittsburgh: University of Pittsburgh Press, 1981.

Chabram-Dernersesian, Angie. "'Chicana? Rican? No, Chicana-Riquena!' Refashioning the Transnational Connection." In *Between Woman and Nation: Nationalisms, Transnational Feminisms, and the State,* ed. Caren Kaplan, Norma Alarcón, and Minoo Moallem, 264–95. Durham, N.C.: Duke University Press, 1999.

———. "I Throw Punches for My Race, but I Don't Want to Be a Man: Writing Us—Chica-nos (Girl, Us)/Chicanas—into the Movement Script." In *Cultural Studies,* ed. Lawrence Grossberg, Cary Nelson, and Paula Treichler, 81–95. New York: Routledge, 1992.

Cheah, Pheng. "Given Culture: Rethinking Cosmopolitan Freedom in Transnationalism." In *Cosmopolitics: Thinking and Feeling Beyond the Nation,* ed. Pheng Cheah and Bruce Robbins, 290–328. Minneapolis: University of Minnesota Press, 1998.

Cheah, Pheng, and Bruce Robbins, eds. *Cosmopolitics: Thinking and Feeling Beyond the Nation.* Minneapolis: University of Minnesota Press, 1998.

Conde, Rosina. *Arrieras somos . . .* Culiacán: DIFOCUR, 1994. Translated as *Women on the Road,* ed. Gustavo V. Segade, introduction by Sergio D. Elizondo. San Diego: San Diego State University Press, 1994.

―――. *De infancia y adolescencia.* Mexico: Panfleto y Pantomima, 1982.

―――. "¿Dónde esta la frontera?" *El acordeón* 7 (1992): 50–52.

―――. *Embotellado de origen.* Aguascalientes: Instituto cultural de Aguascalientes, 1994.

―――. *En la tarima.* Mexico: U Autónoma Metropolitana, 1984.

Cortázar, Julio. *Rayuela.* Buenos Aires: Sudamericana, 1973.

Cortés Bargalló, Luis. *Baja California piedra de serpiente: prosa y poesía (siglos XVII–XX).* Mexico: Consejo nacional para la cultura, 1993.

Cosgrove, Dennis, and Mona Domosh. "Writing the New Cultural Geography." In *Place/Culture/Representation,* ed. James Duncan and David Ley, 25–38. New York: Routledge, 1994.

Cunningham, Hilary. *God and Caesar at the Rio Grande: Sanctuary and the Politics of Religion.* Minneapolis: University of Minnesota Press, 1995.

Davies, Carole Boyce. *Moving Beyond Boundaries,* vol. 2, *Black Women's Diasporas.* New York: New York University Press, 1995.

de Certeau, Michel. "Californie, un théâtre de passants." *Autrement* 31 (1981): 10–18.

―――. *Heterologies: Discourse on the Other.* Translated by Brian Massumi. Foreword by Wlad Godzich. Minneapolis: University of Minnesota Press, 1986.

Derrida, Jacques. *Aporias.* Translated by Thomas Dutoit. Stanford, Calif.: Stanford University Press, 1993.

―――. "Economimesis." *Diacritics* 11, no. 2 (1981): 3–25.

―――. *Memoires for Paul de Man.* Translated by Cecile Lindsay, Jonathan Culler, and Eduardo Cadava. New York: Columbia University Press, 1986.

Díaz-Diocaretz, Myriam. "'La palabra no olvida de dónde vino': Para una poética dialógica de la diferencia." In *Breve historia feminista de la literatura española (en lengua castellana) I. Teoría feminista: discurso de la diferencia,* ed. Myriam Díaz-Diocaretz and Iris Zavala, 77–124. Barcelona: Anthropos; Madrid: Dirección General de la Mujer/Consejería de Educación de la Comunidad de Madrid, 1993.

Díaz-Diocaretz, Myriam, and Iris Zavala, eds. *Breve historia feminista de la literatura española (en lengua castellana) I. Teoría feminista: discurso de la diferencia.* Barcelona: Anthropos; Madrid: Dirección General de la Mujer/ Consejería de Educación de la Comunidad de Madrid, 1993.

Domínguez, Christopher. Review of *Peregrinos de Aztlán. Vuelta* (August 1989): 88.

Eakin, Paul John. Foreword to Philippe Lejeune, *On Autobiography,* trans. Katherine Leary, vii–xxviii. Minneapolis: University of Minnesota Press, 1989.

Esquivel, Laura. *Como agua para chocolate.* Mexico, DF: Planeta, 1989.

Flores, Juan, and George Yúdice. "Living Borders/Buscando America: Languages of Latino Self-formation." *Social Text* 8, no. 2 (1990): 57–84.

Foucault, Michel. *The Archaeology of Knowledge and the Discourse on Language.* Translated by Alan M. Sheridan. New York: Pantheon, 1972.

————. "Discourse on Language." In *The Archaeology of Knowledge and the Discourse on Language,* trans. Alan M. Sheridan, 215–37. New York: Pantheon, 1972.

Fox, Claire F. *The Fence and the River: Culture and Politics at the U.S.-Mexico Border.* Minneapolis: University of Minnesota Press, 1999.

Fregoso, Linda. "*Born in East L.A.* and the Politics of Representation." *Cultural Studies* 4, no. 3 (1990): 264–80.

Fuentes, Carlos. *La frontera de cristal.* Mexico: Altaguara, 1995.

García Canclini, Néstor. *Culturas híbridas: Estrategias para entrar y salir de la modernidad.* Mexico: Grijalbo, 1989. Translated by Christopher Chiappari and Silvia L. López as *Hybrid Cultures: Strategies for Entering and Leaving Modernity.* Minneapolis: University of Minnesota Press, 1995.

Gaspar de Alba, Alicia. *Beggar on Cordoba Bridge.* In Alicia Gaspar de Alba, María Herrera Sobek, and Demetria Martínez, *Three Times a Woman.* Tempe, Ariz.: Bilingual Review Press, 1989.

————. "Malinchista, A Myth Revised." In *Infinite Divisions: An Anthology of Chicana Literature,* ed. Tey Diana Rebolledo and Eliana S. Rivero, 212–13. Tucson: University of Arizona Press, 1993.

————. *The Mystery of Survival and Other Stories.* Tempe, Ariz.: Bilingual Press, 1993.

Girven, Tim. "Hollywood's Heterotopia: U.S. Cinema, the Mexican Border and the Making of Tijuana." *Travesía. The Border Issue. Journal of Latin American Cultural Studies* 3, nos. 1–2 (1994): 93–133.

Golubov, Nattie. "La crítica literaria feminista contemporánea: Entre el esencialismo y la diferencia." *Debate feminista* 5, nos. 9–10 (1994): 116–26.

Gómez Montero, Sergio. *The Border: The Future of Post-Modernity.* San Diego: San Diego State University Press, 1994.

Gómez-Peña, Guillermo. "From Borders: Myths and Maps." In *Borderlands Literature: Towards an Integrated Perspective,* ed. Harry Polkinhorn, José Manuel Di-Bella, and Rogelio Reyes, 77–79. San Diego: Institute for Regional Studies of the Californias, 1990.

————. *Warrior from Gringostroika.* Minneapolis: Gray Wolf Press, 1993.

Grossberg, Lawrence. *We Gotta Get Out of This Place: Popular Conservatism and Postmodern Culture.* New York: Routledge, 1992.

Guerra-Cunningham, Lucía. "Desentrañando la polifonía de la marginalidad: hacia un análisis de la narrativa femenina hispanoamericana." *Inti* 24–25 (Fall 1986–Spring 1987): 39–59.

Gusdorf, Georges. "Conditions and Limits of Autobiography." In *Auto-*

biography: *Essays Theoretical and Critical*, ed. James Olney, 28–48. Princeton: Princeton University Press, 1980.

Gutiérrez-Jones, Carl. "Desiring B/orders." *Diacritics* 25, no. 1 (1995): 99–112.

Haraway, Donna J. *How Like a Leaf*. Interview with Thyrza Nichols Goodeve. New York: Routledge, 2000.

Hayman, David. *Re-forming the Narrative: Toward a Mechanics of Modernist Fiction*. Ithaca, N.Y.: Cornell University Press, 1987.

Herrera-Sobek, María. "The Corrido as Hypertext: Undocumented Mexican Immigrant Films and the Mexican/Chicano Ballad." In *Culture Across Borders Mexican Immigration and Popular Culture*, ed. David R. Maciel and María Herrera-Sobek, 227–58. Tucson: University of Arizona Press, 1999.

———. *Northward Bound: The Mexican Immigrant Experience in Ballad and Song*. Bloomington: Indiana University Press, 1993.

Hicks, Emily. *Border Writing: The Multidimensional Text*. Minneapolis: University of Minnesota Press, 1991.

Hutcheon, L. *Politics of Postmodernism*. New York: Routledge, 1993.

Iglesias Prieto, Norma. *Beautiful Flowers of the Maquiladora: Life Histories of Women Workers in Tijuana*. Translated by Michael Stone with Gabrielle Winker. Foreword by Henry Selby. Austin: University of Texas Press, 1997.

———. *Entre yerba, polvo y plomo, lo fronterizo visto por el cine mexicano*. 2 vols. Tijuana, B.C.: El Colegio de la Frontera Norte, 1991.

Jameson, Fredric. "Reification and Utopia in Mass Culture." *Social Text* 1 (1979): 130–48.

Jameson, Fredric, and Masao Miyosi, eds. *The Cultures of Globalization*. Durham, N.C.: Duke University Press, 1998.

Johnson, David E. "The Time of Translation." In *Border Theory: The Limits of Cultural Politics*, ed. Scott Michaelsen and David E. Johnson, 129–65. Minneapolis: University of Minnesota Press, 1997.

Johnson, David E., and Scott Michaelsen. "Border Secrets: An Introduction." In *Border Theory: The Limits of Cultural Politics*, ed. Scott Michaelsen and David E. Johnson, 1–39. Minneapolis: University of Minnesota Press, 1997.

Kaminsky, Amy K. *Reading the Body Politic: Feminist Criticism and Latin American Women Writers*. Minneapolis: University of Minnesota Press, 1993.

Kaplan, Caren, Norma Alarcón, and Minoo Moallem, eds. *Between Woman and Nation: Nationalisms, Transnational Feminisms, and the State*. Durham, N.C.: Duke University Press, 1999.

Kristeva, Julia. *Powers of Horror: An Essay on Abjection*. Translated by Leon S. Roudiez. New York: Columbia University Press, 1982.

Larsen, Neil. *Reading North by South: On Latin American Literature, Culture, and Politics.* Minneapolis: University of Minnesota Press, 1995.

Leal, Luis. "Mexico's Centrifugal Culture." *Theoretical Studies in Media and Culture* 18, nos. 1–2 (1995–96): 111–21.

Lejeune, Philippe. *On Autobiography.* Foreword by Paul John Eakin. Translated by Katherine Leary. Minneapolis: University of Minnesota Press, 1989.

Lionnet, Françoise. "Of Mangoes and Maroons: Language, History and the Multicultural Subject of Michelle Cliff's Abeng." In *De/colonizing the Subject: The Politics of Gender in Women's Autobiography,* ed. Sidonie Smith and Julia Watson, 321–48. Minneapolis: University of Minnesota Press, 1992.

Lomelí, Francisco A. "En torno a la literatura de la frontera: ¿Convergencia o divergencia?" *Plural* 15–16, no. 179 (August 1986): 24–32.

Ludmer, Josefina. "Mujeres que matan." *Revista iberoamericana* 62, nos. 176–77 (1996): 781–97.

———. "Tretas del debil." In *La sartén por el mango,* ed. Patricia Elena González and Eliana Ortega, 47–54. Río Piedras, P.R.: Huracán, 1985.

Lugones, María. "Hablando cara a cara/Speaking Face to Face: An Exploration of Ethnocentric Racism." In *Making Face, Making Soul: Haciendo Caras/ Creative and Critical Perspectives by Women of Color,* ed. Gloria Anzaldúa, 46–54. San Francisco: Aunt Lute, 1990.

Luna, Francisco. "Visiones fronterizas." In *Literatura fronteriza de acá y allá,* ed. Guadalupe Beatriz Aldaco, 79–84. Hermosillo: Instituto sonorense de cultura, 1994.

MacEoin, Gary. "The Constitutional and Legal Aspects of the Refugee Crisis." In *Sanctuary: A Resource Guide for Understanding and Participating in the Central American Refugees' Struggle,* ed. MacEoin, 118–29. San Francisco: Harper and Row, 1985.

———, ed. *Sanctuary: A Resource Guide for Understanding and Participating in the Central American Refugees' Struggle.* San Francisco: Harper and Row, 1985.

Maciel, David R., and María Rosa García-Acevedo. "The Celluloid Immigrant. The Narrative Films of Mexican Immigration." In *Culture Across Borders: Mexican Immigration and Popular Culture,* ed. David R. Maciel and María Herrera-Sobek, 149–202. Tucson: University of Arizona Press, 1999.

Malcolm, Marion. "Overcoming Paternalism in the Sanctuary Movement." *Basta!* (March 1987): 21–25.

Malcuzynski, M. Pierrette. *Sociocríticas. Prácticas textuales/Cultura de fronteras, teoría literaria: texto y teoría.* Amsterdam-Atlanta: Rodopi, 1991.

Martínez, Demetria. *MotherTongue.* Tempe, Ariz.: Bilingual Press, 1994.

Martínez Sánchez, Fernando. *Innovación y permanencia en la literatura coahui-lense.* Mexico: Consejo nacional para la cultura, 1993.

McClintock, Anne, Aamir Mufti, and Ella Shohat, eds. *Dangerous Liaisons: Gender, Nation, and Postcolonial Perspectives.* Minneapolis: University of Minnesota Press, 1997.

McLeod, Anne. "Gender Difference Relativity in GDR-Writing or: How to Oppose without Really Trying." *Oxford Literary Review* 7 (1985): 41–61.

Melas, Natalie. "Versions of Incommensurability." *World Literature Today* (Spring 1995): 275–80.

Menocal, María Rosa. *Shards of Love: Exile and the Origins of the Lyric.* Durham, N.C.: Duke University Press, 1994.

Michaelsen, Scott, and David E. Johnson, eds. *Border Theory: The Limits of Cultural Politics.* Minneapolis: University of Minnesota Press, 1997.

Mignolo, Walter D. "Globalization, Civilization Processes, and the Relocation of Languages and Cultures." In *The Cultures of Globalization,* ed. Fredric Jameson and Masao Miyosi, 32–53. Durham, N.C.: Duke University Press, 1998.

―――――. *Local Histories/Global Designs: Coloniality, Subaltern Knowledges, and Border Thinking.* Princeton, N.J.: Princeton University Press, 2000.

―――――. "Posoccidentalismo: El argumento desde América Latina." *Cuadernos americanos* 12, no. 67 (1998): 143–65.

Mohanty, Chandra T. "On Race and Voice: Challenges for Liberal Education in the 1990s." In *Between Borders: Pedagogy and the Politics of Cultural Studies,* ed. Henry A. Giroux and Peter McLaren, 38–53. New York: Routledge, 1994.

Molloy, Sylvia. *En breve cárcel.* Barcelona: Seix Barral, 1991.

Monsiváis, Carlos. "De la cultura mexicana en vísperas del TLC." In *La educación y la cultura ante el Tratado de Libre Comercio,* ed. Julio López et al., 189–209. Mexico: Nueva Imagen, 1992.

―――――. "La cultura de la frontera." *Esquina baja* 5–6 (May–August 1988): 41–55.

Montalvo, Garci Rodríguez de. "Las sergas de Esplandián." In *Libros de caballerías,* vol. 40, *Biblioteca de autores españoles,* ed. Pascual De Gayangos y Arce. Madrid: Real academia española, 1950. Translated by William Thomas Little as *The Labors of the Very Brave Knight Esplandián.* Binghamton, N.Y.: Renaissance and Medieval Texts and Studies, 1992.

Montes, Elizabeth. "Rosario Sanmiguel: Callejón Sucre y otros relatos." *Revista de literatura Mexicana Contemporánea* 1, no. 5 (April–July 1997): 94–100.

Moreno de Alba, José. "Observaciones sobre el español en la frontera norte de México." In *La frontera del norte: Integración y desarrollo,* ed. Roque González Salazar, 85–94. México, D.F.: El Colegio de México, 1981.

Morris, Edmund. *Dutch.* New York: Random House, 1999.

Nathan, Debbie. *Women and Other Aliens: Essays from the U.S. Mexico Border.* El Paso, Tex.: Cinco Puntos, 1991.

Nelson, Irina. "A Feminine Discourse in the Mexican North: Identity and Authority in the Narrative of Rosina Conde." Master's thesis, King's College, London, 1994.

Novaro, María. *El jardín del Edén.* Macondo Cine Video, 1994.

Olalquiaga, Celeste. "Vulture Culture." In *Rethinking Borders,* ed. John C. Welchman, 85–100. Minneapolis: University of Minnesota Press, 1996.

Onetti, Juan Carlos. *La vida breve.* Buenos Aires: Sudamericana, 1968.

Ortega y Gasset, José. *The Revolt of the Masses.* New York: W. W. Norton, 1957.

Ortiz, Orlando. *Tamaulipas: Una literatura a contrapelo.* Mexico: Consejo nacional para la cultura, 1994.

Ortiz Taylor, Sheila, and Sandra Ortiz Taylor. *Imaginary Parents.* Albuquerque: University of New Mexico Press, 1996.

Paz, Octavio. *El laberinto de la soledad.* 1959; Mexico: Fondo de Cultura Económica, 1980. Translated by Lysander Kemp as *The Labyrinth of Solitude.* New York: Grove, 1961.

Polkinhorn, Harry. "Alambrada: Hacia una teoría de la escritura fronteriza." In *Borderlands Literature: Towards an Integrated Perspective,* ed. Harry Polkinhorn, José Manuel Di-Bella, and Rogelio Reyes, 29–36. San Diego: Institute for Regional Studies of the Californias, 1990.

Polkinhorn, Harry, José Manuel Di-Bella, and Rogelio Reyes, eds. *Borderlands Literature: Towards an Integrated Perspective.* San Diego: Institute for Regional Studies of the Californias, 1990.

Pratt, Mary Louise. *Imperial Eyes: Travel Writing and Transculturation.* New York: Routledge, 1992.

Rangel Gómez, María Gudelia. Untitled, unpublished manuscript, 1996.

Rebolledo, Tey Diana. "The Politics of Poetics: Or, What Am I, a Critic, Doing in This Text Anyhow." In Gloria Anzaldúa, *Borderlands/La Frontera: The New Mestiza,* 346–55. San Francisco: Aunt Lute, 1987.

"Resources on Beginning and Maintaining Sanctuary." In *Sanctuary,* ed. Gary MacEoin, 198–205.

Richard, Nelly. "Cultural Peripheries: Latin America and Postmodern De-Centering." In *The Postmodern Debate in Latin America,* ed. John Beverley, José Oviedo, and Michael Aronna, 217–22. Durham, N.C.: Duke University Press, 1995.

———. "De la literatura de mujeres a la textualidad femenina." In *Escribir en los bordes. Congreso Internacional de Literatura Femenina Latinoamericana,* ed. Carmen Berenguer et al., 39–52. Chile: Editorial Cuarto Propio, 1990.

———. "¿Tiene sexo la escritura?" *debate feminista* 5, nos. 9–10 (1994): 127–39.

Robbins, Bruce. "Comparative Cosmopolitanisms." In *Cosmopolitics: Think-*

*ing and Feeling Beyond the Nation,* ed. Pheng Cheah and Bruce Robbins, 246–64. Minneapolis: University of Minnesota Press, 1998.

Robinson, Cecil. *No Short Journeys: The Interplay of Cultures in the History and Literature of the Borderlands.* Tucson: University of Arizona Press, 1992.

Rocha, Gilda. *Sonora: un siglo de literatura.* Mexico: Consejo nacional para la cultura, 1993.

Rodriguez, Richard. *Days of Obligation: An Argument with My Mexican Father.* New York: Viking, 1992.

Rodríguez del Pino, Salvador. *La novela chicana escrita en español: Cino autores comprometidos.* Ypsilanti, Mich.: Bilingual Press, 1982.

Roderíguez Lozano, Miguel. "El espacio narrativo de Callejón Sucre y otros relatos de Rosario Sanmiguel." *Tema y variaciones de literatura* 12 (1998): 229–48.

Romero, Rolando. "Border of Fear, Border of Desire." *Borderlines* 1, no. 1 (1993): 36–70.

———. "Postdeconstructive Spaces." *Siglo XX/Twentieth Century* 11 (1993): 225–33.

Rouse, Roger. "Mexicano, Chicano, Pocho: La migracion mexicana y el espacio social del postmodernismo." *Unomásuno, Página Uno* literary supplement (December 31, 1998): 1–2.

Rulfo, Juan. *Pedro Páramo.* Mexico, D.F.: Fondo de cultura económica, 1955.

Saenz, Benjamin Alire. "In the Borderlands of Chicano Identity." In *Border Theory: The Limits of Cultural Politics,* ed. Scott Michaelsen and David E. Johnson, 68–96. Minneapolis: University of Minnesota Press, 1997.

Saldívar, José David. *Border Matters: Remapping American Cultural Studies.* Berkeley: University of California Press, 1997.

———. *The Dialectics of Our America: Genealogy, Cultural Critique, and Literary History.* Durham, N.C.: Duke University Press, 1991.

Sánchez, Rosaura. "Ethnicity, Ideologies, and Academia." *Cultural Studies* 4, no. 3 (1990): 294–302.

Sánchez-Tranquilino, Marcos, and John Tagg. "The Pachuco's Flayed Hide: Mobility, Identity, and Buenas Garras." In *Cultural Studies,* ed. Lawrence Grossberg, Cary Nelson, and Paula Treichler, 556–70. New York: Routledge, 1992.

Sanmiguel, Rosario. *Callejón Sucre y otros relatos.* Chihuahua: Ediciones del Azar, 1994.

Sanson d'Abbeville, Nicolas. *America 1667.* Translated by Pauline Carson Bloch and Robert Martinon. Edited by Louis M. Bloch Jr. Cleveland: Bloch and Company, 1959.

Saravia Quiroz, Leonardo. "Cultura y creación literaria en la frontera: Notas para un paisaje." *La línea* 1 (1988): 45–56.

Spillers, Hortense. "Who Cuts the Border? Some Readings on 'America.'" In

*Comparative American Identities: Race, Sex, and Nationality in the Modern Text,* ed. Hortense Spillers, 1–25. New York: Routledge, 1991.

Spivak, Gayatri Chakravorty. "Can the Subaltern Speak?" In *Marxism and the Interpretation of Culture,* ed. Cary Nelson and Lawrence Grossberg, 271–313. Chicago: University of Illinois Press, 1988.

———. *Outside in the Teaching Machine.* New York: Routledge, 1993.

———. "Subaltern Studies: Deconstructing Historiography." In Spivak, *In Other Worlds: Essays in Cultural Politics,* 197–221. New York: Routledge, 1988.

Stoler, Ann Laura. "Making Empire Respectable: The Politics of Race and Sexual Morality in Twentieth-Century Colonial Cultures." In *Dangerous Liaisons: Gender, Nation, and Postcolonial Perspectives,* ed. Anne McClintock, Aamir Mufti, and Ella Shohat, 344–73. Minneapolis: University of Minnesota Press, 1997.

Stoll, David. *I Rigoberta Menchú and the Story of All Poor Guatemalans.* Boulder, Colo.: Westview, 1999.

Swain, Regina. *La señorita Superman y otras danzas.* Mexico: Fondo editorial tierra adentro, 1993.

Tabuenca Córdoba, María Socorro. "Aproximaciones críticas sobre las literaturas de las fronteras." *Frontera norte* 9, no. 18 (1997): 85–110.

———. "Viewing the Border: Perspectives from 'The Open Wound.'" *Discourse* 18 (1995–96): 146–68.

Trigo, Abril. "Fronteras de la epistemología: epistemologías de la frontera." *Papeles de Montevideo* 1 (June 1997): 71–89.

Trinh T. Minh-ha. "An Acoustic Journey." In *Rethinking Borders,* ed. John C. Welchman, 1–17. Minneapolis: University of Minnesota Press, 1996.

———. *Woman, Native, Other: Writing Postcoloniality and Feminism.* Bloomington: Indiana University Press, 1989.

Trujillo Muñoz, Gabriel. "La literatura bajacaliforniana contemporánea: El punto de vista femenino." In *Mujer y literatura mexicana y chicana: Culturas en contacto* 2, ed. Aralia López González et al., 177–87. Tijuana: Colegio de la Frontera norte, 1990.

———. "La literatura en Baja California: tendencias y propuestas." *Trazadura* 4 (1992): 15–20.

———. "Mi generación: poetas bajacalifornianos nacidos entre 1954–1964." In *Literatura fronteriza de acá y allá,* ed. Guadalupe Beatriz Aldaco, 269–81. Hermosillo: Instituto sonorense de cultura, 1994.

———. *Un camino de hallazgos: Poetas bajacalifornianos del siglo veinte.* Mexicali: U. Autónoma de Baja California, 1992.

Valcárcel, Amelia. *Sexo y filosofía: Sobre "mujer" y "poder."* Barcelona: Anthropos, 1991.

Valdés-Villalva, Guillermina. "La desmitificación de la frontera." In *Entre*

*la magia y la historia. Tradiciones, mitos y leyendas de la frontera,* ed. José
   Manuel Valenzuela Arce, 249–59. México, D.F.: Programa Cultural de las
   Fronteras; Tijuana, B.C.: El Colegio de la Frontera Norte, 1992.

Vila, Pablo. "Sistemas Clasificatorios y narrativas identitarias en Ciudad Juárez
   y El Paso." In *Voces de frontera. Estudios sobre la dispersión cultural en la
   frontera México-Estados Unidos,* ed. Víctor Zúñiga, 137–220. Monterrey:
   Universidad Autónoma de Nuevo León, 1998.

Villarreal, José Javier. *Nuevo León: Entre la tradición y el olvido.* Mexico: Consejo nacional para la cultura, 1993.

Villarreal, Minerva. *Nuevo León: Brújula solar.* Mexico: Consejo nacional para
   la cultura, 1994.

Viramontes, Helena María. "Dance Me Forever." *L.A. Weekly,* June 24–30,
   1988, G20.

———. "The Jumping Bean." In *Pieces of the Heart: New Chicano Fiction,* ed.
   Gary Soto, 122–32. San Francisco: Chronicle Books, 1993.

———. "Miss Clairol." *Americas Review,* special issue on "Chicana Creativity and Criticism: Charting New Frontiers in American Literature," ed.
   María Herrera-Sobek and Helena María Viramontes, 15, nos. 3–4 (1987):
   101–5.

———. *The Moths.* Houston: Arte Publico, 1985.

———. "Spider's Face." *Americas 2001* 1, no. 5 (March/April 1988): 33–34.

———. "Tears on My Pillow." In *New Chicana/o Writing,* ed. Charles M.
   Tatum, 110–15. Tucson: University of Arizona Press, 1992.

Welchman, John C. "The Philosophical Brothel." In *Rethinking Borders,* ed.
   John C. Welchman, 160–86. Minneapolis: University of Minnesota Press,
   1996.

———, ed. *Rethinking Borders.* Minneapolis: University of Minnesota Press,
   1996.

Wilson, Robin. "A Challenge to the Veracity of a Multicultural Icon." *Chronicle of Higher Education,* January 15, 1999, 114–16.

Wittig, Monique. "The Mark of Gender." *Feminist Issues* 5 (1985): 3–12.

Woolf, Virginia. *A Room of One's Own.* 1929. New York: Harcourt Brace Jova-
   novich, 1957. Translated by Laura Pujol as *La habitación propia.* México:
   Seix Barral, 1986.

Zavala, Iris. "Las formas y funciones de una teoría crítica feminista. Femi-
   nismo dialógico." In *Breve historia feminista de la literatura española (en
   lengua castellana) I. Teoría feminista: discurso de la diferencia,* ed. Myriam
   Díaz-Diocaretz and Iris Zavala, 27–76. Barcelona: Anthropos; Madrid:
   Dirección General de la Mujer/Consejería de Educación de la Comunidad de Madrid, 1993.

# Permissions

The poems "Malinchista, A Myth Revised," "Making Tortillas," and "Letters from a Bruja," by Alicia Gaspar de Alba, are reprinted in chapter 2 by permission of the author. The copyright for these poems belongs to the author.

The poem "Refugee Ship," by Lorna Dee Cervantes, from *Emplumada,* is reprinted in chapter 4 from *A Decade of Hispanic Literature: An Anniversary Anthology* (Houston: Arte Público Press—University of Houston, 1982); reprinted with permission of Arte Público Press.

Poetry from *Mother Tongue,* by Demetria Martínez, reprinted in chapter 7, copyright 1994 by Demetria Martínez. Used by permission of Ballantine Books, a division of Random House, Inc.

Portions of chapter 1 were previously published in an earlier version as "Border Theory and the Canon," by Debra A. Castillo, in *Postcolonial Literature: Expanding the Canon,* edited by Deborah L. Madsen (London: Pluto Press, 1999); copyright 1999 by Pluto Press; reprinted with permission. Portions of chapter 1 were also drawn from "Viewing the Border: Perspectives from the 'Open Wound,'" by María Socorro

# Index

Sánchez-Tranquilino, Marcos: and
John Tagg, 163
Sanctuary (U.S. Sanctuary Movement), 168–72, 241–42n2
Sanmiguel, Rosario, 7–8, 20, 61–65;
"Callejón sucre," 65–68; *Callejón
sucre y otros relatos,* 29–30; "La
otra habitación," 79–91; "Paisaje
en verano," 73–79; "Un silencio
muy largo," 68–73
Sanson d'Abbeville, Nicolas: *America
1667,* 191
*Señorita Superman y otras danzas, La*
(Swain), 32, 218–25
*sergas de Esplandián, Las* (Montalvo),
190–91, 220–22, 224, 243n8
"silencio muy largo, Un" (San-
miguel), 68–73
Soldado, Juan, 214
"Sonatina" (Conde), 127–31
"Spider's Face" (Viramontes),
158–61, 162–63
Spillers, Hortense, 166
Spivak, Gayatri Chakravorty, 83,
168, 228–29
Stoler, Ann Laura, 39, 206
Stoll, David, 94
Swain, Regina: *La señorita Superman
y otras danzas,* 32, 218–25

Tagg, John. *See* Sánchez-Tranquilino,
Marcos
Taller de Arte Fronterizo. *See* Border
Arts Workshop
"Tears on My Pillow" (Viramontes),
156–57
*testimonios,* 98, 171, 178, 186
"¿Tiene sexo la escritura?" (Richard),
83

*Tijuana: La casa de toda la gente*
(García Canclini), 198, 218
TLC (Tratado de Libre Comercio).
*See* NAFTA
"Tretas del debil" (Ludmer), 78
Trigo, Abril, 35–36
Trinh T. Minh-ha, 38, 139, 160
Trujillo Muñoz, Gabriel, 21, 125

Valcárcel, Amelia, 239n6
Valdés-Villalva, Guillermina, 60
*vida breve, La* (Onetti), 80–81, 83
Villa, Pancho, 120–21
Villarreal, José Javier, 20
Villarreal, Minerva, 19, 20, 26
Viramontes, Helena Maria: "Dance
Me Forever," 161; "Jumping
Bean," 163–64; "Miss Clairol,"
151–56, 165, 166–67; *The
Moths,* 149; "Paris Rats," 157–58;
"Paris Rats in East L.A.," 30–31;
"Spider's Face," 158–61, 162–63;
"Tears on My Pillow," 156–57

*Warrior from Gringostroika* (Gómez
Peña), 12
warrior image, 242n3; in Martínez,
173–74; in Viramontes, 158–59
Welchman, John C., 5, 194
Wild West, border as, 39, 194,
197–99
Wittig, Monique, 131
Woolf, Virginia: in Conde, 128;
*A Room of One's Own,* 239n8;
in Sanmiguel 79–80

Yúdice, George. *See* Flores, Juan

Zavala, Iris, 63–64

**Debra A. Castillo** is Stephen H. Weiss Presidential Fellow and professor of Romance studies and comparative literature at Cornell University. She is the author of *Easy Women: Sex and Gender in Modern Mexican Fiction* (Minnesota, 1998); *The Translated World: A Postmodern Tour of Libraries in Literature*; and *Talking Back: Strategies for a Latin American Feminist Literary Criticism.*

**María Socorro Tabuenca Córdoba** is a fronteriza from the Juárez–El Paso area. She is dean of the northwest region and regional director of El Colegio de la Frontera Norte in Juárez. She is the author of *Mujeres y fronteras: una perspectiva de género* and (with Ricardo Aguilar) *Lo que el viento a Juárez: un testimonio de una ciudad que se obstina.*